SOCIETY AND POLITICS
UNIFORMITY AND DIVERSITY
IN MODERN DEMOCRACY

SOCIETY AND POLITICS
UNIFORMITY AND DIVERSITY IN MODERN DEMOCRACY

David R. Segal
The University of Michigan

SCOTT, FORESMAN
INTRODUCTION TO MODERN SOCIETY SERIES

Albert J. Reiss, Jr.
Harold L. Wilensky
Editors

Scott, Foresman and Company
GLENVIEW, ILLINOIS   BRIGHTON, ENGLAND

For Mady and Eden

Library of Congress Catalog Card Number: 73–91227
ISBN: 0-673-07840-X

Copyright © 1974 Scott, Foresman and Company, Glenview, Illinois.
Philippines Copyright 1974 Scott, Foresman and Company.
All Rights Reserved.
Printed in the United States of America.

Regional offices of Scott, Foresman and Company are located in Dallas, Texas;
Glenview, Illinois; Oakland, New Jersey; Palo Alto, California; Tucker, Georgia;
and Brighton, England.

Foreword

Modern societies are complex territorial organizations whose populations are more-or-less integrated by economic, legal, military, and political institutions and by the meda of mass communication and entertainment. Sociology reflects this complexity. It is often packaged in separate sociologies such as those of work, religion, minorities, politics, and the community.

By looking at modernization as a process, and urban-industrial ("modern" "affluent") society as a distinctive social system, this series hopes to avoid fragmentation into separate sociologies and at the same time provide intensive treatment of major institutional areas (economy, polity, kinship), units of social organization (society, community, complex organization, family), and of processes that cut across all institutional areas (social differentiation and stratification, social control, demographic and technological change). The series is "relevant" in that all authors address themselves to a single question: "What is modern about modern society?" It is comparative in that all authors know that we cannot answer that question unless we compare the different shapes of modern and premodern societies and of contemporary nations, totalitarian and pluralist, "capitalist" and "socialist." Our abiding concern is the macroscopic, comparative analysis of social structure and change.

Each book in this series can stand alone for specialized courses; each can also be used in combination with others as a flexible substitute for conventional textbooks.

Society and Politics: Uniformity and Diversity in Modern Democracy brings together materials from political science, psychology, history, and anthropology, as well as sociology, to uncover what is sociologically interesting in political institutions, and what is politically relevant in nongovernmental institutions. Its author, David R. Segal, recognizes modern politics as the complex interplay of group interests, party organization, elite social composition, and the mass media of communication. He emphasizes the developmental dynamic to which "modern" as well as "modernizing" nations must adapt, and the sociopolitical strains inherent in increased societal complexity.

Segal balances his concern with the political implications of social strain and conflict with an equally intense preoccupation with social solidarity. He is concerned both with the diverse interests that seek to pull society in several directions at once, and with the threads that hold society together. The result is a sensitive analysis of the eternal problem of cleavage and consensus.

Segal argues that political decisions are constrained not only by the current wishes of the population in the political community, but also by history—the inertia of decisions made in the past—and by events in the international system that are beyond the control of domestic interests.

In coverage, *Society and Politics* is a synthesis of theory (the market model of politics, the idea of structural and ideological convergence in the politics of rich countries, critical elections, the military-industrial complex) and data (voting behavior, socialization and political attitudes, social mobility and status inconsistency, political representation).

Albert J. Reiss, Jr.
Harold L. Wilensky

Preface

One of my major frustrations with the field of political sociology has been the lack of communication among the several disciplines whose members study the social organization of politics: sociology, political science, psychology, economics, anthropology, history, geography. Common concerns appear in all of these sciences, but disciplinary boundaries seem to mitigate against cross-fertilization.

In *Society and Politics* I have tried to bring to bear on problems of political organization a variety of disciplinary perspectives. Some sociologists will doubtlessly feel that I have violated disciplinary orthodoxy, and some communicants of neighboring sciences will feel that as economist, psychologist, anthropologist or historian I am a rank amateur. I plead guilty to both charges, albeit less proudly to the latter than to the former.

Society and Politics is not intended to provide the final answers to questions of social and political organization. If it can sensitize students to the ways in which the resources of several social science disciplines can be utilized to identify important questions and to define strategies for seeking answers to them, it will have served its intended purpose.

This book was conceived as a collaborative enterprise with Morris Janowitz. That other responsibilities forced him to withdraw from the project decreased, but did not negate, his influence on the final shape of the volume. The mark of others who influenced the way I think about politics while I was at the University of Chicago, particularly David Easton, Nathan Leites, and Duncan Macrae, may be less obvious both to the reader and to those scholars, but I find my intellectual debt to them reflected in these pages.

I came to the University of Michigan from Chicago with a framework for political analysis. It was at Ann Arbor that much of the detail was filled in. If there are riches in these pages, the credit should be shared with friends and colleagues in the departments of sociology, political science, and psychology. I owe particular debts to Phil Converse, Sam Eldersveld, Bill Gamson, Dan Katz, Ron Inglehart, Edward Laumann, Warren Miller, Tom Smith, Don Stokes, and Charles Tilly.

The reason for writing a book such as this is students. Several students who have worked closely with me at Michigan will see the results of our discussions and arguments in these pages: Mark Felson, Jerry Hikel, David Knoke, Steve Wildstrom, and John Woelfel in particular. Countless other students who served as guinea pigs as I experimented with early drafts of these chapters in my courses in political sociology, public opinion, social movements, and military sociology must settle for my collective thanks rather than individual recognition. My debt to them is great, for they made the enterprise worthwhile. *Society and Politics* has benefited greatly from the insights of series editor Harold L. Wilensky.

I have dedicated this book to my wife and my daughter. By making it difficult to finish this task, they made it more important to do the job well, and they contributed to that end.

D. R. S.
Arlington, Va.

CONTENTS

1

The Political Function
in Social Systems

POLITICS AS RESOURCE ALLOCATION

Human desires pose a potential problem for every society. The sum of the wants and needs of the individuals and groups within the society may, and usually will, exceed the resources available for distribution to them. The pessimistic Enlightenment philosopher Thomas Hobbes saw that this situation, unchecked, would result in a war of all against all, with each man using violent means against his neighbor to protect his self-interest.[1] In order to avoid this "state of nature" and control his conflicts, Hobbes argued, man in his wisdom invented the sovereign state.

John Locke, a more optimistic philosopher of the Enlightenment, argued that human society had an existence independent of that of the state as a political unit. The state evolved as a convenience for the enforcement of the social contract. For Locke, the state of nature was one of cooperation rather than conflict.[2]

Hobbes and Locke differed in their conceptions of the nature of human life in the absence of political institutions, but they

[1] Thomas Hobbes, *Leviathan* (London: Crooke, 1651).

[2] John Locke, *Two Treatises of Government* (London: Churchill, 1690).

shared a view of the polity as a conflict-regulating institution. Although modern American social science tends to follow in the tradition of Locke, and assume that in the absence of political institutions life might be inconvenient but not savage, there is concern with the Hobbesian problem of order nonetheless. This concern is rooted in the functionalist realization that, in an important sense, politics and war can serve as alternative means for distributing the resources of society. Carl von Clausewitz, a noted philosopher of human warfare, has in fact suggested that war is a "continuation of State policy by other means."[3]

The study of politics, then, is the study of that set of social structures and social processes by which humans resolve their conflicting interests without going to war. In its most elementary form, it is concerned with the processes that determine who gets what, when, and how.[4] David Easton suggests a more refined conceptualization, defining the polity as that social system within which the authoritative allocation of values takes place.[5] By authoritative, he means that the people within the political system recognize the state as the legitimate arbitrator of their differences. People or groups who are competing for the same resources (values) will compete on the basis of the rules of the political system in which they operate. Having chosen to compete on the basis of those rules, they are bound to abide by the final resolution of their differences, even if the other party is awarded what they both wanted.

Four important conditions for the smooth operation of the polity in the regulation of conflict must be noted. First, conflicting interests and differing points of view must be allowed legitimate expression. To the extent that individuals and groups are not allowed to make demands on the resources of the society, or the norms of the system preclude peaceful resolution of differences, unregulated and perhaps violent conflict will be difficult to avoid. It might be argued, for example, that in certain Latin American republics revolutions and coups fulfill the same social functions that elections fulfill in the United States. They provide a means for changing the personnel in power. In such systems, violence is part of the normative social order.

[3] Carl von Clausewitz, *On War,* trans. J. J. Graham, ed. Col. F. N. Maude, vol. 1 (London: Pelican, 1968), p. xxiii.

[4] Harold D. Lasswell, *Politics: Who Gets What, When, How?* (New York: World Publishing Co., 1958).

[5] David Easton, *The Political System* (New York: Alfred A. Knopf, Inc., 1953).

Second, given the legitimacy of conflicting interests, the interested parties must feel that the political system will give them a fair chance to realize their goals. They will not agree to "work within the system," i.e., to resolve differences by politics rather than by violence, if they feel that they have no chance of success within the constraints of that system.

Third, the political system must not be an undifferentiated entity. It must be possible to support some elements of it without supporting the system as a whole. Easton conceptualizes the polity in terms of three levels: the political authorities, the political regime, and the political community.[6] The government officials currently in power comprise the political authorities. The constitutional structure and rules of the game comprise the regime. The political community consists of all the actors involved in the political process, usually within some set of defined geographical boundaries.

Easton suggests that withdrawal of support from the political system takes place at the most specific level first, and only later at the more general level. In the American political system, a dissatisfied person or group would be most likely to withdraw support from the authorities, and argue that the current President, Congress, Supreme Court, or leadership of the major political parties was not upholding the basic tenets of our constitutional democracy. If changing the personnel at the top of the structure failed to correct the wrongs of the system as he perceived them, he might at that point withdraw support from the regime, and argue that under the American constitution a good society cannot be achieved. Only in the most extreme circumstances will large numbers of persons or groups withdraw support from the political community as a whole. The most radical dissenters from the American system want to change both the regime and the authorities. Rarely are sentiments in favor of the abolition of the United States of America as a political unit heard.

A fourth condition for the effective regulation of political conflict concerns the scope of power struggles. The relationships of power that peacefully determine who gets what, when, and how are not confined to the context of the state. Power relationships supported by social norms exist in families, in businesses, in educational institutions, in religious institutions, and so on. To this extent, all of these institutions are political.

---

[6] David Easton, *A Systems Analysis of Political Life* (New York: John Wiley & Sons, Inc., 1965).

POWER AND AUTHORITY

The concepts of *power* and *authority,* mentioned above, are central themes in political sociology. *Power* is the ability of one person to get others to behave the way he wants them to, even if they themselves do not want to behave that way.[7] In the Hobbesian state of nature, power is determined by brute strength. The stronger enforce the compliance of the weaker through coercion.

Coercive force is both an unpleasant and an unstable means of maintaining order. Through the establishment of the state, however, power in the hands of governmental agencies is transformed into *authority.* Governmental decisions are obeyed not merely, or even primarily, because the government is strong. Rather, they are obeyed because the government is presumed to act for the common good. The government, of course, has the means to enforce its decisions through the application of physical force, i.e., by restricting the freedom of or otherwise punishing noncompliers. To the extent that the governmental decisions themselves are seen as furthering the common good, physical manifestations of power used to punish noncompliers are regarded as legitimate.

The nature of power has itself been the subject of theoretical debate in political sociology. Some theorists, such as C. Wright Mills, see it as a "zero-sum game."[8] That is, they see the amount of power available in a social system as fixed. If one person or group gains power, it must be at the expense of some other person or group.

Other theorists see the supply of power in a social system as elastic. Talcott Parsons, for example, argues that just as the amount of money available in an expanding economy will increase, so will the amount of power available in an expanding polity. Where Mills sees the centralization of power as a social evil, Parsons sees it as a potential good because of the resource mobilization it can lead to.[9]

A zero-sum perspective on power is adopted in this book because I believe that, although the polity can generate new power

---

[7] See Max Weber, *Wirthschaft und Gesellschaft,* vol. 2. (Koln: Kiepenheuer & Witsch, 1964), p. 691, and Leon Mayhew, *Society: Institutions and Activity* (Glenview, Ill.: Scott, Foresman and Co., 1971), p. 127.

[8] C. Wright Mills, *The Power Elite* (New York: Oxford University Press, 1959).

[9] Talcott Parsons, *Structure and Process in Modern Society* (New York: The Free Press, 1960).

and thereby improve its total welfare, individuals or groups, without losing any absolute power, may nonetheless become *relatively* weaker through an inflationary spiral of power. For example, there is no reason to believe that segregationist interests in the American South have become weaker in any absolute sense as a result of the civil rights movement. At the same time, the accumulation of new power in the hands of blacks decreases the worth of the power held by white segregationists. The latter might maintain the same degree of control they had previously over the three branches of the federal government, but they now wield less direct control over the behavior of black Americans. In another context, there is no reason to believe that the success enjoyed by the women's liberation movement will reduce the absolute amount of power held by men, vis-á-vis, for example, political authorities. At the same time, however, men will be found to exert less control over political decisions in those areas in which they are opposed by the new power held by women, such as the kinship system.

THE UNIVERSALITY OF POLITICS

There has been some debate among anthropologists regarding the possible existence of apolitical human societies. Redfield has argued that in the simplest societies there was nothing that was political, if politics is conceived of as a set of institutions and procedures for the formal public enforcement of either the common will or the will of a ruler.[10] In this tradition, Sharp describes the Yir Yiront as a people whose actions were governed by a complex set of kinship and clan relations. They were, as seen by Sharp, a people without sovereignty, without hierarchy (outside of the family), and without politics.[11]

The more common anthropological view is that all societies have political systems which at the very least regulate the use of force. In no society are all the rules of social organization automatically obeyed. Thus, every society must have some means of securing obedience and dealing with offenders. In societies in

[10] Robert Redfield, "How Human Society Operates," in H. L. Shapiro, ed., *Man, Culture and Society* (New York: Oxford University Press, 1956), p. 361.

[11] Lauriston Sharp, "People Without Politics," in Verne F. Ray, ed., *Systems of Political Control and Bureaucracy in Human Societies* (Seattle: American Ethnological Society, 1958), pp. 1–18.

which formal governmental institutions had not been created, this political function was performed by other elements of the social structure, such as kinship groups.[12] This was apparently the case with the Yir Yiront.

In fact, "prepolitical societies," in part precisely because of their low level of development, had political problems based upon resource shortages. The typical society at this level of development derived its economic support from the food that could be gathered from the land. Food was a scarce resource. The normative system of the society frequently dictated that the women do the gathering. Women were therefore also a scarce resource. What power that existed in such a society was likely to be wielded by the older men, who therefore had preferential access to the strong young women and were frequently allowed more than one wife. The younger men were at a disadvantage in their quest for young, economically productive mates.

These societies were unlikely to have formal governmental structures. The norms that vested power in the hands of old men and work in the hands of young women were evolved in and enforced by other institutions of society: most notably the family and religious institutions. Only in the sense that formal governmental structures were absent could these societies be considered prepolitical. The very fact that they existed on an economic base in which demand was likely to exceed supply, in which female labor was in short supply, and in which methods for resolving conflicting demands for scarce resources had been evolved makes these societies political in terms of our definition. Politics took place in the context of a "society" without a "state," in a sense supporting the position of Locke as against that of Hobbes. Although the greater part of this book will deal with societies that have established formal governmental structures for the resolution of political issues and two or more political parties to link the people to their government, the fact that politics need not be confined to formal political institutions must be kept in mind.

The gathering societies described above existed on a balance of manifest consensus and latent cleavage. There were cleavages of objective interest between the young men and the old men, each of whom could probably think of uses to which the scarce young women could be put, and there were cleavages of objective interest between all the men as a group and all the women over

---

[12] See, for example, M. Fortes and E. E. Evans-Pritchard, eds., *African Political Systems* (London: Oxford University Press, 1940), and L. P. Mair, *Primitive Government* (Baltimore: Penguin Books, Inc., 1962).

who should do the gathering, a task which either or both groups could presumably perform. These cleavages in all likelihood remained latent. That is, they did not emerge in overt conflict. The young men were unlikely to go to war against the old men, or even to demand some share of the young women (although clandestine liaisons probably took place). The women were unlikely to go to war against the men, or even to demand that the men do some of the gathering.

The reason that these cleavages were unlikely to become manifest conflicts was that there was consensual agreement regarding the norms that allocated women and work within the system. These norms were supported by tradition, by religious ideology, and by kinship structure. It is not surprising that the women accepted their role without question when we note how long into the twentieth century it has taken for large numbers of women in industrial societies to begin to question the norms governing *their* roles. The young men, for their part, could hope to escape the high mortality rates in these societies and live to be old enough to enjoy the services of young women. These societies, however, existed before the evolution of the Protestant ethic, and we must surmise that it was the force of norm and custom, rather than the promise of future payoffs, that caused the young men to accept the delay of gratification demanded of them.

CONSENSUS AND CLEAVAGE IN MODERN SOCIETY

The balance between consensus and cleavage is more delicate in modern industrial nations. As societies become more complex, the number of planes of cleavage contained within them increases. Economic differentiation leads to cleavages along class lines. Religious differentiation leads to cleavages along denominational and sectarian lines. Differences between regions within the nation and between ethnic, religious, and racial groups all provide potential sources of conflict. At the same time that the bases of social cleavage increase, the consensual bases of political integration seem to decrease. The justification of allocative decisions on the basis of religious tenet or tradition becomes less acceptable. Rather, people come to recognize the areas in which latent planes of cleavage exist, and to make those areas explicit concerns of the political process. Since there is no single rational calculus to take the place of religion in defining the single best set of values,[13] conflicts must be resolved through political means.

At the very least, in order for the political process to operate smoothly and nonviolently in complex societies, there must be consensual support for the rules that define the process and for the institutions within which they take place. People and groups must agree on what forms of political participation are appropriate, i.e., on how they will make their demands and attempt to influence political outcomes in their favor. They must also agree that decisions emanating from the institutions of the state will be regarded as authoritative, albeit reversible through processes of appeal.

Other more transient and less universal areas of consensus are likely to emerge as well, manifested in political alliances and coalitions. In modern democracies, the major vehicles for communicating demands to the state are the electoral system and the political parties. Elections are a relatively infrequent occurrence, but groups and individuals may continuously use political parties and elected officeholders as channels of communication through which their demands may become known.

POLITICAL PARTIES AND INTEREST GROUPS

While the number of groups and individuals making claims on the resources of the state may be very large in a modern industrial nation, the number of political parties is likely to be small. Thus, modern political parties seek to aggregate issue groups to increase their electoral strength, while the groups themselves must seek representation through parties that have simultaneous commitments to represent other groups. Some of these commitments have a long history and are difficult to reconcile with more contemporary interests. In such cases, the aggregation process sometimes produces strange political bedfellows. For instance, both anti-integration interests in the southern United States and civil rights interests nationally have ties to the Democratic Party. The degree to which the parties can maintain consensus on their own platforms with such diverse constituencies is an interesting and important political problem. George Wallace's third-party participation in recent American presidential politics, "reform" movements within the two major

---

[13] Cf. Robert E. Lane, "The Decline of Politics and Ideology in a Knowledgeable Society," *American Sociological Review* 31 (1965), pp. 874–895.

American parties, and frequent allusions to fourth-party participation in presidential elections of the future all attest to the fragility of aggregated constituencies.

The number of political parties that can effectively take part in the electoral process is in part determined by how many interests must be represented and how divergent they are. More importantly, however, the effectiveness of political parties in representing the interest groups that support them is constrained by the electoral law. Maurice Duverger, in an insightful discussion of party systems, has pointed out the effects of proportional representation, as against majority rule, on the number of parties in a political system.[14] When a political party is guaranteed representation proportional to its vote in an election, less aggregation takes place. Instead, an interest group that constitutes, let us say, 5 percent of a constituency might well form its own political party, relatively secure in the knowledge that 5 percent of the elected officials will be strongly committed to its position. When a majority is required for election, on the other hand, such a group will be forced to enter into a coalition with other small interest groups in order to elect officials committed to their collective interests.

THE FOCUS OF POLITICAL SOCIOLOGY

What are the lines of cleavage that define the critical electoral groups in modern industrial society? How are members of a population mobilized for political action? What are the social and institutional networks that tie individual interests to the political structure? How do political parties aggregate publics subscribing to diverse ideological positions? How well does the political system represent the diverse interests of a modern population? These are the central problems in political sociology today. The following chapters will attempt to define the current state of our search for their answers.

[14] Maurice Duverger, *Political Parties* (London: Methuen and Co., Ltd., 1954).

2

Communication
as an Integrating Force
in the Polity

DEMOCRACY AND ECONOMIC DEVELOPMENT

How do large numbers of people become mobilized for participation in a democratic political system? What are the social conditions under which democratic political institutions develop?

One of the major research traditions in the study of the evolution of democratic institutions focuses on economic development. In seeking to explain why some societies have developed democratic institutions for solving their resource allocation problems, these scholars argue that the more affluent a society is, the more democratic its political institutions will be.

Seymour Martin Lipset hypothesizes that the extent of democracy in a nation is correlated with its industrialization, wealth, level of education, and degree of urbanization.[1] His study

[1] Seymour Martin Lipset, "Some Social Requisites of Democracy," *American Political Science Review* 53 (March 1959), pp. 69–105. See also his *Political Man* (New York: Doubleday and Co., Inc., 1960), Chapters 2 & 3.

suggests that, on the basis of these factors, one can distinguish between stable democracies on the one hand and regimes that are either dictatorial or unstably democratic on the other. Lipset argues that much of the economic support for democratic institutions is derived from the emergence of a large middle class: a structural phenomenon dependent upon a high level of affluence, industrialization, and urbanization.[2]

Lipset's study was the first to empirically test the hypothesized relationship between economic development and democracy. However, it suffered from methodological shortcomings. Phillips Cutright attempted to correct these, and to generalize Lipset's findings. Where Lipset sought merely to demonstrate that economic development was a *prerequisite* to the emergence of political democracy, Cutright attempted to show that political democracy developed as the economy matured.[3] Like Lipset's study, however, Cutright's analysis clearly distinguished between "underdeveloped," largely nondemocratic countries on the one hand and industrialized, multiparty democracies on the other hand, but did not measure variations within the set of democratic nations.

A more recent study has tried to deal with this problem.[4] Drawing on theories of democratic politics formulated by Anthony Downs and by Robert Dahl, Neubauer constructed an index of democratic development by measuring the amount of electoral equality and competition in political systems.[5] In a study of twenty-three democratic countries, he then showed that the degree of democracy in a country is unrelated to its economic development. He suggested that some level of economic development is necessary as a threshold for the emergence of democracy, but once this threshold is reached, further economic development will not necessarily presage further maximization of democratic practice.

---

[2] Seymour Martin Lipset et al., *Union Democracy* (New York: The Free Press, 1956).

[3] Phillips Cutright, "National Political Development," *American Sociological Review* 27 (April 1963), pp. 253–264.

[4] Deane E. Neubauer, "Some Conditions of Democracy," *American Political Science Review* 61 (December 1967), pp. 1002–1009.

[5] See Anthony Downs, *An Economic Theory of Democracy* (New York: Harper & Row, Publishers, 1957), and Robert A. Dahl, *A Preface to Democratic Theory* (Chicago: The University of Chicago Press, 1956).

COMMUNICATION AND DEMOCRACY

Neubauer, and Cutright before him, did demonstrate a strong relationship between the level of communication in a social system and democratic performance. This relationship reflects a second approach to the study of political development, an approach that emphasizes not economic development, but rather the development of a system of communication capable of integrating the political system. Scholars adopting this approach tend to place primacy on a modern communications technology that can overcome the parochialism of traditional society.[6] Prior to the development of modern media of communication, however, traditional modes of communication, carrying messages tied to the traditional values of society, had an integrative function. It is the fact of communication, rather than the particular media used, that ties people to the polity. Indeed, there are instances, to be discussed below, in which the development of modern social structures hinders the development of political democracy by disrupting traditional channels of social communication without replacing them.

Developmental studies are often undertaken with the assumption that the various institutions of a developing society change at similar rates. This approach overlooks the fact that different social institutions change at different rates, requiring adaptations in other institutions that may delay the total developmental process.[7] If we are to seriously consider the impact of social communication on the development of political democracy, we must attend to alternative ways in which the communication function can be performed, and learn how the institutions of communication, be they traditional or modern, relate to other sectors of society.

There is no doubt that the integration of political systems requires the linkage of large numbers of individuals through channels of social communication. Through social communication the heritage associated with the common characteristics of the members of the system may be shared and may provide the basis for symbolic identification.[8] Cybernetic models of the polity

[6] See, for example, Daniel Lerner, *The Passing of Traditional Society* (New York: The Free Press, 1958).

[7] See William F. Ogburn, *Social Change* (New York: The Viking Press, Inc., 1960).

[8] Karl W. Deutsch, *Nationalism and Social Communication*, 2nd ed. (Cambridge, Mass.: MIT Press, 1966), pp. 86–106.

have suggested that communication is the cement that binds together the units of political organization.[9]

COMMUNICATION AND POLITICAL DEVELOPMENT

Although political development is a complex phenomenon, recent literature has conceptualized it as consisting of three phases: the traditional, the transitional, and the modern. In the first phase, there is a low degree of differentiation in the local political community. The definition of the citizen role is based upon common occupational, religious, ethnic, or regional backgrounds, and political communication takes place through networks of interpersonal contacts. This model of traditional political communication is not restricted in its applicability to the "third world." Even in early America, Alexis de Tocqueville noted that the activities of political notables were a common topic of conversation.[10]

In a modern system, on the other hand, the populace is greatly differentiated, and the definition of the citizen role becomes more cosmopolitan in the sense that it comes to include as fellow citizens people who are members of different occupational groups, ethnic stocks, religious denominations, and so forth. This increased social complexity has two major consequences for the flow of political communication. First, the range of interpersonal contacts among individuals is more limited. Persons who are in close touch with political matters come into personal contact with others who are similarly knowledgeable about politics. Individuals who are less involved with politics, on the other hand, are insulated from interpersonal political communication. Research on the flow of interpersonal communication in the United States has been unable to confirm that people discuss public affairs among themselves to any significant degree,[11] and a survey taken in Detroit in 1964 revealed that 63 percent of the sample had neither asked for nor been asked opinions on any major news

[9] See, for example, Karl W. Deutsch, *The Nerves of Government* (New York: The Free Press, 1963), p. 77.

[10] Alexis de Tocqueville, *Democracy in America*, vol. 1 (New York: Alfred A. Knopf, Inc., 1945), pp. 248–249.

[11] Elihu Katz and Paul F. Lazarsfeld, *Personal Influence* (New York: The Free Press, 1955).

topic during the week or two prior to being interviewed.[12] The evidence suggests that people in modern societies don't talk much about politics among themselves.

A second consequence of the increased differentiation in modern society is the growth of a communications industry which steps in to fill the gap in political communication left by the demise of political conversation. While the relatively low level of interpersonal political communication which persists cannot provide the integrative force necessary in a complex modern society, the agencies of mass communication can and do serve this function.

The characteristics of the transitional stage cannot be delimited as clearly as those of the traditional and modern stages. Indeed, transitional society has largely been defined in terms of the other two. Thus, Lucian Pye suggests that the key structural consideration in the transitional stage is the mixed nature of the communications system. In part, such a system is urban centered and based upon modern communications technology. At the same time, however, separate networks of face-to-face contacts persist among the less urban sectors of the society.[13]

Where this approach errs is in assuming that as soon as urban centers develop, agencies of mass communication spring up and are immediately capable of fulfilling the integrative function of political communication. The concentration of dense populations from a variety of backgrounds in urban centers creates the *necessity* for agencies of mass communication. However, there is a lag between the development of this necessity, or demand, and its fulfillment. Rather than viewing the evolution of politically integrative communications media as a linear development, then, it becomes necessary to recognize that there may be a point at which the political community has become too differentiated to be successfully integrated by face-to-face political communication, but agencies of integrative mass communication have not yet evolved.

In discussing the fact that different institutions change at different rates and may not be well adapted to each other at a particular time, Wilensky notes that

[12] Verling C. Troldahl and Robert Van Dam, "Face-to-Face Communications About Major Topics in the News," *Public Opinion Quarterly* 29 (Winter 1965–1966), p. 628.

[13] Lucian W. Pye, ed., *Communications and Political Development* (Princeton, N.J.: Princeton University Press, 1963), pp. 26ff.

the closest meshing of mass society and mass culture may appear neither in modern pluralist countries nor in modern totalitarian countries, but instead in the new nations of Africa and Asia, where demagogic politicians, on radio, on television, in the village square, inveigh against imperialists and colonialists, manipulating a population torn loose from traditional tribal ties.[14]

At such times there may be a *decrease* in the level of political involvement of a population and an *increase* in the amount of power wielded by the government, rather than by the people. That is, there may be less popular participation in decisions affecting resource allocation.

INTEGRATIVE COMMUNICATION AND VOTING PARTICIPATION

One of the most basic measures of popular participation in the political process is voting turnout. Let us examine the effects of communication on voting turnout under varying conditions of economic development.

In the course of development, populations shift from rural to urban areas, the economic system becomes more complex, and traditional networks of political communication are disrupted. It is generally assumed that the written media (newspapers and magazines) step in to replace the traditional media.

It must be recognized that those segments of the population that are highly educated and literate enough to understand the political content of the written media are also likely to be those that are overrepresented in the elite niches of the social structure. They maintain contact with political events through the emergence of new (and restricted) interpersonal networks. Thus, the written media are superimposed upon a set of face-to-face relations for the upper social strata, while the less literate lower social strata have neither interpersonal nor media contacts with political

---

[14] Harold L. Wilensky, "Mass Society and Mass Culture," *American Sociological Review* 29 (April 1964), p. 178.

events. Even in the United States, with its relatively high level of literacy, we find the lower social strata reporting little political information obtained through the mass media, and in fact expressing a distrust of the written media.[15]

Exposure to television is, in the modern age, both more widespread and more intense than exposure to the written media. It therefore seems that television, rather than the written media, should be viewed as technology's substitute for personal human communication.

How is television ownership related to voting turnout under varying conditions of economic development? If we take urbanization and level of industrialization as measures of economic development, we find that the relationship between television and voting turnout varies as a function of economic development. Urbanization, of course, is not a perfect indicator of economic development or increased social complexity. In some contexts it merely reflects dense but undifferentiated concentrations of people.[16] When this is the case, and when traditional patterns of face-to-face communication are maintained, voting turnout probably increases even in the absence of modern communications media. Concentrated populations are relatively easy to mobilize. The average distance between home and the polling place is much shorter in urban than in rural areas.

At the same time, when television exists in the absence of a high degree of urbanization, it might be taken as indicative of a complex social structure's replacing a traditional communication system with a more modern system without the facilitating effects of population concentration. The combined effect of the breakdown of a traditional system of integrative communication and a lack of urban institutions could lead to *reduced* political participation. The data, in fact, bear out this expectation. When we look at the developing nations of the world, we find that in those with low levels of urbanization, the more television sets there are, the lower the average voter turnout is. Among those with higher levels of urbanization, however, the more television sets there are available, the higher the average voting turnout. The same results

---

[15] See Robert E. Lane, *Political Life* (New York: The Free Press, 1959), pp. 82–83, and V. O. Key, Jr., *Public Opinion and American Democracy* (New York: Alfred A. Knopf, Inc., 1965), pp. 345–369.

[16] See Lerner, *The Passing of Traditional Society,* p. 87.

emerge when we use industrialization rather than urbanization as our measure of economic development.[17]

Two limitations on generalizing from these findings must be noted. First, the studies discussed above all assume that in every national context, the development of a mass communication technology will mobilize the population. This was certainly the case in nations in which the emergence of a modern communication system was associated with the drive for independence, and was generated by pressures from the nationalist revolutionary movements and intellectuals, rather than from colonial governments. This was the case in much of Africa, where such communication systems were aimed at attaining high levels of mass participation in order to achieve very basic structural changes in the form of government. In the postcolonial era, however, the impetus for the development of modern communications has come from newly independent governments, and the goal of these systems has been political control, rather than popular mobilization.

The second limitation on generalizing from these studies is that they are cross-sectional, and hence give us no way to measure the diffusion of communication technologies. They implicitly assume that either the masses, in a quest for political change, or the elites, in a quest for political control,[18] will provide the impetus for the development of modern communications. Yet we know that diffusion is a far more important source of communication technologies than is independent invention, and that the communication pattern that develops in a new state will be shaped at least as much by the patterns existing in other states that are willing to offer help in this area as by internal demand.[19] A nation that receives technical assistance from the Soviet Union in the communications area is likely to develop a more highly centralized media system than will a nation that receives technical assistance from the United States.

---

[17] David R. Segal, "Differential Institutional Development in Transitional Society," *Journal of Developing Areas* 4 (January 1970), pp. 154–172. See also Donald J. McCrone and Charles F. Cnudde, "Toward a Communications Theory of Democratic Political Development," *American Political Science Review* 61 (March 1967), pp. 72–79.

[18] See Paul Kecskemeti, "Totalitarian Communications as a Means of Control," *Public Opinion Quarterly* 14 (Summer 1950), pp. 224–234.

[19] This issue is discussed by Daniel Lerner in "International Cooperation and Communication in National Development," in Daniel Lerner and Wilbur Schramm, eds., *Communication and Change in the Developing Countries* (Honolulu: East-West Center Press, 1967), pp. 103–125.

COMMUNICATION AND CITIZEN POWER

The relationship of communication to politics is important not only in the transitional societies of the "third world." America itself was once a "developing society," and has in fact been referred to by Lipset as "the first new nation."[20] As such, it has experienced many of the same problems as have more recent new nations.[21] More to the point, the American states themselves vary in their levels of economic development and in the structure of their communication systems. These factors may relate to political differences among the states in ways similar to the ways in which they relate to politics among nations.[22]

We have thus far discussed politics in terms of popular participation. A society may, however, be explicitly committed to participatory democracy on an ideological level, while at the same time having a totalitarian government which serves as the "sole value-producing, distributing, and consuming institution."[23] This has been referred to in the literature as "broad scope of government." We do not expect to find among the American states a government that is totalitarian in any absolute sense. We can, however, expect to find variations in the degree to which power is exercised by the government, rather than by the people or by other social institutions.

A study by John Crittendon of comparative political development in the United States provides us with data for studying the effects of economic development and communication on the scope of governmental power in the American context.[24] Crittendon factor-analyzed thirty-three characteristics of the states. Factor analysis is a technique that groups together, into clusters or factors, sets of variables that are related to each other.[25]

---

[20] Seymour M. Lipset, *The First New Nation* (New York: Basic Books, Inc., 1963).

[21] For example, the role of the preelectronic media in integrating the American colonies is discussed in Richard L. Merritt, *Symbols of American Community* (New Haven: Yale University Press, 1966).

[22] See Edward Silva, "A Note on Cross-Societal Propositions and American State Data," *Economic Development and Cultural Change* 14 (April 1966), pp. 355–357.

[23] Robert E. Agger, Daniel Goldrich, and Bert E. Swanson, *The Rulers and the Ruled* (New York: John Wiley & Sons, Inc., 1964), p. 7.

[24] John Crittendon, "Dimensions of Modernization in the American States," *American Political Science Review* 61 (December 1967), pp. 989–1001.

[25] For a discussion of factor-analytic techniques, see Harry Harmon, *Modern Factor Analysis* (Chicago: The University of Chicago Press, 1960).

Three factors resulting from Crittendon's study are of interest to us. Government structure may be measured by his "scope of government" factor. Among the variables comprising this factor are tax level per capita, tax level per income unit, spending level per capita, and proportion in government employment. It is interesting and important to note that this factor does not measure degree of democracy. Both voting and party competition are relatively unrelated to this factor.

Systemic complexity, which we measured in the developing nations in terms of urbanization and industrialization, appears in Crittendon's analysis as "metro-urbanism." Among the variables comprising this factor are urbanization, population, executive salaries, ethnic diversity, and proportion in white-collar occupations.

The integrative communication function appears in Crittendon's study as "integrative message exchange." Among the variables which make up this factor are education, television sets, telephones, and automobiles. It is notable in terms of our earlier discussion on the written media that newspaper circulation does not relate strongly to this factor, suggesting that interpersonal contact (e.g., via telephone) and television share an integrative quality not characteristic of the written media.

Studying the relationships among these three factors reveals patterns akin to those observed in the developing nations discussed above. Scope of government is highest under conditions of imbalance between economic and communications development, i.e., where metro-urbanism is low and integrative message exchange high, and where metro-urbanism is high but integrative message exchange low. In the former case, the government can use a complex communication technology to reach a low-density, agrarian population. In the latter, people are gathered in larger groups and are therefore a more important potential political force, but they do not have the means to share among themselves information on what the government is doing.

COMMUNICATION AND MASS SOCIETY

One of the theoretical concerns of modern political sociology is the evolution of "mass society."[26] In this kind of society, the members of the polity are not linked to each other by common

---

[26] William Kornhauser, *The Politics of Mass Society* (New York: The Free Press, 1959), p. 33.

backgrounds and interests, nor by social networks. Rather, they are tied together by responsibility to a common authority. For this reason, in the absence of local involvements to insulate them from that central authority, they are subject to manipulation by the elites of society through nationally centralized organizations and the mass media.[27]

We shall see in future chapters how interpersonal ties may mitigate against the development of a "mass society." Our concern here is with the role of the mass media. William Kornhauser, in his formulation of the theory of mass society, does not argue that the growth of large-scale communications necessarily expedites manipulation of the masses by the elites. Indeed, it has been suggested above that when the impetus for the modernization of communication technologies comes from a movement toward independence, rather than being imposed on a society by a ruling elite, the structure of the mass communications network may mitigate against highly concentrated power. However, it is assumed that as the total social structure becomes more differentiated and complex, political institutions themselves will, as a matter of course, increase in complexity and scope. In the absence of mediating influences, then, a great deal of power—power generally justified as being utilized in the public interest—will come to be concentrated in political institutions not responsible to a popular electoral base.[28] However, when institutions exist that allow the members of the polity to relate to each other, rather than merely to a common political authority, then power is shared by the electorate. Kornhauser points out the importance of voluntary associations in providing a context for allowing such contact to take place. Worthy of note is the fact that it is the communication function, rather than the social context within which it takes place, that prevents the emergence of the mass society.

From this perspective, Kornhauser's general typology of political systems can be conceived as a developmental one. Kornhauser classifies societies on the basis of how accessible the elite are to pressures from below, and how available the general population is for mobilization by the elite.[29] Integrative communication, to the degree that it is not controlled by the elite, may be assumed to facilitate the accessibility of the elite. They may be

[27] Ibid., pp. 93–101.

[28] See Mills, *The Power Elite*, pp. 298–324.

[29] Kornhauser, *The Politics of Mass Society*, p. 40.

reached and influenced by public opinion. Increased social structural complexity, on the other hand, especially the concentration of populations in large cities and large-scale productive organizations, increases the availability of nonelites. Those societies characterized by low social differentiation will have low availability of nonelites and low accessibility of elites. This form of social organization appears in Kornhauser's theory as "communal society."

Since systems of social stratification and mass communication may develop from this communal base independently of each other, a society may go through a transitional phase in which the modern media of communication may not be developed enough to adequately integrate the society's new structural complexity. This situation, in which traditional forms of communication among people within the system have been disrupted and not replaced, is mass society.

If the institutions of modern communication develop to the point at which they can successfully integrate a highly differentiated society, the mass society phase is passed. Depending upon the locus and the degree of centralization of control of the communication networks, society can then be characterized in Kornhauser's terms as "totalitarian" (with available nonelites and inaccessible elites), or as "pluralistic" (with unavailable nonelites and accessible elites).

I do not mean to suggest that mass society is a phase through which every developing nation must pass. The lag between industrialization and the development of communication media may not in fact be great. Kornhauser's theory of mass society focuses on the degree to which nonelites are "atomized," or devoid of social linkages to other members of the system. We know that in every modern social system there are people whose lives are not woven into the fabric of society and who might be characterized as alienated or atomized. It is indeed questionable whether any society has ever had the ability to successfully integrate all of its members. However, we tend to regard people cut off from social communication with others as exceptional cases. Wilensky points out that even as the centralized state and the mass media of communication develop, older forms of cultural diversity that serve integrative functions persist.[30] Thus, the social isolation of large numbers of individuals, which is characteristic of the hypothetical mass society, is unlikely to occur.

[30] Wilensky, "Mass Society and Mass Culture."

3

The Polity as a Marketplace

THE ECONOMIC ANALOGY

Given a level of economic development sufficient to sustain democratic institutions, and a communication system that ties people to the polity in a participatory manner, what are the mechanisms by which the interests represented by members of the population affect decisions on the allocation of resources? Many theorists have argued that these processes involve exchanges between political leaders and followers that are analogous to exchange relationships in the economic marketplace.

Much of the popularity of the market analogy in the political system is due to its use by David Easton.[1] Early research on the application of economic market principles to the polity, however, was done in the 1920s by economist Harold Hotelling. Hotelling was concerned with the question of why two competing businesses are often in adjacent positions near the center of the market in which they operate.[2] Driving into small towns in America, we

---

[1] See David Easton, "An Approach to the Analysis of Political Systems," *World Politics* 9 (April 1957), pp. 383–408, and Leon Mayhew, *Society: Institutions and Activity* (Glenview, Ill.: Scott, Foresman and Co., 1971), pp. 142–145.

[2] Harold Hotelling, "Stability in Competition," *Economic Journal* 39 (1929), pp. 41–57.

frequently find that Woolworth's and Kresge's are not at opposite ends of town, but right next door to each other, or directly across the street from each other, in the middle of Main Street.

Hotelling assumed that (1) such stores operate in a market system with geographical boundaries, (2) buyers are uniformly distributed within the market, (3) buyer demand is constant, (4) buyers will go to whichever store is closer to them, and (5) each store will attempt to fix its prices and location so as to maximize its profits.

Hotelling argued that, by analogy, one could think of voters as buyers and political parties as firms. The voters, as buyers, are distributed not within the geographical boundaries of a town, but within the ideological boundaries of a polity. That is, there are presumed to be a range of ideological positions acceptable within a democratic polity, and all of these are presumed to be represented in an electorate. The ideological space that Hotelling was concerned with was bounded at its extremes by the positions of liberalism and conservatism. He argued that just as Woolworth's and Kresge's move to the center of town to maximize their share of the economic market by being as physically close as possible to the largest number of buyers, so the two major American political parties have converged to adjacent ideological positions near the center of the liberalism-conservatism spectrum, where the masses of voters are assumed to be.

More recent economic thought has revised Hotelling's model by suggesting that demand is, at least in part, a function of price. Price, in turn, depends in part on transportation costs. For a person living at the edge of town, the long walk to Woolworth's makes it more costly for him to shop there than for someone who lives closer to the center of town. Thus, firms are under pressure not only to move toward the center of the market, but also to retain peripheral support. If a firm is too near the center, transportation costs to and from the hinterlands rise, decreasing demand.[3]

By analogy, in the polity, if both major parties occupy moderate positions, close to each other on the liberalism-conservatism (or indeed any other) dimension, voters at the ideological hinterlands will find it too costly to travel the ideological distance between their own positions and the positions of the parties. Instead, they will fail to participate in the political process, or will participate in ways other than voting. Were

---

[3] See Arthur Smithies, "Optimum Location in Spatial Competition," *Journal of Political Economy* 49 (1941), pp. 423–457.

Hotelling correct, the only interests that would be represented by the party system would be those that were close to a majority position. The revised model, on the other hand, predicts that political parties would diverge ideologically in order to attract and maintain support in the ideological hinterlands. In this view, a wider range of positions would be represented by the party system.

Elements of both models are found in Anthony Downs' economic theory of democracy.[4] Rather than assuming, as Hotelling did, that buyers are uniformly distributed within the market, he suggested that the ideological distribution might vary from one political system to another, or from one time to another, and that this distribution would determine the ideological positions of the parties. Thus, when the bulk of the electorate is located at the extremes of liberalism and conservatism, the parties will diverge ideologically. When there is a bell-shaped distribution, however, the political parties will converge ideologically.

IDEOLOGY AS A DETERMINANT OF POLITICAL DEMAND

These spatial models of party competition have been shown not to correspond with data on how modern electorates and political leaders actually behave politically.[5] One of their major weaknesses is their dependence on the left-right, or liberalism-conservatism, dimension in defining ideological space. While this dimension may have been adequate to explain European political patterns in the nineteenth century, its applicability in the twentieth century is far more limited.

Research earlier in the twentieth century suggested that for educated populations the left-right dimension is not only relevant, but is distributed in the bell-shaped curve that in Downs' theory would predict the ideological convergence of political parties.[6] More recent research has demonstrated that the liberal-

---

[4] Anthony Downs, *An Economic Theory of Democracy* (New York: Harper & Row, Publishers, 1957).

[5] See Donald E. Stokes, "Spatial Models of Party Competition," in Angus Campbell, Philip E. Converse, Warren E. Miller, and Donald E. Stokes, *Elections and the Political Order* (New York: John Wiley & Sons, Inc., 1966), pp. 161–179.

[6] See Stuart A. Rice, *Quantitative Methods in Politics* (New York: Alfred A. Knopf, Inc., 1928).

ism-conservatism dimension continues to be relevant to the educated strata of Western societies.[7]

For the total political system in the twentieth century, however, Edward Shils suggests that it is incorrect to conceive of liberalism-conservatism as a one-dimensional ideological space, given current political realities. Rather, he suggests that the spectrum goes full circle, with democracy somewhere along its middle range, and both extremes shading into totalitarianism.[8] Thus, we can think of socialism shading into Stalinist-type communism on the left and conservatism shading into fascism on the right, with Stalinism and fascism sharing many structural characteristics. Lipset presents an alternative formulation. He suggests that there are two liberalism-conservatism dimensions, one based on economic and the other on noneconomic attitudes. A person who is liberal with regard to one dimension may well be conservative with regard to the other.[9] A manual worker in favor of government welfare programs such as social security, for example, might oppose civil rights legislation that enables minority-group members to compete with him for work.

Other scholars have moved away from the use of labels like "liberalism" and "conservatism," and have tried to define the demands made by people on the government through political parties in terms of specific policy areas.[10] We shall discuss this approach in greater depth later in this chapter.

LIBERALISM-CONSERVATISM IN
THE AMERICAN POLITICAL MARKET

For the moment, let us focus on those segments of the population who find the labels "liberal" and "conservative" politically meaningful, and who relate to the party system in terms of them.

[7] See J. A. LaPonce, "Note on the Use of the Left-Right Dimension," *Comparative Political Studies* 2 (January 1970), pp. 481–502.

[8] Edward A. Shils, "Authoritarianism: 'Right' and 'Left,' " in R. Christie and M. Jahoda, eds., *Studies in the Scope and Method of "The Authoritarian Personality"* (New York: The Free Press, 1954), pp. 24–49.

[9] See Seymour Martin Lipset, *Revolution and Counterrevolution* (New York: Basic Books, Inc., 1968).

[10] See, for example, Angus Campbell, Philip E. Converse, Warren E. Miller, and Donald E. Stokes, *The American Voter* (New York: John Wiley & Sons, Inc., 1960).

In 1969, interviews were conducted with 640 residents of the Detroit metropolitan area. Among other questions, all persons interviewed were asked their party preferences. If they indicated support for the Democratic or Republican Party, they were asked whether they were strong or weak partisans. If they initially said that they were Independents, they were asked if they generally leaned more toward the Democratic Party or the Republican Party. The people interviewed were also asked whether they thought their own views were more liberal or more conservative than those of the Democratic and Republican parties.

Not surprisingly, the plurality of the sample (44.6 percent) reported themselves to be Democrats. Only 22.4 percent called themselves Independents. To some extent, the Democratic plurality reflects the American electorate as a whole. The Democratic Party has in recent years been supported by a greater proportion of the population than has the Republican Party. This of course does not mean that all elections are won by Democratic candidates. The votes of Independents carry great weight, people sometimes vote for a party other than the one they generally support, and Republicans generally profit from higher turnout among their supporters than among Democratic supporters. As we shall see in the next chapter, Republicans tend to come from higher socioeconomic strata than do Democrats, and people from higher strata are more likely to go to the polls.

The proportion of Democrats in our sample also reflects the fact that the study was done in Detroit. Labor unions play an important role in Detroit politics, and in recent years American unions have tended to support the Democratic Party.

The proportion of political Independents in this sample (22 percent) is greater than comparable figures obtained in previous surveys in the Detroit area. It is understandable, however, in view of the disruptive effect of the 1968 presidential election on the partisan stability of the American electorate. Unhappiness with their party's candidates in 1968—Nixon and Humphrey—caused large numbers of voters to weaken their ties to the traditional two-party system.[11]

This weakening of partisan ties is not only reflected in the number of Independents in the Detroit sample. Voters who identified with one of the major parties were more likely to say that they were "not strong" supporters than that they were

[11] See Philip E. Converse, Warren E. Miller, Jerrold G. Rusk, and Arthur C. Wolfe, "Continuity and Change in American Politics: Parties and Issues in the 1968 Election," *American Political Science Review* 63 (December 1969), pp. 1083–1105.

"strong" supporters of their parties, and those people who called themselves Independents were more likely to see themselves leaning toward neither major party than leaning toward either.

Far fewer of the people interviewed were able to use the terms "liberal" or "conservative" to define their political positions than were willing to use party labels. Clearly, position on the left-right spectrum is not a major determinant of political party choice for most people. Of the 640 respondents, only 197, or about 31 percent, placed themselves on a liberalism-conservatism continuum relative to both of the major parties. Since this group represents almost a third of the electorate, it is worthy of our attention. At the same time, we must keep in mind that the traditional ideological cleavage between the left and right seems unimportant in determining the political party choices of over two thirds of the electorate. Later chapters will discuss alternate lines of cleavage that define the other interests the major parties represent.

One of the most commonly held assumptions regarding the American party system is that the Republican Party is more conservative than the Democratic Party. This assumption was clearly shared by the respondents in the Detroit survey. Those who saw themselves as more liberal than the Democratic Party recognized that, almost by definition, they were more liberal than the Republican Party as well. Similarly, those who said that they were more conservative than the Republican Party regarded themselves as more conservative than the Democratic Party also. In the middle of the political spectrum were those voters who regarded themselves as more liberal than the Republican Party, but more conservative than the Democratic Party.

It is interesting to note that only a small proportion of the "ideological" voters who used the terms "liberal" and "conservative" to describe their political positions felt that they were as liberal (or as conservative) as either of the major parties. Only 18 percent felt that either party subscribed to their ideological positions. The remainder saw themselves as being to the left of both parties, between them, or to the right of both ideologically. Thus, whatever similarities exist between the two major American parties can be in part explained by the fact that about a third of the ideological electorate (as estimated from our Detroit data) sees itself as more liberal than one, but more conservative than the other. This is a force for convergence. People who feel that they are more conservative than both parties may refuse to go to the polls if the Republican Party adopts a more liberal platform to appeal to voters at the center of the ideological spectrum. However, they are unlikely to vote for the Democratic Party. Similarly, people who feel they are more liberal than both parties are unlikely to abandon the Democratic Party to become Republican. It is a problem for democracy to keep such people integrated into the political and social structure in such a situation, when there seem to be forces at work to prevent their position from being represented by a major political party.

THE REPRESENTATION FUNCTION IN CONGRESS

By studying the relationship that people see between their own political positions and the positions represented by the major political parties, we begin to see how the market operates, with voters making ideological compromises in order to gain representation through political parties, and the parties in turn trying to find an ideological position that will attract sufficient support in the electorate to produce success at the polls. The market operates at other levels as well. Political party conventions, for example, serve as arenas in which delegates join coalitions in return for payoffs.[12] Perhaps the most visible linkage in the market, however, is that between the constituency and its elected representatives. Mail received by political leaders, letters to the editors of local newspapers, and future success at the poll all indicate how well voters feel they are being served by the men in office.

The linkage between the congressman and his constituency is one of the most interesting in this regard. In Congress, policies bearing on both domestic and international affairs must be agreed upon by the representatives of extremely diverse constituencies. The representatives are, of course, constrained to some degree by the positions of their parties, as well as by the attitudes of their constituents. Thus, the market is a complex one. The congressman must attend to the wishes of his supporters, to his own evaluation of what is best to do, to the influence of fellow members of Congress, and to the position of his party. In this complex market, how much voice does the individual voter, or even the collective constituency, have? Does democracy really work as a means of representing the views of the people?

---

[12] See William A. Gamson, "Coalition Formation at Presidential Nominating Conventions," *American Journal of Sociology* 68 (September 1962), pp. 157–171.

One of the most important studies of congressional representation in the United States was conducted by Warren E. Miller and
Donald E. Stokes.[13] Miller and Stokes were concerned with two
fundamental problems of political representation. The first was
the applicability of Edmund Burke's theory of representation to
the American Congress. Burke argued that a representative should
serve the *interests* of his constituents, but not their *will*.[14] The
politician, in day-to-day contact with political events, was
thought to be a better judge of the people's interests than were the
people. The second concern was the existence in the United
States of responsible national parties that would put forward
platforms on a national level and, if elected, transform them into
national policy.

The notion that a congressman should reflect the attitudes of
his constituents stands in opposition both to Burke's theory and to
the concept of nationally responsible parties. On the one hand, it
suggests that the people do know what they want, and that their
representatives should attend to their will, rather than merely
their interests. On the other hand, it suggests that officeholders
elected as representatives of national political parties with national platforms must nonetheless be attentive to local rather than
national constituencies. If the legislator is to be responsive to his
constituency, then the Democratic congressman from Vermont
must vote against a bill that was a major plank in his party's
national platform if the Democratic voters in Vermont oppose the
bill.

The data used by Miller and Stokes were collected by the
Survey Research Center at the University of Michigan immediately after the 1958 congressional campaign, which was the midterm
election during Dwight D. Eisenhower's second term in the
presidency. A nationwide sample of the electorate, clustered in
116 election districts, was interviewed. Interviews were also held
with the incumbent congressmen and their major-party opponents from these same districts. To these data were added the
roll-call votes of the congressmen who were interviewed and
census data about their congressional districts.

We noted the low level of political information of the average

[13] Warren E. Miller and Donald E. Stokes, "Constituency Influence in Congress," in Campbell,
Converse, Miller, and Stokes, *Elections and the Political Order*, pp. 351–372.

[14] See Heinz Eulau et al., "The Role of the Representative: Some Empirical Observations on
the Theory of Edmund Burke," *American Political Science Review* 53 (September 1959), pp.
742–756.

member of the American electorate in Chapter 2. How can congressmen be attentive to people who are uninformed about legislative issues? Research suggests that congressmen themselves judge proposals on the basis of their views toward government action in fairly general areas, rather than on the basis of the specific proposal in question.[15] It was on the basis of such general areas that Miller and Stokes sought to compare representatives and their constituents. In our previous discussion of ideology, we alluded to research traditions that reject the liberalism-conservatism dimension. The study by Miller and Stokes, concerned with issue areas, represents such a rejection.

Three broad dimensions were identified in the Congress study: (1) approval of government action in the social welfare field, (2) approval of federal action to protect the civil rights of blacks, and (3) support for American involvement in foreign affairs. These dimensions are more general than comparison of attitudes on specific bills would be. At the same time, they are more specific than the abstract notions of liberalism and conservatism.

Miller and Stokes were concerned with how much control, or power, constituents had over their representatives in these three policy areas. In each policy area, they found that there was not total agreement between the attitudes of congressmen and their roll-call voting records, indicating that something other than personal preference was important in determining voting behavior on the floor of Congress.

In analyzing the degree of agreement between congressmen and their constituents, Miller and Stokes found differences among policy areas. The highest agreement was in the area of civil rights. There was also considerable agreement regarding social and economic welfare. On questions of foreign affairs there was very little agreement, indicating perhaps that congressmen are responsive to party policy, the national constituency, and international affairs when issues of a nondomestic nature are involved.

THE DYNAMICS OF CONSTITUENCY INFLUENCE

Miller and Stokes posit three conditions for constituency influence in the Congress. First, the representative must be able to

---

[15] See Duncan MacRae, Jr., *Dimensions of Congressional Voting: A Statistical Study of the House of Representatives in the Eighty-First Congress* (Berkeley: The University of California Press, 1958).

determine his behavior as a legislator on the basis of his own policy views or his perception of the views of his constituents. If he is held, for example, to a strict party position, he is not free to represent the will of his constituency. Second, the attitudes that the representative holds, or his perceptions of the views of his constituents, must agree substantially with the views that his constituents do in fact hold. That is, he must either be like them or have a good idea of what they are like politically, and he must vote in Congress on that basis. Third, the constituency must take the policy views of candidates into account in choosing a representative. In a sense, the district must not only elect a representative; it must also elect to be represented.

This last condition is the weak link in the chain.[16] The low level of political information in the American public precludes the kind of rational decisions on the part of the electorate that would lead to constituency influence in the best of all possible worlds. Yet just as the automobile market operates in the presence of large numbers of consumers who know nothing about how automobiles work, so does the political market operate in the presence of voters who know little or nothing about political issues.

Miller and Stokes, like other scholars before them, confirmed the low level of political communication in America. Of the constituents living in congressional districts in which there was a contest between the major parties in 1958, fewer than 20 percent of those interviewed said that they had read or heard something about both candidates. More than half said that they had read or heard nothing about either candidate. Most voters choose their congressmen on the same basis as they buy automobiles—by brand name. About 84 percent of the vote in 1958 was cast by party identifiers voting their usual party line. If they bought Democratic before and were relatively satisfied, they bought Democratic again.

However, interviews with congressmen indicated that they *believed* that their constituents were familiar with their records.[17] Ironically, it is this misperception that makes representatives

---

[16] See Joseph A. Schumpeter, *Capitalism, Socialism and Democracy* (New York: Harper & Row, Publishers, 1950), Chapter 22.

[17] For a discussion of this phenomenon in other political contexts, see John W. Kingdon, "Politicians' Beliefs About Voters," *American Political Science Review* 59 (March 1967), pp. 137–145.

responsible to their constituencies. In a sense, the congressman's perception is biased by the social networks that tie his constituency to him. The people who write him letters, who visit him in Washington, or who attend meetings when he is back home are those who do have an interest in and knowledge about politics. Since he does not see the ones who are uninvolved, he takes the views of those he does hear from to be representative.

That congressmen are misled by the small but visible politically involved segment of the electorate is a major reason that the electoral marketplace functions. Ford and General Motors do not compete for the whole automobile-buying public. They compete for marginal increments in their sales. In much the same way, elections are won or lost on the basis of marginal increments, and the politically aware voters may provide that margin. Each party may get the support of 40 percent of the voters who turn out on the basis of party loyalty alone. It is the way that the other 20 percent of the vote is split that will determine the election. The way that the incumbent has responded to the demands of this vocal 20 percent, in turn, will affect the division of its vote.

The first two conditions suggested by Miller and Stokes receive more direct empirical support than the last. Their data indicated that the attitudes of a representative and his perception of the attitudes of his constituents each contributed to the determination of his voting pattern in Congress. Thus, to the extent that a congressman shared the political attitudes of his constituents or correctly perceived what those attitudes were, the will of the constituency was represented.

The degree of correspondence between a representative's attitudes and perception of his constituents' attitudes, on the one hand, and the true attitudes of his constituents, on the other, varied greatly among the three issue areas considered. Congressmen were most likely to correctly perceive the attitudes of their constituents, and to agree with those attitudes, in the area of federal action to protect the civil rights of black Americans. Agreement was lower, and misperception of constituent attitudes higher, in the area of social welfare. It was lower still with regard to American involvement in foreign affairs.

This study suggests that congressmen are indeed responsive to constituent demands when they participate in congressional deliberations in the area of civil rights. When the issue shifts to social welfare, however, the attitudes of the local constituency decrease in importance and the position of the political party on a national level comes to the fore. Democratic congressmen are likely to favor, and Republican congressmen to oppose, the extension of the welfare state.

In the area of foreign affairs, congressmen in 1958 were not very responsive either to constituency interests or to national party platforms. Rather, legislative initiative in this area on the whole was low, and the executive branch of the government had preempted this arena, making bipartisan foreign policy that was routinely approved by the Congress. This turn of events led Miller and Stokes to suggest that there were parallels between the political roles of elites and masses, as perceived by Edmund Burke, and the political roles of the president and Congress in the area of foreign affairs in 1958. Just as Burke's representative was presumed to act in the interest of his constituents on the basis of information and skills that were not available to them, so is the president able to summon resources, frequently in the form of classified intelligence reports, that are not widely available either to the voters or to their congressmen. Whether this reflects a trend in American politics or a cyclical fluctuation, or indeed random movement, remains to be seen. Congressional action early in the 1970s on foreign aid appropriations and military expenditures certainly suggest an attempt on the part of the Congress to once again share initiative in the field of foreign affairs with the executive branch of the government.

CONGRESSIONAL REPRESENTATION AND THE STRUCTURE OF IDEOLOGY

Two approaches to the study of attitudes in the political marketplace have been suggested in this chapter. One posits the applicability of a single liberalism-conservatism dimension. It assumes that all of a person's attitudes on political issues will be consistent with his position on this dimension. The other suggests consistency within issue areas, and leaves open the question of consistency among areas. While the issue of attitude structure in the political sphere is as yet unresolved, we may look at the current state-of-the-art and discuss its implications for the linkages between constituencies and their representatives.

There is in fact a contradiction between the linkages Miller and Stokes presumed to exist between the electorate and the Congress in specific issue areas, on the one hand, and research on attitude organization among the mass electorate, on the other. In particular, several studies have suggested that popular attitudes are not structured highly within issue areas that Miller and Stokes postulate to exist. In addition, recent research on legislative voting behavior suggests that the dimensions of economic and noneconomic liberalism noted above may better describe the pattern of roll-call voting in Congress than do the issue areas used by Miller and Stokes.[18]

Many of the discrepancies in descriptions of the structure of political attitudes come from independent analyses of the same bodies of data. One analysis of a major survey of the 1956 presidential election, for example, produced measures of attitudes toward domestic welfare and foreign policy issues that suggested a structuring of attitudes within these domains.[19] A later analysis of the same data, using somewhat different statistical techniques, failed to uncover the same structure.[20] Instead, a cluster of interrelated items was discovered that included domestic welfare and nonwelfare issues and foreign policy issues. The author defined this cluster of items as a measure of "populism."

The most intensive attempt to identify the structure of political attitudes held by the electorate is a study by Philip Converse.[21] Converse analyzed the data collected in the Survey Research Center's 1958 congressional election study in an attempt to discover the degree of mutual constraint among political attitudes. That is, he was interested in the association between holding one attitude regarding a specific issue and holding other attitudes on other issues. He did show that attitudes within the domestic policy area or within the foreign policy area were more strongly related to each other than were relationships between attitudes that crosscut the domestic-foreign difference. However, even the relationships within domestic or foreign arenas were weak. This finding is consistent with other research on attitudes

---

[18] See Aage R. Clausen, "Measurement Identity in the Longitudinal Analysis of Legislative Voting," *American Political Science Review* 61 (December 1967), pp. 1020–1035. For another analysis building on the work of Miller and Stokes, see Charles F. Cnudde and Donald J. McCrone, "The Linkage Between Constituency Attitudes and Congressional Voting," *American Political Science Review* 60 (1966), pp. 66–72.

[19] Campbell, Converse, Miller, and Stokes, *The American Voter.*

[20] Robert Axelrod, "The Structure of Public Opinion on Policy Issues," *Public Opinion Quarterly* 31 (Spring 1967), pp. 55–60.

[21] Philip E. Converse, "The Structure of Belief Systems in Mass Publics," in David Apter, ed., *Ideology and Discontent* (New York: The Free Press, 1964), pp. 206–261. For a general discussion of the structure of belief systems, see Giovanni Sartori, "Politics, Ideology and Belief Systems," *American Political Science Review* 63 (June 1969), pp. 398–401.

toward international relations which has shown, for instance, that even in the relatively narrow field of national security, electoral attitudes are not highly structured.[22] It is, however, inconsistent with a wide range of social psychological theory which suggests strains toward consistency in the attitudes held by a person.[23]

A third analysis of the 1958 congressional election data yielded yet another cluster of interrelated attitudes, including one item from each of the three areas discussed by Miller and Stokes: social welfare, civil rights, and internationalism.[24] All three items concerned the degree to which government should participate in these three areas of life. They thus provide a measure of attitudes toward scope of governmental power. Moreover, they do so in such a way as to discriminate positions on the liberalism-conservatism dimension as defined by Downs.[25] We have therefore come full circle in our discussion of the organization of political attitudes.

In order to study the relationship between liberalism-conservatism so conceived and legislative behavior, the average scores of constituents were computed in the thirty-six districts studied in which twenty or more respondents were interviewed. Miller and Stokes had studied all 116 districts in which interviews were taken, but they weighted the districts differentially in terms of the number of people interviewed. Therefore, these thirty-six districts were the most important ones in their analysis.

The mean constituency scores in these districts were compared with the ways the congressmen from these districts had voted on moves to limit federal spending in 1958, another measure of scope of government or liberalism-conservatism. In the six districts in the sample that elected someone other than the incumbent to Congress in November 1958, the correlation between the two measures was −.63. Since this figure was based on only six cases, it must be interpreted with great caution. It does

[22] See Davis B. Bobrow, "Organization of American National Security Opinions," *Public Opinion Quarterly* 33 (Summer 1969), pp. 223–239.

[23] See, for example, William N. McPhee et al., "Attitude Consistency," in William N. McPhee and William A. Glaser, eds., *Public Opinion and Congressional Elections* (New York: The Free Press, 1962), pp. 78–120. Also Roy T. Bowles and James T. Richardson, "Sources of Consistency of Political Opinion," *American Journal of Sociology* 74 (May 1969), pp. 676–684.

[24] David R. Segal and Thomas S. Smith, "Congressional Responsibility and the Organization of Constituency Attitudes," *Social Science Quarterly* 51 (December 1970), pp. 743–749.

[25] Downs, *An Economic Theory of Democracy*.

suggest, however, that where there is a bad fit between a constituency's political attitudes and the voting record of its representative in Congress, that representative will be replaced. Among the thirty districts that returned their incumbent congressmen for another term in 1958, the correlation was .43, suggesting some relationship between congressional responsiveness and reelection. Thus we find that, even with alternative ways of conceptualizing constituency opinion, there is evidence that the congressman, either because he shares the attitudes of his constituents or because he correctly perceives their attitudes, does reflect their wishes.

4

Social Cleavage
in Modern Democracy

THE ABSENCE OF ISSUE SALIENCE

We have seen in the preceding chapter that only a minority of American voters view the political world in terms of a left-right ideological spectrum. More generally, we know that political issues do not explain people's party preferences at election time. On any given issue, only a minority of the American electorate is likely to express an opinion and perceive that the political parties differ in their positions.[1] Even where people hold positions on issues that are consistent with their political-party identification (and many people do),[2] their voting behavior seems to be based on their identification with a party, and not on the basis of their issue positions. Given the fact that people are tied to the polity through identification with a political party, the question we must ask is what determines party identification.

At a very elementary level, most individuals learn their party preference from their parents at a very young age and carry it with

---

[1] For example, see Campbell, Converse, Miller, and Stokes, *The American Voter*, Chapter 8.

[2] See Key, *Public Opinion and American Democracy*, p. 445.

them through their lives. This phenomenon of political socialization will be dealt with in a later chapter. To take it as the answer to the question before us now would require that we explain the party identification of the parental generation, which in turn could also be explained by socialization, leading us no closer to an answer. At present, we cannot concern ourselves with why a particular *individual* identifies with the Democratic Party or the Republican Party. Rather, we must be concerned with why certain *social groupings* are aligned with one of the major parties, while other groupings are aligned with the other.

Some studies have sought to demonstrate that the American electorate does behave rationally, casting ballots in order to elect officials who will favor given policy positions.[3] The shortcoming of this approach is that, at best, it demonstrates that most of the members of the electorate have some issues in mind at election time.[4] It has *not* been shown that the same issues are important to large numbers of voters in the same election, or that the same issues are going to be salient to a group of voters over time. Thus, while this approach can explain why some voters cast their ballots in a particular manner in a particular election, it cannot explain the persisting ties between groups of voters and political parties. To explain these ties, we must look at the social structure of American society.

SOCIAL STRUCTURE AND POLITICAL CLEAVAGE: THREE APPROACHES

The study of the social bases of political cleavage has gone through three somewhat overlapping periods in the twentieth century. The first, lasting roughly until the middle of the century, emphasized social stratification as the basis of political cleavage. A wide range of approaches to the study of stratification were prevalent, but the dominant concern was whether, and to what degree, the political system reflected the class or status systems of modern society. Much of political sociology during those years

[3] See, for example, V. O. Key, Jr., *The Responsible Electorate* (Cambridge: Harvard University Press, 1966).

[4] David E. RePass, "Issue Salience and Party Choice," *American Political Science Review* 65 (June 1971), pp. 389–400.

was concerned with research at the local community level and/or the analysis of aggregate census-type data and voting records, and inferences regarding the national political system were difficult, although they were attempted. The second stage, reflecting the political calm of the mid-twentieth century, focused on the decline of class conflict, the "end of ideology," and the dawning of an era of political consensus, all of which were thought to have been brought on by the maintenance of high levels of affluence and concomitant changes in social stratification in the industrial nations of the West. Sociologists of the third era, beginning in the late 1960s, have been forced to concern themselves with the question of why, in these affluent states, consensus has not been achieved, and why political conflict is widespread.

SOCIAL STRATIFICATION AND POLITICS

The theoretical underpinnings of the first era were drawn from the works of Karl Marx and Max Weber. For Marx, class conflict was an enduring state of human life. Class conflict in industrial society, in the Marxian view, is a stage in the historical progression of conflict in which the "manifold gradation of social rank" prevalent under earlier forms of social organization, such as feudalism, is simplified into a dichotomization of social rank based upon ownership of the means of production. Thus the population of an industrialized society is presumed to be composed of two classes, the owners, who are employers, and the nonowners, who are employees. These groups are presumed to have opposing interests. In the Marxian view, the economy is the substructure, or base, of the entire social organization. Politics, as a superstructure, merely reflects the economic system.[5] Thus, the political party system is seen as a reflection of these class-based antagonisms, with one party representing the interests of the owners, or capitalists, and another representing the interests of labor, or the proletariat. In the extreme case, the state itself is seen as the tool of the capitalists, and the only way that labor may have its interests represented by the government is through revolution. Early empirical research in the United States did not assume the

---

[5] See Karl Marx, *Capital,* 3 vols. (Moscow: Foreign Languages Publishing House, 1962), especially Vol. 3. Also, Karl Marx and Friedrich Engels, *The Communist Manifesto* (New York: International Publishers Co., Inc., 1948).

necessity of revolution, but did focus on the relationship between economic interests and political power.[6]

Much of the recent work done within a neo-Marxian framework assumes that the working class can exert leverage on the state through the normal operations of the electoral system and its political parties. Seymour Martin Lipset, for example, wrote:

> More than anything else the party struggle is a conflict among classes, and the most impressive single fact about political party support is that . . . the lower income groups vote mainly for parties of the left, while the higher income groups vote mainly for parties of the right. . . . The leftist parties represent themselves as instruments of social change in the direction of equality; the lower income groups support them in order to become economically better off, while the higher income groups oppose them in order to maintain their economic advantage.[7]

Lipset's own research, and that of other scholars, shows political parties in the Western world developing as instruments of class interests. One cross-national study, for example, finds Australia and Great Britain to be "class-polarized" political systems, with voting determined by occupation, union membership, and subjective social class identification. Political parties in these countries are viewed as representing economic class interests.[8]

The perspective derived from the work of Max Weber differs from that built on Marxian bases in three important ways. First, Weber had a more differentiated view of the economic system than Marx did. Class, for Weber, derived both from the possession of material goods and from the opportunity to get them. These opportunities, in turn, were determined by a person's positions in the economic markets. Unlike Marx, who saw the labor market as the key to economic organization, Weber considered the operation of three markets. In each market, one could be in either a superior

---

[6] Among the studies in this tradition, see Arthur N. Holcombe, *The Political Parties of Today* (New York: Harper & Row, Publishers, 1924); John D. Barnhart, "Rainfall and the Populist Vote in Nebraska," *American Political Science Review* 19 (1925), pp. 527–40; William F. Ogburn and Lolagene C. Coombs, "The Economic Factor in the Roosevelt Elections," *American Political Science Review* 34 (1940), pp. 719–727.

[7] Seymour Martin Lipset, *Political Man* (New York: Doubleday & Co., Inc., 1963), p. 239.

[8] Robert Alford, *Party and Society* (Chicago: Rand McNally & Co., 1963).

or a subordinate position. In the labor market, the employer is superior to the employee; in the credit market, the creditor to the debtor; in the commodity market, the producer to the consumer.[9] Second, Weber, unlike Marx, recognized that status, or social honor, does not correlate perfectly with economic position. Weber pointed out that there is a relationship between economic class and social status, but that status groups cut across class lines. The university professor, for example, is not self-employed and is not a producer of goods, yet he may share the same social status as a member of the landed gentry. Unlike economic classes based on similar market position, status groups, to Weber, were characterized both by a sense of membership and by a common life-style.

Third, where Marx stressed the composition of economic classes holding divergent values and supporting ideologically opposed political parties, to the exclusion of other considerations, the Weberian perspective includes an organizational or institutional component. Rather than viewing political parties as mere reflections of economic interest groups, this perspective takes formal and informal party leadership into account. The party organization is viewed as an independent and voluntaristic component of political change, exerting influence over its base of support, rather than merely reflecting group interests. Thus, the Weberian view includes the composition of the elite and the technologies of the mass media as elements of political analysis.[10] We have already discussed linkages between officeholders and their constituents, and some political functions of the media of mass communication. Themes such as these will recur in this book.

STATUS POLITICS

The concept of class politics is easier to grasp than is the concept of status politics. In the former, material well-being is at stake, and most people can easily see how groups might fight for their economic interests in the political marketplace. It is less intuitively clear what is at stake in status politics, and how it differs, in form or content, from class politics.

[9] Max Weber, *Economy and Society*, ed. Guenther Roth and Claus Wittich (Totowa, N.J.: Bedminster Press, 1968), pp. 952 ff.

[10] For a discussion of this difference between Marxist and Weberian perspectives, see Morris Janowitz, *Political Conflict* (Chicago: Quadrangle Books, Inc., 1970), pp. 7–9.

The concept of status politics in the American case has most commonly been used to explain waves of right-wing political sentiment during periods of economic affluence. Historian Richard Hofstadter, for example, has argued that in times of economic discontent, depression, or national emergency, the issues of politics have to do with material interests. In times of economic well-being, on the other hand, political cleavages come to reflect status politics, "the clash of various projective rationalizations arising from status aspirations and other personal motives."[11] These strivings, as Hofstadter conceived of them, are only partially conscious, and are manifested by two very different segments of society.

Long-established Anglo-Saxon Protestants, who were once far more dominant in American politics than they are today, feel that they have a claim to status by virtue of their ancestry, but are being deprived of their rightful place in the American social structure. At the other end of the social spectrum, recent immigrant groups experience status anxieties associated with establishing themselves as true Americans, partly because they have been made to feel inferior by "native Americans." Both the old Yankees and the new immigrants, in seeking assurance that they have a place in American society, become defenders of what they perceive to be the principles for which America stands, and opponents of the enemies of the American way of life—communists, and, by extension, socialists, liberals, and political nonconformists.

Seymour Martin Lipset parallels Hofstadter's discussion in his own analysis of the radical right in American politics. Lipset sees status politics giving rise to political movements rooted in the strivings of groups or individuals seeking to either maintain or improve their social status. Such groups come to the fore in periods of full employment and inflation, when many people are able to improve their economic positions and to rival groups that had previously established themselves economically.[12] In such times, status anxiety is experienced by people who have advanced themselves economically and must strive to be accepted *socially* at their new economic levels. It is also experienced by groups who have inherited prestigious positions in American society and are

[11] Richard Hofstadter, "The Pseudo-Conservative Revolt," in Daniel Bell, ed., *The Radical Right* (New York: Doubleday & Co., Inc., 1969), p. 84.

[12] Seymour Martin Lipset, "The Sources of the Radical Right," in Bell, ed., *The Radical Right*, pp. 307–371.

suddenly confronted by newcomers who, on the basis of recent economic gains, claim to be their equals.

The political consequences of status anxiety are very different from those of economic class interests. An economic class can rationally pursue its goals in the political marketplace because its goal is clear and because governmental policy can affect its fulfillment. It wishes either to bring about a redistribution of economic resources or to maintain the status quo. Once relative economic well-being has been redistributed through economic prosperity, there is little the political parties or the government can do about the distribution of status. The response of status-anxious groups, therefore, has been the irrational persecution of groups that symbolize the status threat: political enemies, minority ethnic or religious groups, etc. Thus, the American Protective Association of the late nineteenth century opposed the Catholics, the Progressive movement of the early twentieth century opposed immigrants, and the Ku Klux Klan opposed Jews, Catholics, and blacks.

Seven years after Hofstadter and Lipset published their respective thoughts on status politics and the right wing, Hofstadter had second thoughts. "It now seems doubtful," he wrote in 1962, "that the term 'status politics' . . . is an adequate term for what I had in mind. . . . The term 'status' requires supplementation. If we were to speak of 'cultural politics,' we might supply part of what is missing."[13] What he was referring to was the presence in the body politic of differences in religious and moral convictions, ethnic differences, and other sources of subcultural variations. In specifying that there was no single status dimension in the American system, Hofstadter was anticipating recent theoretical and empirical work on the relationship between ethnicity and politics. As we shall see in later sections, there is an important ethnic component in American political alignments. And the best evidence available suggests that it is the persistence of subcultural differences, rather than the status ordering of ethnic groups, that best explains these alignments.

SOCIAL STRATIFICATION AND COMMUNITY POWER

One of the earliest and most influential studies of the association between social stratification and community power was

---

[13] Richard Hofstadter, "Pseudo-Conservatism Revisited," in Bell, ed., *The Radical Right*, pp. 98–99.

Floyd Hunter's analysis of decision makers in Atlanta, Georgia, in the 1940s.[14] Hunter compiled a list of over 175 people who were leaders of civic, professional, fraternal, business, and governmental organizations, or who represented local "society," or "wealth." The persons on this list were rated by a group of "judges," who selected the top forty persons on the total list. Interviews were then held with the leaders to determine, among other things, relative rankings and degree of contact among them. A small group of men, primarily presidents of companies or chairmen of boards of directors, were identified as occupying the apex of the "power pyramid" in Atlanta. Thus, business was seen to dominate civic affairs. The lower level of the power structure, men concerned with the execution rather than the formulation of policy, was composed of leaders of voluntary associations. The voluntary associations, then, could be seen as a training ground for public policy making. The voluntary-association leader, however, could not expect to move up to the top policy-making stratum unless he held a major position in the economic structure. Hunter viewed the decision-making process very much in terms of a Marxian model of economic determinism.

A somewhat different view of community power and its relationship to social stratification is manifested in Robert Dahl's developmental analysis of political power in New Haven, Connecticut.[15] Dahl saw New Haven politics as dominated by its economic elite (which was elite in every other area of social life as well) in the period from 1784 to 1842, but he argued that, over time, political power came to be more widely shared.

In the early period, New Haven was run by its "established families." The typical mayor of New Haven in those years came from one of these families, had been educated at the local university (Yale), and spent most of his life in public affairs. Thus, wealth, education, social status, and political office were all concentrated in the hands of a small proportion of the population. This group was conservative and socially homogeneous, had virtually complete control of the community, and operated in a social climate conducive to the maintenance of that control. The local political model was one of "town-meeting democracy," in which citizens could make their views known. In this model, voting was not by secret ballot, but by voiced preferences. A

---

[14] Floyd Hunter, *Community Power Structure* (Chapel Hill: The University of North Carolina Press, 1953).

[15] Robert A. Dahl, *Who Governs?* (New Haven: Yale University Press, 1961).

person disagreeing with the preferred policies of the local elite would have to say so publicly, in its presence. It is not surprising that the solid middle-class shopkeepers of the town agreed, at least publicly, with the elite bankers, who held mortgages on their properties. The artisans, who perhaps manifested a more egalitarian ideology, were disenfranchised because of property requirements. The maintenance of control by the elite was supported, moreover, by the dominant Calvinist ideology, according to which the "established families" were classified as members of "the elect."

The demise of this power structure did not occur of an instant. After 1800, the structures and processes that concentrated control in the hands of the established families of New Haven began to deteriorate. With politics at the national level dominated by the Jeffersonians, strength of numbers became an important political resource. With the advent of the secret ballot, the spread of suffrage, the decline of property requirements for voting, the growth of population, the mobilization of voters by evolving political parties seeking mass bases of support, and the spread of an egalitarian political ideology, the dominance of public life by the established families decreased. From 1842 to 1900, a new kind of wealth came to dominate local politics—the new wealth of the self-made man. The new political elite, like the old, came from old families, but not from *wealthy* old families. In Marxian terms, this transformation of the elite might be seen as the triumph of the industrial bourgeoisie over the old aristocracy. As the American political-party system evolved into Democratic and Republican organizations, both parties sought to nominate industrialists to public office in New Haven.

Karl Marx proposed that capitalism sows the seeds of its own destruction by creating an industrial proletariat that will eventually revolt against the repression of the capitalist bourgeoisie. The industrialization of New Haven, while giving capitalist entrepreneurs the dominant position in local politics in the short run, did pave the way for the ascendence of the urban proletariat in the polity. This rise, however, took place without revolution.

As industry expanded in America and entrepreneurs turned new wealth into political power, the labor force also grew, largely through immigration. In New Haven, as the population swelled with immigrants of diverse ethnic backgrounds, local politics became ethnic politics. As the ward system evolved and aldermen were elected to city government to represent local territorial units, immigrants found their way into politics, representing wards with high concentrations of fellow immigrants. Once in office, they were able to help open up channels of social mobility for themselves and for other members of their ethnic group.

Dahl suggested a three-stage model of ethnic political assimilation. In the first stage, the members of the immigrant group are almost exclusively working class, and the interests of the immigrants are homogeneously class-based interests. In the second phase, the group becomes more socioeconomically heterogeneous, as some members attain white-collar occupations through upward social mobility. The ethnic issues in this stage are cultural rather than socioeconomic. In the last stage, the ethnic group becomes assimilated in the great American melting pot, and ethnic politics becomes irrelevant. In later sections, we shall see how the cleavage between blue-collar and white-collar occupations is not as severe as it was formerly, how social mobility among ethnic immigrants may be regarded as a curse as well as a blessing, and how the final stage of ethnic assimilation seems not to have been attained, Dahl's theory notwithstanding. For the moment, however, let us focus on the processes that produced ethnic politics and the political ascendancy of the working class in New Haven.

As the electoral base of immigrant ethnic groups in New Haven grew, both the Democratic and Republican parties, which had previously directed their appeals at the industrialists, made overtures to the ethnic communities. The Democratic Party established ties with the Irish Catholic communities, while the Republican Party moved somewhat later into the Italian wards. Note that contrary to the "common knowledge" that Catholics tend to be aligned with the Democratic Party, we find the political allegiances of New Haven's Catholics divided along ethnic lines.

Early in the twentieth century, the Irish in New Haven controlled both the Democratic and the Republican parties, and by 1933 the Irish were the most numerous group on the city payrolls. Using their political position to create channels for social mobility, they managed to occupy 50 percent of the city jobs, although only 13 percent of the families in New Haven were Irish. By midcentury, the Irish were moving rapidly into business and professional positions in New Haven. Manufacturers and executives of large corporations, in the meanwhile, were excluded from the top elective offices in the city.

In 1945, an Italian Catholic won the mayoralty as a Republican, manifesting the upward mobility of a second immigrant ethnic group. The dominance of the Irish in governmental jobs made it difficult for more recently arrived immigrants to use the civil service as a channel of social mobility, but through the 1940s Italians were moving into powerful positions in the Republican Party, and, Dahl argued, the Italian community reached the second stage of political assimilation. Ethnic politics, he suggested, was declining. After 1953, the Democratic Party actively competed with the Republican Party for the Italian vote.

Ethnic politics appears in Dahl's formulation as an intervening stage between class politics dominated by the upper classes, old and new, and class politics dominated by the offspring of ethnic immigrant groups. However, it is not clear that the last stage of class politics has arrived. Although class has become a more salient issue in New Haven politics, according to Dahl, the politics of ethnicity are still very much in evidence on the New Haven scene.

Our discussion of the structure of community power, in comparing Hunter's Atlanta with Dahl's New Haven, has thus far been confined to differences in their evaluations of the role of economic class in the polity. Hunter saw dominant economic position as the primary political resource, while Dahl saw first old wealth, then new wealth, and finally strength of numbers as the primary resource. This difference in perceptions of the role of social stratification is reflected in differences in strategies for studying the decision-making process itself.

Hunter presumed that decisions were made by the social and economic elite of Atlanta. Therefore, he felt that the formal structure of politics and government would not reveal the true decision-making process in the community. Dahl, on the other hand, having demonstrated the decline of social and economic dominance, proceeded to analyze decision making in three issue areas in New Haven: the nomination process within political parties, decisions regarding urban redevelopment, and decisions regarding public education. He found that, contrary to the picture presented by Hunter, very few social notables participated overtly in public affairs. Some were active with regard to urban redevelopment, and indeed one would expect them to be on the basis of self-interest. As property owners they were concerned with property values. However, they did not dominate the political arena.

Economic notables in the community participated more in public affairs than did social notables. They too were concerned mostly with urban redevelopment, and like the social notables, they did not dominate the political scene. The decision-making model that emerges from Dahl's analysis is one in which decisions are made by people in elective or appointed decision-making positions in the political party and governmental structures, and groups or individuals whose self-interests are at stake have the opportunity to try to influence the process in their own favor. This would seem to be a reasonable form of the operation of democratic politics to which to aspire.

Scholars interested in community power structure have been disturbed by the discrepancy between Hunter's model and that suggested by Dahl.[16] However, it is not difficult to imagine that Atlanta did in fact have a different power structure in the 1940s than New Haven did in the 1950s. Given the fact that the ascendance of the working classes to political power in New Haven was based on industrialization, one might in fact expect that Atlanta, industrializing somewhat later, would experience a later political mobilization as well. Indeed, a later study of Atlanta did suggest that many important business and economic personalities in that city exercised relatively little political power, and that the city was not ruled, as Hunter had found, by a highly cohesive economic elite. Rather, it was the people who occupied clearly political positions who played the major role in decision making.[17]

The passage of a decade in all probability did account for change in the power structure of Atlanta, Georgia. It is also important to recognize, however, that the methods one uses to study community power structures seem to have some impact on the kind of power structure one discovers. A study of Burlington, North Carolina, combined Hunter's "reputational method" (asking people to list and rank-order the most powerful members of the community) and a method based on leaders.[18] These data taken together suggested three different types of community leaders, which in turn had different configurations across the stratification dimensions of class, status, and power.

First, there were *visible leaders,* who were regarded as leaders by nonleaders and other leaders alike. That is, they played leadership roles, and were recognized as playing these roles by

---

[16] See, for example, William E. Connolly, *Political Science and Ideology* (New York: Atherton Press, Inc., 1967). For an overview of the field, see Nelson W. Polsby, "The Study of Community Power," in David L. Sills, ed., *International Encyclopedia of the Social Sciences,* vol. 3 (New York: Crowell Collier and Macmillan, Inc., 1968), pp. 157–163.

[17] M. Kent Jennings, *Community Influentials* (New York: The Free Press, 1964).

[18] Charles M. Bonjean, "Community Leadership," *American Journal of Sociology* 68 (May 1963), pp. 672–681.

the population. This type had a uniformly high configuration across the dimensions of class, status, and power.

Second, there were *symbolic leaders.* These were people who were regarded as leaders by the population, but who did not have as much power as the community attributed to them. They were high in class and status, but low in power. Such people, for example, tended to be wealthy, but not to participate in political decision making.

Third, there were *concealed leaders.* These people were regarded as members of the leadership stratum by other leaders, but their leadership roles were not recognized by the public at large. They were low in class and status, but high in power. Although not holding visibly high positions in the stratification system, they influenced political decisions.

An alternative typology emerged from a study of community power in Syracuse, N.Y.[19] Here five factors were used: reputation, decision-making ability, social position, voluntary activity, and organizational participation. These varying procedures did not indicate a single set of leaders. However, there was overlap among the elite strata defined by these varying methods. The pattern of this overlap suggested three basic types of leaders.

First, there were those who were revealed by reputational study to be regarded as the top leadership of the community. As was the case in Hunter's study, these people tended to be the heads of economic organizations, and were categorized as *institutional leaders.* These institutional leaders, however, tended not to be active participants in community affairs. They were thus similar to the reputational *symbolic leaders* of Burlington.

The major burden of effecting community change in Syracuse was carried by the *effectors*—government personnel and professional participants, as well as middle-management personnel in the large corporations. A somewhat less effective role was played by the *activists:* officeholders in voluntary organizations, community service organizations, and clubs. These people were similar to those who appeared at the lower strata of the power elite in Hunter's study of Atlanta.

The picture that emerges from these studies of the relationship between social stratification (and particularly economic class) and community power is one of change. The portion of Dahl's study devoted to the early years of New Haven and the

---

[19] Linton C. Freeman, Thomas J. Fararo, Warner Bloomberg, Jr., and Morris H. Sunshine, "Locating Leaders in Local Communities," *American Sociological Review* 28 (October 1963), pp. 791–798.

early study of Atlanta both suggest control of the local political system by economic dominants. The portion devoted to the later years of New Haven and the studies of Burlington, Syracuse, and other communities[20] suggest some persistence of the image of economic dominants acting as political dominants as well. The real functioning of politics and government, however, at least at the local community level, seems to be directed by political officials and government employees, with latitude for representatives of interest groups to enter the political arena and influence the authoritative allocation of values.

STRUCTURAL CHANGE AND THE POLITICS OF CONSENSUS

The above section indicates a movement away from class-based models of political life at the local community level. In like manner, in the mid-twentieth century the general theoretical trend of Western political sociology was away from models of class conflict, and toward consensual models of political life.[21] The years from 1945 to 1965 were seen as a period of "deideologization."[22] In the following section we shall deal with some of the changes in social structure, and concomitant changes in political ideology, that were thought to underlie the politics of consensus.

THE CONVERGENCE THEME

Twentieth-century models of class conflict, as they appeared in Western political sociology, assumed a Marxist notion of class structure. That is, they assumed great differentials between the economic interests and well-being of the working class and those of the middle class. They also assumed the relevance of a major political ideology manifesting the interests of each group: communism and socialism emphasizing the interests of the working

---

[20] See especially Robert O. Schulze, "The Bifurcation of Power in a Satellite City," in Morris Janowitz, ed., *Community Political Systems* (New York: The Free Press, 1961).

[21] See, for example, Ulf Torgerson, "The Trend Toward Political Consensus," in Erik Alardt and Stein Rokkan, eds., *Mass Politics* (New York: The Free Press, 1970), p. 93.

[22] Stein Rokkan, "International Cooperation in Political Sociology," in Alardt and Rokkan, eds., *Mass Politics*, p. 20.

class, and capitalism reflecting the interests of the middle class. In the European nations with multiparty systems, this range was completely represented. In the United States, in the absence of major communist and socialist contenders for political power, it was assumed that the Democratic Party leaned in a more socialistic or welfare-state direction, while the Republican Party leaned in a more capitalistic direction.

The cleavage between left and right in any given national context was seen as a reflection of the cleavage between the capitalist and communist blocks in the international system. Indeed, the promise of communism for the working class was the progress of a communist revolution and the dominance of a communist ideology, in theory if not in practice, in the USSR, one of the two superpowers. In symbolic terms, at least, the aspirations of workers with leftist political sentiments in noncommunist nations were tied to the success of communism in communist nations. Conversely, increased similarity between political systems associated with communistic and capitalistic economies would theoretically erode the underpinnings of ideological differentiation between left and right in any given national context.

The convergence of social structures in communistic and capitalistic societies was anticipated by economist Joseph Schumpeter. Schumpeter argued that, for a variety of reasons, the institutional structures of capitalist society would eventually collapse under the weight of the success of that very system.[23] By routinizing innovation, the capitalist entrepreneur would be denied his social role. Through increases in the scale of productive enterprise, property would become depersonalized and the entrepreneur would become alienated. By educating an intelligentsia that throve on criticism and was not dependent on an aristocracy for financial support, capitalism was providing the leadership that would mobilize the hostility of the masses toward the capitalist system.

Schumpeter's analysis has Marxian undertones in its anticipation of widespread hostility among the masses who are alienated from property. It departs from Marx in expecting the capitalist bourgeoisie, which has begun to function in a collectivist and routinized manner, to join with the masses in questioning the capitalist ethic. The trend that Schumpeter anticipated philosophically and thought he saw evolving historically was

---

[23] Schumpeter, *Capitalism, Socialism and Democracy.*

toward socialism, with control over productive enterprise being wielded collectively, as in mature, postentrepreneurial capitalism. In Schumpeter's view, this collective control would be in the public, rather than the private, sector. The obsolescence of a capitalist bourgeoisie, and the recognition of that obsolescence by the bourgeoisie, would eliminate one of the major economic bases of class conflict. A second major base of antagonism between social classes would be removed as well if, under democratic socialism, a redistribution of income could be achieved through rational programs of social welfare.

While the capitalist nations were posited to be moving in a socialist direction, communist nations were also thought to be moving toward democratic socialism. Scholars interested in communist society have argued that, in a system of increased literacy and affluence, the highly centralized "command economy" system of Stalinist Russia will prove untenable and the society will accept alternative forms of economic and political organization.[24]

This approach to structural convergence accepts the Marxian assumption of economic determinism, but it rejects Marx's prognosis for relationships between economic classes in industrial society. Rather than seeing capitalism leading to the increasing polarization of classes, this approach sees industrialization, whether capitalistic or communistic, leading to a decrease of existing differentials in income, in wealth, in social status, and in political power.[25] That is, this approach, while accepting Marxian sociology, rejects Marxian economics.

It is this hypothesized convergence in systems of social stratification between capitalistic and communistic societies that underlies the "age of consensus" that political sociologists not too long ago saw dawning. Before proceeding with our discussion of this age, however, let us note briefly two dissenting positions on the theme of structural convergence.

First, the assumption of economic determinism has been pointed out as a weak link in convergence theory, just as it is in orthodox Marxism. By emphasizing industrial organization generally and deemphasizing the nature of that industrial organization

[24] For discussions of the convergence phenomenon, see Peter Wiley, "Will Capitalism and Communism Spontaneously Converge?" in Morris Bornstein and Daniel Fusfield, eds., *The Soviet Economy* (Homewood, Ill.: Dorsey Press, 1966); and Jan S. Prybyla, "The Convergence of Western and Communist Systems," *Russian Review* 23 (January 1964), pp. 3–17.

[25] See, for example, Alex Inkeles, "Social Stratification in the Modernization of Russia," in Cyril E. Black, ed., *The Transformation of Russian Society* (Cambridge: Harvard University Press, 1960).

in specific national contexts, this approach underestimates the degree to which purposive social action can shape specific industrial societies and therefore contribute to structural differentials among industrial societies. In turn, as the role of purposive action is played down, so is the effect of values and ideologies which may motivate such action. That is, the social and cultural dynamics of individual societies are disregarded.[26]

A second critique of convergence theory accepts the possibility of economic determinism, but makes a pessimistic prognosis for modern society. Unlike theorists who consider the natural outcomes of industrialization to be liberalization and democratization, scholars in this tradition see both capitalistic and communistic societies converging on alienated bureaucratic, rather than democratic, social structures.

Milovan Djilas subscribes to this approach in his analysis of social stratification in communist society. The growth of bureaucracy, Djilas argues, produces a new oppressor class, composed of bureaucrats, to replace the bourgeoisie of capitalist society.[27] In this view, the decline of capitalism does not change the nature of class relations in industrial society, although it does change the composition of the classes. Bureaucracy is functional as a system of economic organization because it achieves efficiency through centralization of control. If, as in the case of democratic politics, one wishes to maximize widespread political participation and is willing to accept costs in terms of efficiency, then bureaucracy is a most unsuitable form for political organization.

One variant of the bureaucratization model foresees the military as the dominant bureaucratic structure in the political system.[28] We will consider this point of view at a later point, when we discuss the structure of the "military-industrial complex."

THE CONVERGENCE OF CLASSES IN AMERICA

The trends in social stratification anticipated in the capitalist and communist nations by the convergence theorists were noted

[26] See John H. Goldthorpe, "Social Stratification in Industrial Society," in Reinhard Bendix and Seymour Martin Lipset, eds., *Class, Status and Power,* 2nd ed. (New York: The Free Press, 1966), pp. 648–659.

[27] Milovan Djilas, *The New Class* (New York: Praeger Publishers, Inc., 1957). See Alfred G. Meyer, "Theories of Convergence," in Chalmers Johnson, ed., *Change in Communist Systems* (Stanford, Calif.: Stanford University Press, 1970).

[28] Stanislaw Andreski, *Military Organization and Society* (Berkeley: The University of California Press, 1968).

in the American context by Thorstein Veblen. Veblen had a very different view of social stratification from those put forth by Marx and Weber. Both of these latter theorists assumed large social and economic gaps between the working and middle classes. The numerically small bourgeoisie possessed property and skills, were employers of labor, had high income and advanced educations. The laboring masses, on the other hand, were primarily unskilled, uneducated, propertyless, and had different life-styles from those of the middle class. Veblen saw these differences between classes disappearing as the lines of demarcation between classes became vague and people aspired to, and achieved, the style of life enjoyed by higher social strata.[29]

The processes leading to the breakdown of rigid class boundaries in the United States are easy to specify. New technologies of production have created demands for manual workers to achieve higher levels of skill and education. The strength of labor unions has improved the economic well-being of manual workers, and increasingly enlightened social welfare and taxation policies have eroded the economic disadvantages of the working class.

In the middle class, the increased scale of production units and the increasingly specialized skills required to run them have replaced the independent entrepreneur, who dominated the early years of the industrial revolution, with a bureaucratic managerial class that, in terms of property ownership, is as alienated from the means of production as the workers are.[30] With the maturation of the American economy and the rapid expansion of the tertiary sector (service industries) relative to the primary (extractive) and secondary (manufacturing) sectors, a large corps of bureaucratic white-collar functionaries have appeared who, despite their white-collar status, have relatively low incomes.

In 1910, 11.6 percent of the United States civilian labor force was in unskilled manual occupations. By 1956 this figure had fallen to 5.5 percent. During this same period, the proportion of the total work force involved in urban manual-labor occupations increased slightly, primarily in the categories of skilled and semiskilled, rather than unskilled, labor. At the same time, there

---

[29] See Thorstein Veblen, *The Theory of the Leisure Class* (New York: The Viking Press, Inc., 1931).

[30] See C. Wright Mills, *White Collar* (New York: Oxford University Press, 1951), pp. 71–72. Of course, the argument must also be noted that, with the growth of bureaucracy, power becomes vested in the hands of the managerial class, and it is power, not ownership of property per se, with which we should be concerned. See A. A. Berle, *Power Without Property* (New York: Harcourt Brace Jovanovich, Inc., 1959).

was almost a doubling of the proportion of the labor force in white-collar occupations. In 1910, 22.3 percent of the labor force was involved in professional, managerial, clerical, and sales occupations. By 1956 this figure had increased to 39.8 percent.[31] A little over half of this latter figure was accounted for by clerical and sales personnel.

The structure of the American labor force, and the labor forces of other industrial nations undergoing the same processes, has come to be characterized by a concentration of workers in upper-working-class (skilled craftsmen such as those in the printing and building trades, foremen, and highly paid operatives) and lower-middle-class (clerical, sales, semitechnical, and semiprofessional) occupations, or a large "middle mass."[32] This is a very different structure than the polarized proletariat and bourgeoisie envisaged by Marx. One may argue either that, through affluence, the working class has undergone a process of *embourgeoisement,* or that, through being deprived of ownership of the means of production, the middle class has been absorbed by the proletariat. Either interpretation reflects a convergence of the labor force on the middle range of the occupational-prestige hierarchy.

THE END OF IDEOLOGY

We have noted above that not all writers have seen the structural trends associated with industrialization resulting in social democracy. One broad inquiry into the political ideologies of the first half of the twentieth century was conducted by Harold Lasswell and his associates and rooted in Lasswell's concern with the "world revolution of our time."[33] Lasswell saw the international system moving away from democracy and toward the establishment of "garrison states."[34]

The study involved the content analysis of editorials in the prestige newspapers in five industrial nations: the U.S., Britain,

[31] See Harold L. Wilensky and Charles N. Lebeaux, *Industrial Society and Social Welfare* (New York: The Free Press, 1965), p. 92.

[32] See Harold L. Wilensky, "Orderly Careers and Social Participation," *American Sociological Review* 26 (August 1961), pp. 521–539.

[33] Harold D. Lasswell, *The World Revolution of Our Time* (Stanford, Calif.: Stanford University Press, 1951).

[34] For an explanation of this concept, see Harold D. Lasswell, "The Garrison State," *American Journal of Sociology* 46 (1941), pp. 445–468.

France, Germany, and the USSR. It was assumed that in every country, the ideology of the ruling elite is reflected in the editorial content of the prestige newspapers. The analysis revealed that in the years 1890 to 1950 a change had indeed taken place, and that the values of democracy and internationalism were losing ground, while those of totalitarianism, militarism, conflict, and aggression were gaining.[35]

As the second half of the twentieth century dawned, a contrary trend was noted. In 1955, a conference on "The Future of Freedom" was held in Milan, Italy. The participants from the Western nations, including Daniel Bell, Seymour Martin Lipset, and Edward Shils, arrived at a consensual view on the decline of ideology. Their argument was that, largely because of increasing economic affluence in the Western industrial nations, extremist ideologies appeared to be declining. This decline was reflected in the observation that the extremes of political right and left had been shown to have similarities that were more impressive than their differences.[36] We noted this latter argument earlier in our discussion of the organization of political attitudes. It is significant that, although everyone at the Milan conference agreed that the economic trends thought to underlie the decline of ideology were taking place in all industrial nations, the non-Western scholars insisted on the continued importance of radical ideologies.

Perhaps the most widely read statement of the end-of-ideology hypothesis is Daniel Bell's essay. Bell argues that the ideologies that had emerged from the politics of nineteenth-century Europe were by the 1950s exhausted. The failure of radical ideologies to produce the good societies they promised, the calamities of Nazi and Soviet repression, the liberalization of capitalism, and the rise of the welfare state have all, in Bell's view, contributed to the decline in the attractiveness of radical political ideologies. Bell asserts, "In the Western world . . . there is today a rough consensus among intellectuals on political issues: the acceptance of a Welfare State; the desirability of decentralized power; a system of mixed economy and of political pluralism. In that sense . . . the ideological age has ended."[37]

---

[35] Daniel Lerner, Ithiel de Sola Pool, and Harold D. Lasswell, "Comparative Analysis of Political Ideology," *Public Opinion Quarterly* 15 (Winter 1951–1952), pp. 715–733.

[36] See Edward Shils, "The End of Ideology?" *Encounter* 5 (November 1955), pp. 52–58.

[37] Daniel Bell, "The End of Ideology in the West," in *The End of Ideology*, rev. ed. (New York: The Free Press, 1962), p. 402.

The "end of ideology" does not necessarily portend a disappearance of the traditional relationship between social stratification and political party choice in the industrial nations of the West. It has, however, in the view of Seymour Martin Lipset, changed the nature of class politics. Lipset argues that, on the one hand, the "fundamental political problems" of industrial society have been solved. The working class has achieved basic citizenship rights in the political and economic arenas. The left has recognized that there are dangers inherent in governmental centralization. The right has recognized that it can live with, and sometimes profit from, the welfare state. On the other hand, the electorate still seems to vote, as it has in the past, largely along class lines. "The democratic class struggle will continue," argues Lipset, "but it will be a fight without ideologies, without red flags, without May Day parades."[38]

The transformation, in Lipset's view, is a change from the politics of conflict between hostile and antagonistic economic classes to the politics of collective bargaining. In this latter model, different economic strata still have different and sometimes opposing interests, but the gap between them is diminished. Lipset sees the economic productivity of affluent industrial society bringing about a more equitable distribution of gratifications, material and nonmaterial (e.g., education). This redistribution, in turn, mitigates against interclass hostility and tension.

At the same time, some level of inequality persists in industrial society, and this residue becomes the focus of the politics of collective bargaining. The working class is receiving enough of a payoff so that it doesn't want to overthrow the political and economic system, but it seeks a still larger payoff. The working-class-based parties, therefore, maintain their support, rather than atrophying. They also move toward an ideological moderation, and become less radical in the economic reforms that they espouse. Moreover, this maintenance of support of the left by moderation of ideologies on the left is not the only structural change noted by Lipset at this end of the political spectrum. "If the workers have remained loyal to the parties of their class on election day," he writes, "they show much less commitment to these parties the rest of the year."[39] He notes losses in dues-paying

---

[38] Seymour Martin Lipset, "The End of Ideology?" in *Political Man* (New York: Doubleday & Co., Inc., 1960), p. 408.

[39] Seymour Martin Lipset, "The Changing Class Structure and Contemporary European Politics," *Daedalus* 93:1 (Winter 1964), p. 280.

party memberships and reduced circulation of party newspapers as concomitants of the decline in ideology.

Lipset notes political consequences of change in the middle classes, as well. He sees the emergence of a white-collar class composed of employees—clerks, salesmen, middle management, civil servants, and the like—as a major force for political moderation and stabilization. Such a class can, through the strength of its numbers and its central position in the stratification system, reward moderate political parties both at the polls and through financial support, and it can punish extremist parties. Its members are not bourgeois in the Marxist sense of the term, and while they may differ from manual workers in terms of life-style and values, they share with the working class concerns about social welfare and employee well-being. These common concerns mitigate against class-based conflicts. At the same time, persisting differences have prevented the middle class from abandoning support of the traditionally more conservative political parties. These parties, in turn, in response to structural change, have become more moderate in their conservatism.

THE POLITICS OF CONSENSUS

Robert E. Lane holds a different view of the politics of consensus. Lane agrees with the Marxian assumption that the economic structure underlies the political structure. He also agrees with Lipset in feeling that Marxian economics failed to correctly anticipate the structure of the American economy in the twentieth century.[40]

Lane, taking his lead from economist John Kenneth Galbraith,[41] characterizes the United States as an affluent society. By this he means that the United States has the following important economic characteristics:

1. A high national income, per capita;
2. A relatively equalitarian distribution of income;
3. A favorable rate of growth in GNP, per capita;
4. A functioning system of social welfare;
5. A managed economy.

[40] Robert E. Lane, "The Politics of Consensus in an Age of Affluence," *American Political Science Review* 59 (December 1965), pp. 874–895.

[41] John Kenneth Galbraith, *The Affluent Society*, 2nd ed. (Boston: Houghton Mifflin Co., 1969).

In this context, Lane argues, interpersonal trust will increase, elections will come to have less of a bearing on people's lives, the relationship between ideology and class status will change, religious as well as political ideologies will have less influence on men's secular lives, and there will be a decline in political alienation. The traditional ties between social strata and political parties will remain, in Lane's formulation, but the ideologies associated with positions in the stratification system will diminish, so that political opposition, as manifested through the political party structure, will not be expressed in terms of class antagonisms.

Where Lipset sees ideological politics being replaced by the politics of collective bargaining, Lane sees the emerging model as one of scientific decision making. The same technology that has changed the American stratification system is seen as generating increasingly large quantities of "knowledge"—information about humans, society, and nature collected on the basis of objective standards of truth. "Just as the 'democratic society' has a foundation in governmental and interpersonal relations, and the 'affluent society' a foundation in economics," Lane explains, "so the 'knowledgeable society' has its roots in epistemology and the logic of inquiry."[42]

Lane suggests that one can conceive of the policy process in terms of a model of "pure politics" or in terms of a model of "pure knowledge." In the former case, decisions are determined on the basis of power and electoral advantage. In the latter, they involve the rational calculation of how agreed-upon goals can be realized with the greatest efficiency. He then argues that the political domain is shrinking and the knowledge domain growing. Lane does not deny that politics will continue to exist. Rather, he suggests that even when decisions are made on the basis of self-interest, the perspective of policy-makers will be shaped increasingly by knowledge, with ideology playing an ever diminishing role.

It is possible, in this perspective, that the rational calculus of decision making does not trickle down to the mass electorate, but remains in the domain of the political elite. Thus, the task of the decision-maker, who relies increasingly on scientific information, may change from the making of policy to the making of administrative decisions. At the same time, voters may continue to behave

[42] Robert E. Lane, "The Decline of Politics and Ideology in a Knowledgeable Society," *American Sociological Review* 31 (October 1966), p. 650.

as if interest groups, operating through the political party structure, were the determining forces in the decision-making process.[43]

THE CONSENSUS-AND-CLEAVAGE APPROACH

Despite the political quiescence of the 1950s, it was clear by the late 1960s that an age of political consensus, or of the replacement of politics by rationality, had not come about. Political sociology found itself with a need for a perspective that could account for political cleavages persisting, and even increasing, in the face of affluence.[44]

The "middle mass" model discussed above gives priority to changes in social stratification derived from economic growth. Accordingly, it places less importance on the independent and autonomous roles of political institutions, and emphasizes instead degrees of economic affluence.

In this approach, the social groups that still accept ideological or class-conflict politics are holdouts or residues, and the decline of their political impact is explicitly asserted. The politics of the middle mass, as we have noted above, does not imply the end of the party divisions. It does, however, imply a narrowing of party differences and a decrease in the importance of the differences that do persist.

The newly emerging perspective that seemed better able, in the late 1960s, to account for persisting cleavages and new cleavages that were sometimes ideological in nature was the "consensus and cleavage" approach.[45] In this model, politics and political behavior are still seen as derived from the conflicts of social strata, but political alignments are more than just by-products of social stratification. Political institutions and political leadership, in this view, are more autonomous elements in the process of political change. The social stratification system itself is seen as molded in part by political decisions and by the actions of political parties.

[43] See, for example, A. Hoogerwerf, "Latent Socio-Political Issues in the Netherlands," *Sociologia Nederlandica* 2 (Summer 1965), pp. 161–177.

[44] See Morris Janowitz and David R. Segal, "Social Cleavage and Party Affiliation," *American Journal of Sociology* 72 (May 1967), pp. 601–618.

[45] See Morris Janowitz, "Political Sociology," in *International Encyclopedia of the Social Sciences*, vol. 12 (New York: The Macmillan Co., 1968), pp. 298–307.

Both in placing a greater emphasis on political institutions and in postulating a more complicated pattern of social stratification than does the middle-mass approach, the consensus-and-cleavage model builds on the formulations of Max Weber. The middle-mass approach, as we have noted above, tends to accept Marxist sociology even as it rejects Marxist economics and politics.

In the consensus-and-cleavage perspective, political conflict is based on new and more differentiated social groupings which reflect economic, professional, and bureaucratic interests. Likewise, religious, ethnic, and linguistic differences can persist or emerge as bases of political cleavage which include ideological elements. Advanced industrialization produces a changing stratification system which alters older forms of political conflict and provides the basis for newer forms. These new conflicts are more delimited, but they have deep consequences for collective problem solving, and they may be so aggregated as to produce pervasive strains. In this view, because there are built-in limitations in the trend toward greater social equality, what is crucial is not only the persistence of the social structural bases of political cleavage, but also the capacity of political institutions to adjust to, and to create, the conditions for political consensus.

Moreover, in contrast to the middle-mass model, the consensus-and-cleavage approach places great emphasis on the international context and on the impact of foreign affairs on domestic politics.[46] Neither structural nor ideological convergence between communist and capitalist economic and political systems are assumed. On the contrary, for Western Europe, modern politics is seen as an expression not only of changes in internal social structure, but also of the recent history of adjustment, after intense struggle, with the Soviet Union. The emerging phase of international relations is producing new bases of internal cleavage in the Western European democracies, both as commitments to the European community come into conflict with nationalistic orientations and as neutralist sentiments protrude into domestic political debates. Thus, the consensus-and-cleavage approach is not limited to an extrapolation of the midcentury phenomena that produced an increase in political bargaining. Rather, it seeks to identify those changes in social structure, political institutions, and the international context that can arouse dormant ideological

---

[46] See, for example, Daniel H. Willick, "Foreign Affairs and Party Choice," *American Journal of Sociology* 75 (January 1970), pp. 530–549.

leanings or introduce new rigidities and new conflicts into the political arena.

The differences between the middle-mass and the consensus-and-cleavage positions can be briefly summarized along one crucial dimension of political change in an advanced industrial society. The middle-mass outlook assumes that the social sources of rigid ideological orientation or of political extremism are residues or holdouts which, with additional economic expansion, will be incorporated into the political structure. The consensus-and-cleavage approach sees the sources of rigid ideological orientation not only in a polarized system of social stratification, but in social change and political leadership as well. It is thus oriented toward the detection of new sources of resistance to political consensus. Indeed, one position in the consensus-and-cleavage approach accepts the postulate that a middle mass has emerged in the stratification systems of industrial nations. Rather than contributing to political consensus, however, the middle mass is seen as a potential political combatant, as class conflict in the Marxian sense is replaced by a form of status politics in which the upper-working and lower-middle classes are pitted against the educated and rich above them and the minorities and poor below them.[47] The two extremes of the stratification distribution become forces for change, while the middle of the distribution, in an effort to consolidate past gains, becomes a force of conservatism.

The middle-mass and consensus-and-cleavage approaches do not exhaust the debate on the relationship between social structure and politics in modern industrial democracies, but they do encompass the basic issues involved. In the next chapter we shall investigate the planes of social cleavage, including class, that seem to serve as planes of political cleavage in the industrial democratic nations of the West and especially in the United States.

---

[47] See Harold L. Wilensky, "Class, Class Consciousness, and American Workers," in William Haber, ed., *Labor in a Changing America* (New York: Basic Books, Inc., 1966), pp. 12–43.

5

Dimensions of Cleavage

MANIFOLD CLEAVAGES

The political somnolence of the 1950s was not destined to be followed by a rational-consensual politics anywhere in the industrial West. Student demonstrations in the United States and Europe, working-class counterdemonstrations, racial unrest in America, French separatist agitation in Canada, religious warfare in Northern Ireland, conflict between Flemish and Walloons in Belgium—these and other manifestations of cleavages that seem not to lend themselves to resolution through collective bargaining—suggest that, rather than rejecting models of political conflict, we must recognize that other areas of conflict that have perhaps been overshadowed historically by class-based antagonisms have, with the decline of class conflict, come to the fore.

There has been since the late 1960s a renaissance of interest in the bases of political cleavage in industrialized Western nations. The recognition that changes in modern society have generated new planes of cleavage rather than producing consensus, that social tensions that have existed historically have increased in import, and that we are still confronted by the historical residues of cleavage based upon social class antagonisms has led to renewed interest in the dimensions of political opposition.

Seymour Martin Lipset and Stein Rokkan have attempted to

establish a taxonomy of such cleavages. They suggest that the two major revolutions of modernization—the national revolution and the industrial revolution—have produced four critical dimensions of opposition in Western politics.[1] The national revolution is seen as producing conflicts between subject and dominant cultures. Colonized peoples rebel against imperialism, and repressed ethnic minorities demand political recognition from the governmental structure. The national revolution also produces a conflict between the churches and the governmental institutions of society. Prior to rendering unto Caesar that which is Caesar's and unto God that which is God's, the political community must arrive at a consensual decision on what does belong to Caesar and what to God.

The processes of the industrial revolution, on the other hand, are reflected in a third cleavage, between workers and employers. If we assume that the employers are the owners of economic enterprise, we see that this cleavage was the basis of Marx's political model. And finally, the industrial revolution also produced a cleavage between the primary (extractive) and secondary (manufacturing and commercial) sectors of the economy. This plane of cleavage was in fact treated in Weber's analysis of social class, but has been overlooked by scholars more strongly influenced by the Marxist tradition.

The typology suggested by Lipset and Rokkan does not specify an ordering of the importance of these planes of cleavage on a comparative basis. In the context of specific national historical experiences, one dimension or another can be asserted to have primacy as a function of the temporal unfolding of the national and industrial revolutions. This contrasts with Lipset's earlier work, which asserted that political parties in the West were based primarily on class interests.[2]

A recent comparative study of social structure and political parties in the Western nations has attempted to measure the relative importance of dimensions of political opposition.[3] This study suggests that religious cleavages, i.e., those between proclerical and anticlerical groups, between communicants of differ-

---

[1] Seymour Martin Lipset and Stein Rokkan, *Party Systems and Voter Alignments* (New York: The Free Press, 1967), p. 34.

[2] Seymour Martin Lipset, *Political Man* (New York: Doubleday & Co., Inc., 1960), p. 220.

[3] Richard Rose and Derek Urwin, "Social Cohesion, Political Parties and Strains in Regimes," *Comparative Political Studies* 2 (April 1969), pp. 7–67.

ent churches, or between groups with secular and sacred orientations, rather than class differences, are the major bases of political party differentiation in the West. The authors of this study argue that the typology suggested by Lipset and Rokkan overemphasizes the importance of cultural cleavages—those based on linguistic, ethnic, or nationality differences—and regional differentiation. In support of these assertions, they present data on the claimed constituencies of seventy-six political parties in seventeen nations. Of the seventy-six parties, eighteen are defined as religiously homogeneous and twenty as socioeconomically homogeneous. An additional nineteen parties are seen as being supported by mutually reinforcing loyalties (having supporters who share two or more social characteristics), while the remaining parties are heterogeneous (based upon aggregated publics). Of those supported by mutually reinforcing loyalties, eleven are based on class and religion (sometimes in conjunction with other factors), five are based on religion in conjunction with factors other than class, and only one is based on class in conjunction with something other than religion. Thus, a total of thirty-four parties, or almost 45 percent of all parties considered, are based in whole or in part on religious cleavages. Thirty-two parties are rooted in whole or in part in social class cleavages. Among the other factors considered, regional and cultural differences each figured in the claimed constituencies of eight of the parties supported by mutually reinforcing loyalties.

This analysis supports the contention that there are a plurality of potential planes of political party differentiation, and clearly suggests that in Australia and in the nations of Western Europe and North America, religious and social class divisions are paramount among them. At the same time, for three important reasons, it fails to provide an adequate picture of the social bases of political party differentiation.

First, it underemphasizes the manifold bases of support of the heterogeneous parties, although it acknowledges that the trend in the Western nations is toward support of such parties, increasing their importance in the political arena. Nineteen of the original seventy-six parties, or 25 percent, fell into the heterogeneous category, including both the Democratic and Republican parties in the United States. The size of these parties relative to other political parties in the Western world, their overwhelming importance in the American polity, and the increasing importance of heterogeneous parties generally demand that greater attention be paid to the social structural forms that account for their support.

Second, the claim that religion rather than class is the primary plane of cleavage is not well supported by the finding that two more parties have religious than class bases. These dimensions in particular clearly warrant further exploration.

Third, the authors of this study approach the problem of political cleavage from a political rather than a sociological perspective. Rather than looking for sources of cleavage in the social structure, they take the parties themselves as units of analysis and define the homogeneity of a party largely in terms of the constituency it claims to represent. An alternative view of the operation of modern electoral systems suggests that if one studied the infrastructure of party support within the electorate, rather than studying party organization, one would discover a significant amount of variance in the support bases of "homogeneous" parties. Moreover, one might expect relatively little of this variance to be due to the constituencies the parties claim. The set of parties available for the voters to choose among in the nations of the West has not changed much over the last couple of decades. More importantly, given the inertia of complex organizations, the parties themselves have experienced little internal change. At the same time, the societies in which these parties and party systems operate have in many cases changed dramatically. Therefore, consideration of the ways in which changing cleavages within national electorates adapt to relatively constant party structures, or at least to party structures that change at slower rates, seems crucial.

In the discussion that follows, I shall use the typology suggested by Lipset and Rokkan as an organizing principle. I do so not because this typology represents a unique solution to the problem of defining the planes of cleavage in modern society, but because it gives us a set of categories that on the one hand does not reduce politics to the notion of class conflict and on the other hand enables us to place most empirically defined planes of cleavage into a small enough number of categories to make them comprehensible. My discussion will deal primarily with the American experience. Where appropriate, however, comparative materials will be included.

THE POLITICS OF CULTURE: RELIGION, ETHNICITY, RACE

The United States of America maintains a constitutional separation between sacred and secular institutions, the church and the state. It is ideologically committed to political ecumenicity. Yet researchers repeatedly find a persistent and pervasive relationship between religious orientation and political party choice in America.[4] One major study carried out in Detroit found that 40 percent of the white Protestants in its sample were Republican, as compared to 19 percent of the white Catholics and 2 percent of the Jews.[5]

The United States at its inception was a Protestant nation, as noted in our earlier discussion of community power in New Haven, Connecticut. The Congregationalist Church was the keystone of the social structure of New England, and the Episcopal Church played a similar role in the South. Despite the formal separation of religious and governmental institutions, the early states were in an important sense theocratic. In the early years, communicants of the "high" churches supported the ruling Federalists, while the dissenting Protestant sects—the Methodists and Baptists—supported the Democrats. As noted previously, the dominant Calvinist ethic dictated that the religiously and economically elect became the political elect as well.

Very quickly, however, the achievement orientation of the secular ideology forced a rejection of notions of predestination in favor of an Arminian theology—an acceptance of the doctrine that men can achieve salvation through good works.[6] The rise of the values of achievement and egalitarianism served as a resource to challenge the dominance of the American polity by the high Protestant churches, which came to be affiliated with the Republican Party after the demise of the Federalists. This challenge was supported by the extension of suffrage and the growth of an industrial labor force through successive waves of immigration that, far from building the strength of the high churches, were increasingly composed of non-Protestants and, indeed, non-Christians. By allowing the Democratic Party to gather to its fold a disproportionate share of the growing, religiously mixed urban electorate, the high Protestant Republicans lost the political initiative and their dominance of the governmental structure.[7]

---

[4] David R. Segal, "Classes, Strata and Parties in West Germany and the United States," *Comparative Studies in Society and History* 10 (1967), pp. 66–84.

[5] Gerhard Lenski, *The Religious Factor* (New York: Doubleday & Co., Inc., 1963), pp. 138–139.

[6] Seymour Martin Lipset, *The First New Nation* (New York: Basic Books, Inc., 1963), p. 163.

[7] See E. Digby Baltzell, *The Protestant Establishment* (New York: Random House, Inc., 1964), pp. 77, 227.

The Republican Party eventually followed the lead of the Democratic in broadening its electoral base, but religion remains one of the primary planes of differentiation between the American political parties nonetheless.

The same processes of immigration that produced religious diversity in the United States produced ethnic diversity as well. Much of the early sociological research on immigrant ethnic groups in the United States assumed a series of processes culminating in assimilation, when the unique characteristics of specific ethnic groups would disappear. This approach derived largely from the assimilationist perspective of the University of Chicago's school of urban sociology in the 1920s. The writings of Robert E. Park, Harvey Zorbaugh, and Louis Wirth, among others, present a model of relations between immigrant groups and a dominant society that begins with the cultural isolation of the immigrant community and ends with the complete absorption of the minority people and the loss of their identity.[8] This assimilationist perspective is manifested in Dahl's view of ethnic politics, mentioned earlier.

Just as the assimilationist perspective in general has been received critically by modern American sociology, so has the theory of political assimilation in particular. In one of those instances in which two analyses of a single body of data yield two answers to the same question, Wolfinger has used the New Haven data to challenge Dahl's theory of ethnic political assimilation.[9] Rather than accepting Dahl's assumption that ethnic identification, and therefore ethnic voting, is strongest in an immigrant group's early years in residence in a new society, Wolfinger argues that what is really important is the ethnic relevance of an election. The relevance of the election, in turn, is determined by the presence of fellow ethnic-group members on the ballot. Since people are unlikely to be nominated to candidacy prior to achieving middle-class status, the greatest mobilization of an ethnic vote will occur after an ethnic group has produced a middle class, or during what Dahl regards as the second phase of assimilation. Thus, what is crucial in the Wolfinger model is not so much rank-and-file homogeneity as the ability of the ethnic group to generate a leadership cadre that can link the ethnic group to the political parties. Thus, Wolfinger argues for increasing

[8] See especially Robert E. Park, *Race and Culture* (New York: The Free Press, 1950).

[9] Raymond E. Wolfinger, "The Development and Persistence of Ethnic Voting," *American Political Science Review* 55 (December 1965), pp. 896–908.

mobilization of the ethnic vote over time, rather than for political assimilation.

A second major critique of Dahl's political assimilation theory, which also questions the relevance of Wolfinger's formulation, is offered by Parenti.[10] Parenti's argument is that, since political assimilation in particular assumes the occurrence of social structural assimilation in more general terms, and since the bulk of the evidence suggests that American society does not act as a great melting pot, the issue of political assimilation is an inappropriate question to raise at all. Given the persistence of ethnic subcultures, there is no reason to expect ethnic political assimilation to take place. Of course, the possibility is left open for political assimilation to occur in the future, if cultural assimilation occurs. However, the simple fact of social mobility's taking place within an ethnic community does not, as Dahl suggests, necessarily portend cultural assimilation.

At the very least, these various approaches suggest that particular combinations of ethnicity and social class may have effects upon political behavior that are not predictable on the basis of the main effects of these variables taken independently. Indeed, one study has suggested that when the effects of ethnicity and class on politics are considered together, the former are significant, the latter are not, and the interaction effects are.[11] This study explains these results in terms of a theory of political cross-pressures—a topic that we shall consider in the next chapter.

The current state of our knowledge suggests that ethnic politics have persisted, for whatever reason, in America. Indeed, research has shown that subcultural groups defined in terms of shared religion and ethnicity maintain both group cohesion, as defined by patterns of interpersonal association,[12] and common political attitudes. What is important here is that, given the persistence of a relationship between religion and political party choice, there is ethnic differentiation *within* religious groups. Thus we find that, while Catholics in general are more liberal than are Protestants, German Presbyterians are more likely to identify

[10] Michael Parenti, "Ethnic Politics and the Persistence of Ethnic Identification," *American Political Science Review* 61 (September 1967), pp. 717–726.

[11] Abraham H. Miller, "Ethnicity and Political Behavior," *Western Political Quarterly* 24 (September 1971), pp. 483–500.

[12] See Edward O. Laumann, "The Social Structure of Religious and Ethnoreligious Groups in a Metropolitan Community," *American Sociological Review* 34 (April 1969), pp. 182–197.

with the Democratic Party than are Anglo-American Catholics.[13] For purposes of political analysis, then, subcultural groups in American society should not be identified in terms of either religion or ethnicity alone, but by joint ethnoreligious affiliation.

Discussions of the politics of race in the United States are limited in general to comparisons of whites and blacks. While there is considerable literature on Japanese Americans and American Indians as targets of political persecution, for example,[14] we know little of the political preferences of members of these groups. In recent years, social movements rooted in an emerging sense of ethnic identity have claimed that the American polity has not been responsive to the groups these movements represent. These movements have gone to great lengths to avoid being identified with any one political party.

Historically, blacks have been concentrated primarily in the South and, with the exception of the Reconstruction period, the South has managed to prevent blacks from effectively participating in politics. Only since the Voting Rights Act of 1965 has there been a major mobilization of black voters. At the same time that restrictions on black voting have decreased, the concentration of blacks in urban areas of the North has increased, making this group a major political force in urban areas.

In contrast to the political heterogeneity of the white population, black Americans have comprised an extremely homogeneous voting group in recent years, supporting the Democratic Party. In 1964, for example, analysis of data from a sample of the national electorate revealed that 97 percent of the black respondents who said they had voted had supported the Democratic presidential candidate. The remaining 3 percent refused to indicate whom they voted for. None of these black respondents indicated support for the Republican candidate.[15]

This study suggests that black support of the Democratic Party is not simply a phenomenon of black American culture. Rather, it reflects the perception of blacks that certain currents in the larger American culture are racist. At any given socioeconom-

---

[13] Edward O. Laumann and David R. Segal, "Status Inconsistency and Ethnoreligious Group Membership as Determinants of Social Participation and Political Attitudes," *American Journal of Sociology* 77 (July 1971), pp. 36–61.

[14] See Roger Daniels, *The Politics of Prejudice* (Berkeley: The University of California Press, 1962).

[15] David R. Segal and Richard Schaffner, "Status, Parties, and Negro Americans," *Phylon* 29 (Fall 1968), pp. 224–230.

ic level, blacks in this survey felt that they had lower social status than did whites at the same socioeconomic level. Lower-status groups in American society are more likely to support the Democratic Party. In this case, the Democratic support was due not only to the lower occupational and financial position of blacks in American society relative to whites, but to the fact that, even holding these factors constant, there were status costs to being black in America.

Another study, this one based on a survey conducted in Muskegon, Michigan, in 1966 and 1967, presents a more detailed view of the political ideology of black Americans.[16] Again, blacks were shown to be overwhelmingly Democratic, although a small percentage of the higher-income blacks in Muskegon indicated support of the Republican Party. Moreover, the blacks in this sample indicated a belief that their economic well-being was positively affected by Democratic electoral victories and nega-tively affected by Republican electoral victories. Yet these blacks were less involved in politics than the whites in the sample, their strong loyalty to the Democratic Party notwithstanding. This paradox was due to the fact that the black respondents did not believe that the political parties controlled the government. Rather, they believed that other organizations, not subject to control or influence by the electorate, ran the government.

The notion that there is a "power elite" that controls the government is not uniquely black, and in a later chapter we shall consider the power-elite thesis in greater depth. We note here that *belief* in this political model, as an alternative to a representative democracy model, has real implications for the political par-ticipation of blacks. It leads them to be less active in the party and electoral systems. At the same time, there are clear results that can be attributed to the mobilization of black voters within the electoral system. In the election of 1964, which because of the voting rights provisions of the Civil Rights Act of that year might be considered the turning point in black voter mobilization, 250 blacks were elected to public office. By 1965, about 1800 blacks held elective or appointed positions in federal, state, county, and city governments. In 1967, the Ninetieth Congress of the United States included seven black Americans—the largest number since the Reconstruction.

---

[16] William H. Form and Joan Huber, "Income, Race, and the Ideology of Political Efficacy," *Journal of Politics* 33 (1971), pp. 659–688.

THE SACRED AND THE SECULAR

The second set of planes of cleavage generated by the national revolution—those between religious and governmental institutions—are less clearly manifested in the United States than they are in other nations. In the Latin nations, most notably Italy and France, there are clear conflicts between the Catholic parties, the political ideologies of which are not wholly divorced from religious dogma, and the communist parties, which see religion as the opiate of the people. It has been argued, of course, that communism is itself a religion, although one devoid of a supernatural being other than the natural forces of history. Perhaps for this reason, the conflict between Catholics and Protestants in the American colonies serves as a better example of cleavage between the sacred and the secular, although not a pure type. The cleavage of clerical and anticlerical forces in North America was largely a conflict between French and English colonizers, and hence a form of cultural cleavage that could have been discussed in the previous section as well as in the present one. In addition, it considerably predated partisan politics in America, and was resolved through armed conflict. We noted in the first chapter that war is simply politics carried out by physical means, and we shall use this equation to dramatize the impact of religion on politics.

While the United States was born through rebellion against European domination and established churches (a point that should be remembered when we speak of contemporary violence, revolutionaries, and the rejection of old moral standards), Canada was settled in large measure because of a sense of religious mission, and emerged as a separate nation precisely because she resisted the revolutionary currents that characterized the colonies to the south. Indeed, had the English population in North America not vastly outnumbered the French population, more traditional European political patterns might today characterize both the United States and Canada.

In 1660 there were only about 2,500 Frenchmen on the North American mainland, and Colbert's policies of encouraging and financing immigration to America was unable to raise this number to much over 12,000 by 1680. It is not much of an oversimplification to argue that North America was the object of French missionary colonialism, while the West Indies were of more economic interest to the French.

England, on the other hand, was in the throes of an agricultural revolution that was displacing tremendous amounts of peasant labor. Small tracts previously farmed by peasants were being consolidated into large estates, and many displaced families, who were moving into already overcrowded cities, were willing to accept indentured servitude as a means of reaching the New World. This source of population arrived on the heels of the less numerous Englishmen who had come to establish the trading companies of the British colonies, such as the Massachusetts Bay Company and the Virginia Company. The earlier group was composed primarily of religious dissidents and marginal members of the gentry. Neither wave of English immigrants was likely to support the establishment of a national church. The indentured servants, in turn, were followed by new human resources acquired through even more involuntary means: convicted panderers, paupers, prostitutes, pirates, and highwaymen, for whom deportation was a humane fate; black Africans seized as slaves; and Irishmen seized as prisoners of war. While the early English immigrants came with a view toward making their fortunes and returning with respectable riches to British society, the indentured servants and other involuntary laborers did not view themselves as transients.

By 1640 there were some 20,000 English settlers in the Massachusetts Bay Colony alone. Despite the fact that the French kept their colonies more politically and economically dependent on their homeland than did the English, strength of numbers guaranteed that the model of European life that would be aspired to in North America would be Protestant and dissident.[17] The presence of the French on the continent guaranteed a Catholic and clerical resistance.

Two eighteenth-century wars shaped and reflected the church-state cleavage on the North American continent. The flow toward English hegemony and disestablishment in North America was not based upon waves of immigration alone, but on the expansion of the English territories as well. The Treaty of Utrecht, in 1713, ended twenty years of fighting by granting Newfoundland, Acadia, and the Hudson Bay Territory to the English. The French were left free to develop the interior region from Labrador to the Great Lakes, the Mississippi, and Louisiana. The next thirty years were characterized by rapid economic growth in the French territories and a great deal of trade among these territories, the West Indies, and France.

---

[17] See William H. McNeill, *The Rise of the West* (New York: Mentor Press, 1965), pp. 727 ff.

England during this period had become a major mercantile power, and sought to extend its New World holdings. In 1755, while both nations professed intentions of peace, General Braddock began to plan a campaign against the French, and a fleet of eighteen French ships was sent to defend Canada. British forces attacked French ships on the seas and French forts on land. The French waged counteroffensives on land, although Louis xv maintained a manifest policy of peace and refused to declare war. In June of 1756, however, after a shuffling of alliances that aligned England with Prussia and France with Austria, both Britain and France formally declared war.[18]

France was thus engaged in conflicts in both Europe and North America, while Britain was able to leave the European campaign to her Prussian ally and devote her attention to the colonies. France, preoccupied with the European campaign, was unable to support the brilliant military efforts of Montcalm, and the Seven Years War ended with the capitulation of Montreal in September 1760. The Treaty of Paris, signed in February 1763, ended hostilities between England and France. The entire territory of New France was ceded to England and, in return, George III agreed to allow the Canadians, who were now British subjects, to practice the Catholic faith.

With the cession of Canada, a bicultural colony was established. Historians differ on the degree to which French Canadians accepted their new status as British subjects.[19] It is clear, however, that the newly ceded territory was born with a pervasive social cleavage that polarized the population in terms of religion, culture, language, territory, and economic interests.[20] The French have subsequently been a repressed segment of Canadian society, and the issue of biculturalism persists as a crucial one in Canadian politics.

The second war on the North American continent which drastically changed the structure of social relations was the American Revolution. The British colonists, drawing upon radical political ideas current in Europe and no longer fearful of French expansion in North America, sought their independence from

---

[18] See Gustave Lanctot, *A History of Canada*, Margaret M. Cameron, trans., vol. 3 (Toronto: Clarke, Irwin, 1965) for an insightful, although partisan, account of the Seven Years War.

[19] Ibid., pp. 191–192.

[20] For a discussion of the problems of achieving political integration among linguistic groups, see Ronald F. Inglehart and Margaret Woodward, "Language Conflicts and Political Community," *Comparative Studies in Society and History* 10:1 (October 1967), pp. 27–45.

England in the late eighteenth century. Britain, internally divided and facing a war with France as well, chose not to put its total military resources against the colonials serving under George Washington. The revolution succeeded, and a new nation-state was established based upon political principles very much in opposition to those of the old regime.[21]

Neither the French nor the English in Canada chose to go the way of the revolutionaries, but for very different reasons. The position of the English was a secular one. English Canadians, along with Tories from the United States who migrated north, still considered themselves Englishmen. Indeed, Canada's own loss of colonial status was due to the reluctance of Britain to continue colonial responsibilities in North America after the revolution, rather than a demand on the part of the colonists for independence.

The French, by contrast, might have been expected to utilize the experience of the American Revolution to free themselves from the Protestant British domination that had befallen them in 1763. However, they at least had their right to practice Catholicism guaranteed by treaty, and the French clerics of Quebec were wary of both the religion and the anticlericalism of the New England revolutionaries. Indeed, the French Canadians isolated themselves culturally from France itself when that country experienced its own revolution, out of fear of anticlerical currents. While the issue of clericalism is not of major political import in the United States today, it remains one in Canada.[22]

This is not to say that the clericalism dimension is absent from American politics. Both of the major American parties, as discussed earlier, are ecumenical in the sense of drawing support from more than one church, and we maintain a constitutional separation of church and state. These factors notwithstanding, however, the questions of public support for parochial schools, the responsibility for teaching morality (sex education), and the legalization of abortion are among the issues that have recently brought the interests of religious institutions and/or religious dogma itself into political debate. Note that on these occasions the cleavage has not been a partisan one, but rather has cut across party lines.

---

[21] See Lipset, *The First New Nation.*

[22] See Mildred A. Schwartz, *Public Opinion and Canadian Identity* (Berkeley: The University of California Press, 1967), and Frederick C. Engelmann and Mildred A. Schwartz, *Political Parties and the Canadian Social Structure* (Englewood Cliffs, N.J.: Prentice-Hall, Inc., 1967).

ECONOMIC SECTORS

Just as the historical cleavage between the sacred and the secular in North America is reflected in part today in the existence of two large nations on the continent, so is the historical cleavage between agricultural and mercantile-commercial interests reflected in political regionalism in the United States.

Some historians view the political regionalism of the American South as a product of the Civil War, rather than as a reflection of gross historical differences in the economic development of the colonies and, later, of the states.[23] However, as early as 1614 the economy of Virginia was becoming dependent upon tobacco, and the importance of agriculture in the South increased thereafter. By the late seventeenth century the plantation system, which had been proven an efficient means of producing sugar in the Indies, had spread to the mainland. The organization of tobacco production was changed in Virginia and Maryland to accommodate it to the plantation system. In other Southern colonies the efficient production of cotton and rice, which required economies of scale, became increasingly dependent upon slavery as a social institution. As the Southern economy shifted toward "King Cotton," the importance of slavery increased still further. By 1860 four and a half million black men and women were bound into slavery.[24] During this period, the Southern gentry wielded great influence in the political affairs of the colonies.

As causes of war, the economic strains between the industrial North and the agricultural South prior to the Civil War were far more important than the movement to abolish slavery. Early in the conflict, in fact, President Lincoln offered to recognize the institution of slavery if the states that had seceded would rejoin the Union. It was only as the war progressed that the North increasingly defined its goals in terms of liberty in order to prevent England from intervening in the conflict on the side of the Confederacy.

The culmination of the "irrepressible conflict" between the North and the South in the Civil War, although it reversed the balance of political power between the two sectors of the nation

[23] See, for example, C. Vann Woodward, *Reunion and Reaction,* 2nd ed. (New York: Doubleday & Co., Inc., 1966).

[24] Oscar Handlin, *The Americans* (Boston: Little, Brown and Co., 1963), p. 212.

and led to the abolition of slavery in the South, in no way decreased the regional economic cleavage that characterized the American social structure.[25] The plantation aristocracy of the South was driven from its position of power in the national government by the farmers, laborers, and businessmen of the North and West, but the basic conflicts between the North and the South were aggravated, rather than resolved, by the war and the period of reconstruction that followed it.

President Lincoln had proposed benign programs for the rehabilitation of the South and the readmission of the states of the Confederacy to the Union. However, his successor, Andrew Johnson, was unable to realize those plans. Johnson was overpowered by a Republican Congress, and narrowly escaped being convicted at his impeachment proceedings. He was unable to keep the Congress from dividing the South into military districts under the command of army officers, or from disenfranchising most white Confederates. The contemporary dominance of the Democratic Party among white Southerners must be attributed in large measure to a reaction against the Republican Reconstruction that has been transmitted through the generations.

Not until almost a decade after the states of the Confederacy had been readmitted to the Union were the military occupation of the South and domination by civilian agencies representing the North ended. The imprint of the Civil War has been inscribed indelibly on Southern politics.[26] White Southerners accustomed to regarding blacks, at best, as people who did not have the rights of citizenship were faced with the problem of asserting their dominance in areas in which black majorities had been granted the franchise by the Emancipation Proclamation.

A study of the 1948 and 1952 presidential vote in the Dixiecrat states showed that, at midcentury, color was still *the* political issue in predominantly black areas of the South.[27]

---

[25] See Charles A. Beard and Mary R. Beard, *The Rise of American Civilization*, vol. 2 (New York: The Macmillan Co., 1927), "The Approach of the Irrepressible Conflict," pp. 3–51, and "The Second American Revolution," pp. 52–121.

[26] V. O. Key, Jr., *Southern Politics* (New York: Random House, Inc., 1949), p. 5. See also Alexander Heard, *A Two-Party South?* (Chapel Hill: The University of North Carolina Press, 1952).

[27] William J. Keefe, "Southern Politics Revisited," *Public Opinion Quarterly*, 20 (Summer 1956), pp. 405–412.

Similarly, Converse has argued that, although the two-party political model of the North is being increasingly approximated in Southern cities, the rural South can be expected to retain its traditional one-party structure.[28]

Studies of electoral support for George Wallace in 1968 suggest the continuation of this pattern. An analysis of voting in certain Southern congressional districts revealed that the higher the proportion of the constituency in a congressional district that was black, the higher was the proportion of the vote cast for Wallace.[29] Since it seems reasonable to assume that it was not the black population that was supporting Wallace, the data point to a direct relationship between the presence of a large black population and the continuation of traditional assertions of white supremacy. In this case, the white Southern vote departed from its traditional Democratic alignment in rejection of the liberal Democratic candidate for president. The basis of this rejection, however, was traditional political sentiment. A more refined study of Southern voting patterns in 1968 revealed that voting for Wallace as a reaction against the black electorate was less prevalent in the upper South (Arkansas, Florida, North Carolina, Tennessee, Texas, and Virginia) than in the lower South (Alabama, Georgia, Louisiana, Mississippi, and South Carolina).[30]

This differentiation of the South into subregions is related to the cultural and economic history of the South. The pre-Civil War plantation system was concentrated within the states of the lower South, and these states have tended to have a low degree of urbanization and a high concentration of blacks in their rural areas. By contrast, within the states of the upper South the plantation system was less fully developed, and these states have tended to have a relatively low concentration of blacks in their rural areas. In terms of modern political orientations, recent studies of the South have shown that the two subregions may be broadly differentiated in terms of their orientations toward racial and economic matters and, in particular, in terms of the greater

[28] Philip E. Converse, "On the Possibility of a Major Political Realignment in the South," in Campbell, Converse, Miller, and Stokes, *Elections and the Political Order*, pp. 212–242.

[29] Robert A. Schoenberger and David R. Segal, "The Ecology of Dissent," *Midwest Journal of Political Science* 15 (August 1971), pp. 583–586.

[30] For a discussion of these subregions of the South, see Bernard Cosman, *Five States for Goldwater* (University: The University of Alabama Press, 1966).

fear of blacks by whites in the lower South than in the upper South.[31]

When the relationship between the Wallace vote and the percent of blacks is analyzed by county in the states of the upper and lower South, the relationship is positive in the states of the upper South. In these states, the greater the black proportion of the population of a county, the higher was the vote for George Wallace. In the lower South, because of the concentration of blacks, the correlation was negative.[32] As the percentage of a county population that was black neared 100 percent, there were fewer white voters available to react against the black political presence by voting for Wallace.

The persistence of regional cleavage, of course, is rooted not only in historical differences, but also in the barriers that define regions as unique subcultural entities and limit social transactions between them.[33] That is, regional differences based upon historical occurrences will persist only insofar as cultural exchanges between regions are restricted to prevent cultural assimilation and diffusion.

In terms of political partisanship, for reasons discussed above, the major regional cleavage today is that between the Southern and border states on the one hand and the rest of the nation on the other.[34] This differentiation, in turn, is rooted today in minimal social contact between these regions. Cultural diffusion and assimilation, including the diffusion and assimilation of political culture, would be hastened by net in-migration to the Southern and border states. With few exceptions, however, the Southern and border states have had high rates of net out-migration.[35] The only states in these regions that experienced net gains in population through migration in the decade from 1940 to

---

[31] Donald R. Matthews and James W. Prothro, *Negroes and the New Southern Politics* (New York: Harcourt Brace Jovanovich, Inc., 1966), pp. 169–172, and Donald S. Strong, "Further Reflections on Southern Politics," *Journal of Politics* 33 (May 1971), pp. 239–256.

[32] Ira M. Wasserman and David R. Segal, "Aggregation Effects in the Ecological Study of Presidential Voting," *American Journal of Political Science* 17 (February 1973), pp. 177–181.

[33] See Kevin R. Cox, "On the Utility and Definition of Regions in Comparative Political Sociology," *Comparative Political Studies* 2 (April 1969), pp. 68–98.

[34] Segal, "Classes, Strata and Parties in West Germany and the United States," p. 79.

[35] Henry S. Shryock, Jr., *Population Mobility Within the United States* (Chicago: Community and Family Study Center, 1964), pp. 82–83.

1950 were Florida, which has the unique position of being a resort and retirement center, and Virginia and Maryland, which gained in population as the scale of governmental activities in neighboring Washington, D.C., increased.

In contrast, the loss in population in the west-northcentral states (Iowa, Kansas, Minnesota, Nebraska, North Dakota, and South Dakota) was nowhere near the magnitude of the Southern experience, and the west-northcentral states comprised the only other region that revealed a consistent net out-migration. These areas may, in turn, be compared with the relative stability of population in New England and the great gains of population attributable to migration experienced along the Pacific coast.

There has been some debate in sociological circles on whether the Southern political culture is still distinct from the political culture of the rest of the United States and, if so, whether this distinction can be expected to continue in the future. One school argues quite forcefully that regional cultural differences have in fact persisted.[36] An alternate view argues that, in terms of urbanization, industrialization, occupational redistribution, income, and education, the South has been changing more rapidly than the rest of the nation for the past half-century, and is becoming increasingly indistinguishable from the other regions of the United States.[37] If one accepts an economic-determinist view of politics and relegates historical differences in political culture to a secondary role, one would anticipate on the basis of these changes that the political distinctions between the South and the other regions would break down as well. That the leading scholars in this area do not draw such inferences from these data reflects an awareness of the influences of culture on political stability (or rigidity) and a rejection of the simple deterministic model of politics.

So far I have discussed the political cleavage between sectors of the economy only in the global terms of regional politics. However, the political differences between economic sectors are reflected in survey data on individuals as well. Moreover, where Lipset and Rokkan, writing about economies less developed than that of the contemporary United States, saw the important cleavage existing between the primary sector, based upon extraction

---

[36] See Norvall D. Glenn and J. L. Simmons, "Are Regional Cultural Differences Diminishing?" *Public Opinion Quarterly* 31 (Summer 1967), pp. 176–193.

[37] See John C. McKinney and Linda Brookover Bourque, "The Changing South," *American Sociological Review* 36 (June 1971), pp. 399–412.

(landed interests), and the secondary sector, based upon manufacturing (industrial entrepreneurs), American survey data, reflecting a system with a large tertiary (service) sector, reveal differences across all three major sectors. Thus, for example, location in the secondary sector is related to working-class identification and Democratic Party preference, while location in the tertiary sector is more likely to be related to middle-class identification and Republican Party preference.[38]

ECONOMIC CLASSES

In Chapter 4 we discussed the issue of social class cleavage prior to the 1950s in the industrial nations of the West. In this section we will consider the persistence of class-based cleavages in the 1970s, as well as potential planes of cleavage other than that between employer and employee in the modern economy.

As noted in our earlier discussion on the end of ideology, the correlation between economic class and political partisanship may diminish, but it is not expected to completely disappear in the middle-mass society. There is some evidence that politics in the United States has become less class-based.[39] This seems to be the case in Germany, France, and Italy, as well. The association between class and partisanship in Great Britain, on the other hand, has remained consistently high.[40] The diminution of the extent of class-based politics, in those nations where it is occurring, is notable. At the same time, it is equally important to note first of all that, although diminished, the relationship does persist in all nations in which class was once a dominant plane of cleavage in politics. In the United States, for example, blue-collar workers are still more likely to support the Democratic Party and owners of businesses more likely to support the Republican Party. Secondly, we must keep in mind that in other nations, such as England, there has not even been a diminution of the relationship. The decline of cleavage between the working class and the middle

[38] See Raymond J. Murphy and Richard T. Morris, "Occupational Situs, Subjective Class Identification and Political Affiliation," *American Sociological Review* 26 (June 1961), pp. 303–392.

[39] See Philip E. Converse, "The Shifting Role of Class in Political Attitudes and Behavior," in Eleanor Maccoby, Theodore M. Newcomb, and Eugene L. Hartley, eds., *Readings in Social Psychology* (New York: Holt, Rinehart & Winston, Inc., 1958).

[40] Paul B. Abramson, "Social Class and Political Change in Western Europe," *Comparative Political Studies* 4 (July 1971), pp. 131–155.

class is obviously not a necessary concomitant of mature industrialization, although it is a frequent one.

Considering briefly the major studies carried out in the Western nations, we find that high-income workers in three factories in England, like less affluent manual workers in that country, prefer the Labour Party and give class-based reasons for their preferences.[41] In France, despite the decline in class politics, the working class has retained its leftist character. Indeed, in many ways increased affluence has been related to structural changes that have increased radicalism.[42] Similarly, in Germany, working-class political orientations have been shown to differ from middle-class political orientations, income differences among manual workers notwithstanding.[43] Where the middle-mass theory presented by Lipset sees leftist sentiment in the working class as a historical residue, more recent research suggests that communist parties stand for more extensive redistribution of society's material benefits than do social democratic parties. It has been very much in the economic self-interest of manual workers in Europe to support the former, at least through the 1950s and 1960s.[44] By supporting communist parties, the European worker in the second half of the twentieth century is not necessarily manifesting working-class authoritarianism,[45] nor is he necessarily demonstrating that he is alienated from the polity.[46] Rather, he may be behaving more rationally than we have a right, on the basis of other findings, to expect voters to behave.

Our earlier discussion of planes of political cleavage other than social class should make it clear that the love affair that flourished between political sociology and Marxian models of society in the first half of the century is over. Not only has the

---

[41] John H. Goldthorpe, David Lockwood, Frank Beckhofer, and Jennifer Platt, *The Affluent Worker: Political Attitudes and Behavior* (Cambridge: Cambridge University Press, 1968).

[42] Richard F. Hamilton, *Affluence and the French Worker in the Fourth Republic* (Princeton, N.J.: Princeton University Press, 1967).

[43] Richard F. Hamilton, "Affluence and the Worker: The West German Case," *American Journal of Sociology* 71 (September 1965), pp. 144–152.

[44] Walter Korpi, "Working Class Communism in Western Europe: Rational or Nonrational," *American Sociological Review* 36 (December 1971), pp. 971–984.

[45] See Seymour Martin Lipset, *Political Man* (New York: Doubleday & Co., Inc., 1963).

[46] See E. Allardt, "A Theory on Solidarity and Legitimacy Conflicts," in E. Allardt and Y. Littunen, eds., *Cleavages, Ideologies and Party Systems* (Helsinki: Transactions of the Westermarck Society, 1969).

existence of sources of cleavage other than economic class dictated the abolition of unicausal models, but some scholars have suggested, despite evidence to the contrary, that there is not a significant relationship between economic self-interest and political involvement.[47] The argument has been put forth that, while the rhetoric of economics persists in political analysis in America, it has been adopted merely as a "conventional shorthand" for issues that are in reality political or moral.[48] That is, while issues and interests are described in economic terms, they are not truly economic issues or interests. This argument concludes on the note that the convention has outlived its usefulness, in part because politicians have forgotten that it is a convention and have begun to believe that economics controls politics, and more importantly because the dominant cleavages in American society today do not lend themselves to economic analysis with the same facility that earlier cleavages did.

On the other hand, the relevance of economic notions of social class—and even Marxian notions of class in particular—is still argued by some scholars.[49] We have earlier indicated that many theorists who subscribed to the middle-mass perspective at midcentury rejected Marx's economics while accepting his sociology. More in the tradition of Weberian economics, it has been suggested that Marxian explanations of American politics fail not because Marx's model was economic, but because Marx did not go far enough in seeking out the economic markets that serve as the bases of class conflict.[50]

The increased skill level and bargaining power of the working class may lead to the *embourgeoisement* of the proletariat, and the trend from entrepreneurial to bureaucratic occupations does alienate managers as well as workers from the means of production, thereby diminishing the import of the labor market as a source of social conflict. But differential placement in the credit or commodity markets, which Weber recognized but Marx did not,

[47] Frank Lindenfeld, "Economic Interest and Political Involvement," *Public Opinion Quarterly* 28 (Spring 1964), pp. 104–111.

[48] Peter F. Drucker, "On the 'Economic Basis' of American Politics," *The Public Interest* 10 (Winter 1968), pp. 30–42.

[49] George Lichtheim, "Class and Hierarchy: A Critique of Marx," *European Journal of Sociology* 5 (1964), pp. 101–111. Also, Bertell Ollman, "Marx's Use of Class," *American Journal of Sociology* 73 (March 1968), pp. 573–580.

[50] See Norbert Wiley, "America's Unique Class Politics: The Interplay of the Labor, Credit and Commodity Markets," *American Sociological Review* 32 (August 1967), pp. 529–541.

may serve as a basis for political conflict. Research has demonstrated the conflicting political interests of debtors and creditors,[51] but the notion of political opposition between consumers and producers has not been attended to as seriously. However, the proposition that one's role as a consumer is an important indicator of behavior in noneconomic areas is not a novel one. At least one line of thinking about life in modern industrial nations holds that the relationship between consumer roles and occupational roles is decreasing, and that, whereas the latter was previously the central determinant of behavior, the balance is shifting toward the former.[52] David Reisman clearly subscribes to this view with regard to American society. He writes, "The spread of other-direction has brought to the political scene the attitude of the inside-dopester, originating not in the sphere of work but of consumption."[53]

Research concerned with the effects of these alternative definitions of economic class on political party choice has produced two results of note.[54] First, when compared to other potential planes of cleavage, economic classes came out second best in their ability to explain patterns of partisanship. That is, region, religion, and race were all more powerful predictors of political party choice than were positions in the three economic markets considered. Second, and of perhaps greater interest given the general decline of the importance of the labor market for political alignments, was the fact that position in the labor market bore a weaker relationship to political party choice than did either position in the credit market or position in the commodity market. That is, the decline of the importance of employer-employee or white-collar–blue-collar distinctions does not necessarily mean a decline in the importance of economic categories generally, but rather indicates the necessity of changing one's categories to reflect the changing economic system. In a credit- and consumer-oriented economy, these markets become more important than do traditional labor-market categories.

[51] See, for example, Seymour Martin Lipset, *Agrarian Socialism* (Berkeley: The University of California Press, 1950).

[52] See Helmut Schelsky, "Gesellschaftlicher Wandel," *Offene Welt* 41 (1956), pp. 65 ff.

[53] David Reisman, *The Lonely Crowd* (New Haven: Yale University Press, 1961), p. 180.

[54] David R. Segal and David Knoke, "Political Partisanship: Its Social and Economic Bases in the United States," *American Journal of Economics and Sociology* 29 (July 1970), pp. 253–262.

PARTY COALITIONS

In Chapter 1 we noted that, in polities that elect officeholders on the basis of majority rule rather than proportional representation, the number of major political parties tends to be small (generally two) and each party must recruit support from diverse constituencies. The United States of America is characterized by such a political system, and our two major parties have been based on electoral coalitions.

In this chapter we have indicated some of the major sectors of the American social structure from which the major parties derive support. The Democratic Party tends to be supported by minority religious, racial, and ethnic groups, by the economically disadvantaged, and by Southerners. The Republican Party, in turn, tends to gain support from the major Protestant churches, from whites of Anglo-Saxon background, from the economically advantaged, and from Northerners. There are additional differences between the Democratic and Republican electorates that have not been dealt with in this chapter because they reflect basic economic cleavages that we have dealt with, rather than representing basic antagonisms in their own right. Union members and their families, for example, tend to support the Democratic Party, while families with no trade-union affiliation tend to support the Republican Party.[55] Since white-collar unionism is still weak in the United States, the labor vote largely reflects the political distinction between the working class and the middle class, although it adds something to this distinction as well.[56] Similarly, the central-city areas of major metropolitan regions tend to support the Democratic Party, while suburban and small-town areas have been more likely to vote Republican.[57]

How are these various segments put together to form a party electorate? Given the segmental nature of the electorate, what determines which party will win a given election?

In general, the coalitions that form to support a particular party are fairly stable for some period of time.[58] During such a

---

[55] See Arthur Kornhauser, Harold L. Sheppard, and Albert J. Mayer, *When Labor Votes* (New York: University Books, 1956).

[56] Harold L. Wilensky,"Class, Class Consciousness and American Workers,"in William Haber, ed., *Labor in a Changing America* (New York: Basic Books, Inc., 1966), especially pp. 22–26.

[57] See Key, *Public Opinion and American Democracy.*

[58] V. O. Key, Jr., "A Theory of Critical Elections," *Journal of Politics* 17 (February 1955), pp. 3–18.

period, one party or the other will have the support of a majority of the electorate. Interestingly, that party need not win all of the elections during such a period.[59] Let us consider why this is the case.

There are three major factors in determining the contribution of a segment of the electorate to the support base of a political party: the size of that segment of the electorate, i.e., how many voters are in it; the turnout in that segment of the electorate, i.e., how many of those voters will in fact go to the polls on election day; and the loyalty of that segment to a specific political party.[60] Since no major segment of the American electorate is so politically homogeneous as to give its total vote to one party or the other, the question becomes how much more than 50 percent of the two-party vote of that segment does the favored political party get?

Between the New Deal and at least 1968, the Democratic Party commanded the support of the greater share of the American electorate. Whether this has changed in the years since 1968 will be discussed in Chapter 8. The groups supporting the Democratic Party until 1968 were minorities in their particular realms (wealth, race, religion, region, etc.). The Republican Party was supported by groups that were majorities in their domain, and were characterized by higher voting turnout. However, party loyalty was stronger among the groups supporting the Democrats than among the groups supporting the Republicans. For example, the most Republican segment of the American electorate, composed of Protestants identifying with the middle or upper classes, not affiliated with unions, primarily small businessmen, and located outside the South, was about 57 percent Republican, while the Southern working class was about 25 percent Republican; a much larger deviation from an even split.[61]

The major parameters of the groups making up the Democratic coalition (size, turnout, and loyalty) have undergone some changes in the past two decades. These fluctuations are indications of the ebb and flow of the political resources upon which the

---

[59] David R. Segal, "Partisan Realignment in the United States," *Public Opinion Quarterly* 32 (Fall 1968), pp. 441–444.

[60] Robert Axelrod, "Where the Votes Come From," *American Political Science Review* 66 (March 1972), pp. 11–20.

[61] David R. Segal, "Social Structural Bases of Political Partisanship in West Germany and the United States," in William J. Crotty, ed., *Public Opinion and Politics* (New York: Holt, Rinehart & Winston, 1970), pp. 230–231.

parties can draw, which in turn indicate why the "majority" party may not always win elections.

The importance of the poor to the Democratic coalition has decreased as the size of this group has dwindled. Income redistribution has reduced the size of the group that votes for the Democratic Party solely on the basis of economic deprivation. However, this group has been characterized historically neither by high levels of turnout nor by overwhelming loyalty to the Democrats. Its dwindling, therefore, is not a great loss to the party.

Blacks, on the other hand, have become increasingly important in the Democratic coalition. They have been extremely loyal to the party, and the impact of voting rights and civil rights legislation has been to increase their turnout markedly.

Labor unions, once a backbone of the Democratic coalition, have decreased in size relative to other important segments of the American electorate, and their loyalty to the Democratic Party has declined markedly. In 1972, despite substantial union leadership support for the Democratic Party, a good deal of rank-and-file sentiment seemed to favor a third-party candidacy by George Wallace prior to his incapacitation in an assassination attempt.

The Catholic vote is currently the major segment in the Democratic coalition, but it has been running a weak first. It includes a large segment of the American electorate and has been characterized by high voting turnout, but it experienced a high defection rate in 1972.

The Southern vote likewise seems to have been defecting from the Democratic coalition. In the Eisenhower election of 1956 the Southern vote was evenly split, and of late it has been leaning toward third parties such as George Wallace's American Independent Party.

The central cities are declining in importance for the Democratic coalition, due largely to demographic factors. The flight to the suburbs has left only 10 percent of the American population living in the central cities of our largest metropolitan areas. These are mostly people who would be expected to vote Democratic on grounds other than residence, e.g., they are black, or union members, or have other pro-Democratic characteristics.

The Republican Party operates in a similar electoral marketplace, building its coalition of other groups in the electorate. It should be pointed out that, while we have been viewing these characteristics of voters one at a time, their effects are additive. For example, a Catholic union member is more likely to support the Democratic Party than is either a non-Catholic union member or a Catholic nonunion member. In the next chapter we shall look more closely at how these combinations of characteristics are thought to affect the vote.

6

Politics in Complex Systems

COMBINING ELEMENTS

We have seen that there exists in American society, and in other modern societies, a multitude of potential political cleavages. These cleavages are defined by conflicting interests that bind social groups to the polity by linking them to one or the other of the political parties. Until now we have dealt with the voter as if only one such group membership were relevant to his partisan choice: as if he chose the Democratic Party because he was black, or the Republican Party because he was wealthy, and so on. The effects of group membership may in some cases be additive; since Catholics and union members both tend to support the Democratic Party, a Catholic union member is more likely to support the Democratic Party than is a non-Catholic union member or a Catholic nonunion member. But in other cases, group memberships pull the voter in opposite directions.

In this chapter we shall discuss theories and data that deal with cases in which individual voters or groups of voters have some group affiliations that would lead us to expect them to vote for one party, while at the same time having other group affiliations that would lead us to expect them to vote for another party.

In the Weberian tradition, a person can be considered in a

high economic class in one market (labor, credit, commodity), while in a low economic class in another market. Imagine a two-party political system in which one party represents the interests of employers and creditors, while the other represents the interests of employees and debtors. If a person is an employer but also a debtor, which party will he support? Chapter 4 also noted that the correlation between economic class and social status may be imperfect. If, in a two-party system, one political party represents the interests of the economically advantaged, high-status segments of society, while the other represents the interests of the economically disadvantaged, low-status segments, where will the support of the high-status but economically disadvantaged segments of society be thrown? Recall that early in the political history of New Haven, the high-status families had a virtual monopoly on the local wealth, as well. Through the processes of economic growth and industrialization, however, lower-status segments of the population—recently arrived ethnic groups—gained wealth. This change in the nature of the relationship between status and wealth, in turn, had important implications for the conduct of politics in New Haven.

The first part of this chapter will deal with several theories which try to explain the behavior of voters who belong to groups that hold differing expectations for the voters' political behavior. The main theories are status inconsistency, class inconsistency, social mobility, cross-pressures, and relative deprivation. The most recent and sophisticated research has in most instances refuted the more elegant theories. Because a great deal of the recent literature of political sociology has been devoted to these theories, however, the beginning student in political sociology should be exposed to both the structure of the theories and the nature of the data that have been brought to bear on them. The remainder of this chapter will consider the effects of conflicting group loyalties on the political system, rather than on the individual voter.

STATUS INCONSISTENCY

Of the various theories that attempt to explain the responses of an individual whose several positions contain conflicting expectations, the theory of status inconsistency (or status crystallization or status discrepancy) has probably served as the basis for the greatest amount of research.

In traditional societies, there tends to be a high correlation among the various dimensions of the social stratification system. That is, a person who is of high status on one dimension will tend to be of high status on other dimensions. Similarly, a person who is of low status on one dimension will tend to be of low status on others. Traditional societies also tend to have *ascriptive* stratification systems. That is, individuals pass their relative advantages or disadvantages on to their children. Members of the ascending generation, then, find their place in the social structure not primarily on the basis of their own achievements, but on the basis of the social positions their parents occupied.

With the rationalization of economic systems through the processes of economic development and industrialization, achievement-oriented bases of status become differentiated from traditional bases of status and assume increased importance. Thus, capable people from low-status backgrounds, while still inheriting some of their social status from their parents, may nonetheless distinguish themselves through high levels of educational achievement, the attainment of high levels of income, or entry into high-status occupations.

If there originally was a relationship between social stratification and politics in a society, such multiplications of the bases of status will confound it. Some members of the society who come from families that have little claim to status on the basis of ascriptive criteria, and that have probably been disadvantaged in the past in terms of wealth and political power, will find themselves in high-status political and economic positions through their own achievements. At the same time, some who inherited high ascriptive status from their parents may find themselves economically and politically deprived because of their own intellectual (or other) shortcomings.

Thus, in complex societies, an individual's position on one dimension of social stratification does not necessarily determine or coincide with his location on another dimension. As Pitirim Sorokin explains, "The stratified pyramids of the unibonded groups never consolidate in such a way that all their strata coincide."[1] While there is a *tendency* for different types of status to reach a common level over time,[2] at any given point there are

[1] Pitirim A. Sorokin, *Society, Culture and Personality* (New York: Harper & Row, Publishers, 1947), p. 292.

[2] Emile Benoit-Smullyan, "Status, Status Types, and Status Interrelationships," *American Sociological Review* 9 (April 1944), pp. 151–161.

always individuals whose several statuses are highly inconsistent with each other.

The theory of status inconsistency, as formulated by Gerhard Lenski,[3] sees the status-inconsistent individual as a marginal person,[4] poorly integrated into the social groups he would be expected to belong to by virtue of his statuses. The social marginality of the status-inconsistent individual, in terms of this theory, is due to a discrepancy between his own estimation of his position in the social structure and the evaluation of his position by people with whom he interacts.

The theory assumes that, when an individual is of high status on one stratification dimension but of low status on another, he will optimize his subjective definition of his position by basing that definition on his higher status and disregarding his lower status. If, for example, he is a member of a high-status profession but a low-status religious denomination, he will define himself in terms of his occupation and not include his religion in his estimation of his status. Other people, however, will attempt to optimize their own positions in social encounters with the status-inconsistent individual, and hence will define him in terms of his lower status.[5] In social encounters, then, the status-inconsistent individual expects to receive deference or respect from other people on the basis of his highest status. However, due to the propensity of others to attempt to maximize their own relative advantage in social encounters, these deference expectations are unfulfilled. The status-inconsistent individual is therefore postulated to be frustrated by social contacts, to find them uncomfortable, and to withdraw from social participation.[6]

Moreover, the social discomfort experienced by that status-inconsistent individual is hypothesized to have political consequences. Lenski's original study showed that status-inconsistent people were more likely to prefer the Democratic Party, and that certain types of status inconsistency were more closely related to political liberalism than were others. Specifically, the effect was

---

[3] Gerhard E. Lenski, "Status Crystallization: A Non-Vertical Dimension of Social Status," *American Sociological Review* 19 (August 1954), pp. 405–415.

[4] See Everett V. Stonequist, "The Problem of the Marginal Man," *American Journal of Sociology* 41 (July 1936), pp. 1–12.

[5] Gerhard E. Lenski, *Power and Privilege* (New York: McGraw-Hill Book Co., 1966), p. 87.

[6] Gerhard E. Lenski, "Social Participation and Status Crystallization," *American Sociological Review* 21 (August 1956), pp. 458–464.

manifested most strongly when low ethnic status was combined with high income, educational, or occupational status. Later research suggested that the important combinations of statuses involved low ascribed and high achieved status,[7] and Lenski subsequently incorporated this position into his theory.[8] The status-inconsistent individual who is frustrated by a social system that continues to judge him on ascriptive bases, despite his own success, seeks to change the political system, and in particular supports the Democratic Party in the hope that the party's progressive programs will minimize his ascriptive disadvantage. Other research has suggested that individuals who experience inconsistencies between *achieved*-status dimensions are likely to support right-wing political extremist groups,[9] and attempts to replicate Lenski's findings by looking at people experiencing inconsistencies among achieved statuses have found that such people are not overly likely to support the Democratic Party.[10]

Five major types of criticism have been directed at the status-inconsistency model. First, the assumption that status-inconsistent people define their position in the stratification system at a higher level than do people with whom they interact has been called into question. Research in social psychology has shown that individuals, when presented with inconsistent status attributes of another person and asked to evaluate that person's position, average the several status characteristics of the stimulus person.[11] Status-inconsistency theory suggests that they will focus on the lowest status. Similarly, where inconsistency theory tells us that the status-inconsistent person will emphasize his highest status, research suggests that he, too, will average his several kinds of status.[12] Thus, we have reason to believe that the

[7] Elton F. Jackson, "Status Consistency and Symptoms of Stress," *American Sociological Review* 27 (August 1962), pp. 469–480.

[8] Gerhard E. Lenski, "Status Inconsistency and the Vote," *American Sociological Review* 32 (April 1967), pp. 298–301.

[9] Gary B. Rush, "Status Consistency and Right-Wing Extremism," *American Sociological Review* 32 (February 1967), pp. 86–92.

[10] See William F. Kenkel, "The Relationship Between Status Consistency and Politico-Economic Attitudes," *American Sociological Review* 21 (June 1962), pp. 365–368.

[11] Samuel Himmelfarb and David J. Senn, "Forming Impressions of Social Class," *Journal of Personality and Social Psychology* 12 (May 1969), pp. 38–51.

[12] David R. Segal, Mady W. Segal, and David Knoke, "Status Inconsistency and Self-Evaluation," *Sociometry* 33 (September 1970), pp. 347–357.

status-inconsistent individual and the people with whom he interacts will agree on his status. He is therefore unlikely to hold deference or respect expectations that will be unfulfilled.

Secondly, but not surprisingly, given the weakness of the first assumption, the disruption of social relationships that is presumed to follow from the frustrated deference expectations of the status-inconsistent person has never been empirically demonstrated. Lenski presents only inferential evidence in support of this assumption.[13] More recent research suggests in some cases that status-inconsistent people do not differ from status-consistent people in the stability of their social relationships,[14] and in other cases that status-inconsistent people may actually have more satisfying social contacts than do people who are status consistent.[15]

Third, some critics have argued that when the main effects of the individual statuses are taken into account first, the presumed inconsistency effect has no explanatory power. A series of studies have shown that, when the variance accounted for by the main status effects is carefully measured, little if any additional explanation can be credited to an inconsistency effect.[16] We have seen in the last chapter that ethnicity is related to political party choice, as is occupation. Thus, knowing a person's ethnic background and his occupation, we have a basis for predicting his party choice on the basis of these relationships. Status-inconsistency theory states that, above and beyond the predictive ability that we have on the basis of these relationships, if we know that a person is of low ethnic status and high occupational status, we will have additional predictive ability. In other words, in addition to the additive effects of ethnicity and occupation on political party choice, status-inconsistency theory posits a statisti-

---

[13] See Lenski, "Social Participation and Status Crystallization."

[14] Edward O. Laumann and David R. Segal, "Status Inconsistency and Ethnoreligious Group Membership as Determinants of Social Participation and Political Attitudes," *American Journal of Sociology* 77 (July 1971), pp. 36–61.

[15] Karl E. Bauman, "Status Inconsistency, Satisfactory Social Interaction and Community Satisfaction in an Area of Rapid Growth," *Social Forces* 47 (1968), pp. 45–52.

[16] See Gerard Brandmeyer, "Status Consistency and Political Behavior," *Sociological Quarterly* 6 (1965), pp. 241–256; Robert W. Hodge, "Social Integration, Psychological Well-Being and Their Socioeconomic Correlates," *Sociological Inquiry* 40 (Spring 1970), pp. 182–206; Donald Treiman, "Status Discrepancy and Prejudice," *American Journal of Sociology* 71 (May 1966), pp. 651–664.

cal interaction effect *between* ethnicity and occupation that will also have an effect on political party choice.

Fourth, even when a statistical interaction effect between an ascribed status and an achieved status can be shown to have an effect on political party choice, this effect cannot be equated with an inconsistency effect. There are many possible causes of statistical interaction effects. In order to test for the specific form of statistical interaction predicted by status-inconsistency theory, the magnitude and direction of the effects of the status dimensions themselves, as well as of the interaction effect, should be specified a priori.[17]

Fifth, and most substantively interesting, the effects frequently attributed to status inconsistency have been interpreted by some researchers as being due to ethnic-group membership. One variant of this criticism is concerned with the political effects of ethnic status as a variable in the stratification system. This position is merely a specification of point three above.[18] Indeed, Lenski, as noted above, has argued the importance of low ethnic status combined with high achieved status for explaining political liberalism, and research in this tradition has shown that the political effects of status inconsistency are in general manifested only when the low ascriptive status of the inconsistent individual is socially visible.[19]

Another variant of explanation in terms of ethnicity takes a more subcultural bent. From this perspective, the relative social ranking of ethnic groups in status terms is not important. Rather, primacy is placed upon their subcultural traits regarding political behavior.[20]

An empirical test of the ability of status-inconsistency theory to explain political orientations among members of fifteen ethno-religious groups in the city of Detroit in 1966 failed to provide

[17] Most beginning students need not concern themselves with the technicalities of this statistical problem beyond the recognition of its existence. The reader who is interested in pursuing this issue further, however, would do well to read Hubert M. Blalock, "Status Inconsistency and Interaction: Some Alternative Models," *American Journal of Sociology* 73 (November 1967), pp. 305–315.

[18] See K. Dennis Kelley and William Chambliss, "Status Consistency and Political Attitudes," *American Sociological Review* 31 (June 1966), pp. 375–382.

[19] David R. Segal, "Status Inconsistency, Cross-pressures and American Political Behavior," *American Sociological Review* 34 (June 1969), pp. 352–359.

[20] See Nathan Glazer and Daniel P. Moynihan, *Beyond the Melting Pot* (Cambridge: MIT Press, 1963).

support for the theory.[21] Rather, differences among ethnoreligious groups, when they appeared, were explained more parsimoniously by subcultural differences. Status-inconsistent Jews in the sample behaved the way that status-inconsistency theory predicts members of low-status ethnic groups would behave. However, status-consistent German Presbyterians behaved very much the same way that status-inconsistent Jews behaved—a phenomenon that is in opposition to the predictions of inconsistency theory. Not only do these data suggest a rejection of the status-inconsistency framework, but they also suggest that subcultural patterns among Jewish respondents may explain why some research has produced results that seem to support status-inconsistency theory when crude religious categories are used to identify ascribed status. Most status-inconsistency research in America has coded Judaism as a low status religion. In the context of this definition, effects that were attributed in the past to status inconsistency, such as political liberalism, might better be viewed as characteristics of American Judaism.

To briefly review the current state of status-inconsistency research in several national contexts, we find that, in the United States, Jews and blacks behave the way status-inconsistency theory predicts that members of groups with low ascribed status will, but that their behavior can better be explained by subcultural patterns, rather than by the theory of status inconsistency. In Australia, inconsistency between high achieved status and low ascribed status has been shown to be related to liberal political preferences, as status-inconsistency theory suggests. However, once the main status effects are taken into account, the inconsistency effect, while significant, explains only a small amount of variance in political preference (see the third criticism of the status-inconsistency model stated above), and much of the variance attributed to the inconsistency effect is really shared between that effect and the ascribed religion variable.[22] In Canada, significant inconsistency effects have been demonstrated, but again they have been quite small.[23] In Germany, research has not been able to

---

[21] Laumann and Segal, "Status Inconsistency and Ethnoreligious Group Membership as Determinants of Social Participation and Political Attitudes."

[22] Leonard Broom and F. Lancaster Jones, "Status Inconsistency and Political Preference," *American Sociological Review* 35 (December 1970), pp. 989–1001.

[23] David R. Segal, "Status Inconsistency and Party Choice in Canada," *Canadian Journal of Political Science* 3 (September 1970), pp. 471–474.

identify inconsistency effects on political party choice at all.[24] In sum, while a great deal of attention has been paid to status-inconsistency theory in political sociology, the payoff has not been large at all.

CLASS INCONSISTENCY

A model similar to that of status inconsistency, but with different political outcomes, has been suggested to explain the political behavior of Americans who hold inconsistent economic class positions in the labor, credit, and commodity markets.[25] The class-inconsistent person is by definition a member of the advantaged class in one or two of these markets. Economic advantage, unlike educational attainment, can be lost through liberal, progressive, or radical change in the social structure. Although the class-inconsistent person seeks change to reduce the strain of his inconsistency, he is unwilling to engage in liberal or radical political activity that risks a loss of the advantage he already possesses. Rather than wishing to see the rewards of society distributed more widely, such people wish to see all values consolidated in the hands of those who are already somewhat advantaged. They are therefore hypothesized to support, in the extreme, right-wing political groups, and in more moderate terms, the Republican Party, as a means of halting the spread of the welfare state and "creeping socialism." Like status-inconsistency theory, the theory of class inconsistency has not held up well under the weight of empirical study. Analysis of the effects of class inconsistency on Republican Party preference reveals that only in the case of inconsistencies between credit-market and commodity-market positions are such effects manifested, and even here they are extremely small.[26]

---

[24] Nico Stehr, "Statuskonsistenz," *Kölner Zeitschrift für Sociologie und Social Psychologie* 23 (January 1971), pp. 34–54; David R. Segal and David Knoke, "The Impact of Social Stratification, Social Mobility, and Status Inconsistency on the German Party Infrastructure," *Journal of Political and Military Sociology* 1 (Spring 1973), pp. 19–37.

[25] Norbert Wiley, "America's Unique Class Politics," *American Sociological Review* 32 (August 1967), pp. 529–541.

[26] David R. Segal and David Knoke, "Class Inconsistency, Status Inconsistency, and Political Partisanship in America," *The Journal of Politics* 33 (November 1971), pp. 941–954.

SOCIAL MOBILITY

As was the case with theory and research on the political effects of status inconsistency, social mobility has been viewed by many scholars as a process that isolates people from the social groups that should integrate them into the body politic. In an achievement-oriented system, in which a person can attain a higher (or lower) position in the occupational prestige hierarchy than his parents held, the discrepancy between prestige levels across two generations has been thought to be problematic for the member of the ascending generation and to have implications for his political behavior.

Unlike early theories regarding the political effects of status inconsistency, theories of the relationship between social mobility and politics have hypothesized differences between the United States and the nations of Western Europe, based on the greater assumed openness of American society. These differences have been hypothesized to be most apparent among upwardly mobile individuals.

In their study of social mobility in industrial society,[27] Reinhard Bendix and Seymour Martin Lipset argue that European men from working-class origins who achieve middle-class occupational positions are not accepted by their fellow members of the middle class who come from middle-class origins, i.e., who have not experienced occupational mobility between generations. Faced with this nonacceptance by their peers, upwardly mobile Europeans retain the leftist political orientations of their working-class origins. By contrast, the upwardly mobile in America are accepted in their class of destination, since America is not wedded to a traditional class system and values individual achievement. As a manifestation of the acceptance of the upwardly mobile, and perhaps an expression of gratification for this acceptance, the American upwardly mobile individual adopts the political conservatism of his class of destination, and sometimes overconforms, being more conservative than nonmobile members of the middle class.

The argument can be stated in terms of processes of political socialization. Individuals born into working-class families learn leftist political attitudes from their parents, and learn to identify with the political party of the left at this time as well. During

---

[27] Reinhard Bendix and Seymour Martin Lipset, *Social Mobility in Industrial Society* (Berkeley: The University of California Press, 1959).

adulthood, upwardly mobile people from working-class origins who are accepted by their middle-class peers (the American case) will be resocialized by those peers. Those who are not accepted by their middle-class peers (the European case) will not be resocialized, and will continue to reflect the socialization experience they received from their parents.

The conventional view of the political effects of social mobility also holds that the downwardly mobile individual is, at least in the American context, less likely to be resocialized in his class of destination than is the upwardly mobile individual. The person who moves from a middle-class position to a working-class position may hope to regain his lost status, or he may refuse to discard his middle-class values even if he cannot hope to regain his middle-class position.[28] In either case, because he refuses to accept his new working-class peers, he is not resocialized by them and he continues to manifest more conservative middle-class political ideas than do other members of the working class. Given the difference in the probability of resocialization between the middle class and the working class, Lipset has argued that social mobility favors conservative parties.[29] The downwardly mobile will maintain their middle-class conservatism, while the upwardly mobile may adopt middle-class conservatism. An alternative perspective argues that the downwardly mobile are radicalized by their experience in the stratification system.[30] Were this perspective found to be true, there would be no reason to expect social mobility to benefit only the conservative parties. Recent research has suggested, however, that social mobility has little if any impact at all on political behavior.[31]

As was the case with status-inconsistency theory, the testing of social-mobility hypotheses involves the evaluation of models that posit statistical interaction effects, or mobility effects, versus models that simply posit additive contributions of political learning at point of social origin and point of social destination among mobile people. Social-mobility hypotheses postulate that there is

---

[28] See Harold L. Wilensky and Hugh Edwards, "The Skidder: Ideological Adjustments of Downward Mobile Workers," *American Sociological Review* 24 (1959), pp. 215–231.

[29] Lipset, *Political Man*, p. 257.

[30] Joseph Lopreato and Janet Saltzman Chavetz, "The Political Orientation of Skidders," *American Sociological Review* 35 (June 1970), pp. 440–450.

[31] Mary R. Jackman, "The Political Orientation of the Socially Mobile in Italy," *American Sociological Review* 37 (April 1972), pp. 213–222.

something unique about the politics of people born into working-class families who achieve middle-class occupations that we cannot determine simply by arguing that their political attitudes are influenced to some degree by their working-class parents and to some degree by their middle-class peers. Critics of social-mobility hypotheses expect the political attitudes of such people to be intermediate between those of nonmobile working-class people and those of nonmobile middle-class people. Proponents of these hypotheses expect that the political attitudes of mobile individuals would not be intermediate between the nonmobile working-class and middle-class patterns. Rather, they expect that, in Europe, because the upwardly mobile are not accepted as equals in their class of destination, there would be little difference between the upwardly mobile and the working-class nonmobile, while in the United States there would be little difference between the upwardly mobile and the middle-class nonmobile because the mobile individual is accepted in his class of destination. In neither the U.S. nor Europe would there be much difference between the downwardly mobile and the middle-class mobile.

In recent years, a number of authors have questioned theories that suggest unique effects on politics attributable to social mobility. One analysis of survey data collected in the Detroit area in 1956–1957 found people upwardly mobile from the working-class to the middle-class to be intermediate in their party preferences between working-class nonmobile and middle-class nonmobile respondents.[32] More recently, a study of the effects of social mobility on political party identification and voting across six American presidential elections showed mobile men and women to be intermediate in Republican identification and vote between working-class and middle-class nonmobile.[33] Wilensky has pointed out that, while social mobility is frequently regarded as disruptive of social relationships, in many cases it merely represents the progression of an orderly and continuous career. Moreover, in those cases in which mobility, particularly downward mobility, is a disturbing experience, societies differ in their definitions of the socially appropriate response. The downwardly mobile in Nazi Germany might have been joining the SS while their counterparts in the U.S. were joining the labor movement or

---

[32] David R. Segal and David Knoke, "Social Mobility, Status Inconsistency and Partisan Realignment in the United States," *Social Forces* 47 (December 1968), pp. 154–157.

[33] Kenneth Thompson, "Upward Social Mobility and Political Orientation," *American Sociological Review* 36 (April 1971), pp. 223–235.

participating in the activities of New Deal agencies.[34] Sociological theory lacks the precision to anticipate what effect, if any, mobility will have in a particular national context.

As a result of the refinement of techniques of statistical analysis used to identify mobility effects, sociologists have increasingly come to accept the position that there are no mobility effects per se on political behavior. Rather, socially mobile people are influenced in their party choices by both childhood and adult socialization experiences. The degree to which one of these experiences is dominant over the other varies from individual to individual, from nation to nation, and from one historical period to another. These variations have not been the subject of extensive analysis. However, we shall discuss them in the next chapter, in which we shall deal with socialization and social influence processes in politics.

CROSS-PRESSURES

While both the status-inconsistency framework and the social-mobility framework conceive of the group affiliations that influence party choice in terms of status, the cross-pressure framework is concerned with the case in which an individual belongs to two or more groups that have differing definitions of the forms of political behavior that are appropriate for him. The relative status of these groups vis-à-vis others that the individual does not belong to, or vis-à-vis each other, is unimportant. And while both the status-inconsistency framework and the social-mobility framework see the political effects of these phenomena in terms of support of parties of the left vs. parties of the right, the cross-pressure framework concerns itself with the more elemental issue of partisanship vs. nonpartisanship. The concern here is not so much with how an individual votes as with whether he votes at all.

As a result of data obtained in a study of presidential voting in Erie County, Ohio, in 1940, a team of researchers associated with the Bureau of Applied Social Research at Columbia University, led by Paul Lazarsfeld, proposed that "whatever the source of the conflicting pressures, whether from social status or class identification, from voting traditions or the attitudes of associates,

---

[34] Harold L. Wilensky, "Measures and Effects of Social Mobility," in Neil J. Smelser and Seymour Martin Lipset, eds., *Social Structure and Mobility in Economic Development* (Chicago: Aldine-Atherton, Inc., 1966), pp. 98–140.

the consistent result was to delay the voter's final decision."[35] That is, the voter who in terms of some group memberships was expected to vote Democratic, while in terms of other group memberships was expected to vote Republican, delayed his decision on which party to vote for as long as possible.

The Bureau of Applied Social Research conducted a study in 1948 in Elmira, New York, to follow up some of its earlier findings, among them the cross-pressure phenomenon. This study concluded that "a few cross-pressured voters act like the proverbial donkey and do not vote at all"[36] (we assume that the symbolic reference to the Democratic Party was unintentional), while other cross-pressured voters were able to resolve the issue by assigning weights to the relevant pressures. More recent research on the phenomenon has suggested that withdrawal of psychological affect from political symbols is one method of resolving cross-pressures.[37]

Studies of the cross-pressure phenomenon are not unanimous in their support of the proposition that persons under cross-pressures are less partisan, i.e., make later voting decisions or fail to vote, than are people who are not under cross-pressures. Researchers working for President John F. Kennedy prior to his election, for example, initially assumed the operation of cross-pressure effects, but found that their assumption was not supported by the 1960 presidential election. They had expected that Catholic Republicans, torn between their party identification and the candidacy of a coreligionist on the ticket of the opposition party, would stay away from the polls. Instead, Catholic Republicans tended to cross party lines and vote for Kennedy.[38]

The cross-pressured Catholic voter has frequently been in a stressful situation in the United States. In 1948, he seems to have resolved the stress by not going to the polls, while in 1960, he resolved it by voting Democratic. This difference has been attributed to the fact that in 1948, the Democratic Party was not an attractive alternative. Harry Truman himself was a relatively

---

[35] Paul F. Lazarsfeld, Bernard Berelson, and Hazel Gaudet, *The People's Choice* (New York: Columbia University Press, 1948), p. 60.

[36] Bernard R. Berelson, Paul F. Lazarsfeld, and W. N. McPhee, *Voting* (Chicago: The University of Chicago Press, 1954), p. 200.

[37] Lipset, *Political Man*, p. 211.

[38] Ithiel de Sola Pool, R. P. Abelson, and S. L. Popkin, *Candidates, Issues and Strategies* (Cambridge: MIT Press, 1965), p. 76.

unimpressive candidate, a Protestant, and had been tainted by the image of communism through the Harry Dexter White scandal. Thus, while the individual under cross-pressures might have been motivated by his traditional Democratic tendencies to lean toward the Democratic Party, the party itself did not reinforce this tendency. In 1960, on the other hand, the Democrats, aside from having a strong liberal platform, had an attractive Catholic candidate with whom cross-pressured Catholics could identify strongly. In this case the "push" from the Republican Party created by a conservative platform was reinforced by the "pull" generated by the Democratic Party.

The cross-pressure framework differs from the status-inconsistency framework in the privacy of the stress that the subject voter feels. The black lawyer in the status-inconsistency situation is purported to experience stress because other people identify him as black and lower their estimations of his status. The Republican Catholic voter in an election in which a Catholic seeks office as a Democrat, by contrast, is not defined by others as a Catholic, but rather is likely to see his religion as relevant to his political behavior himself. That is, the stress is intrapersonal, rather than interpersonal.[39] In the absence of interpersonal pressures involving conflicting expectations, the individual may withdraw from the political arena, as he did in 1948, until such time as one of the troublesome pressures becomes politically irrelevant, e.g., until Catholicism ceases to be an issue in presidential politics. However, if one of the alternative sets of expectations has greater short-run payoff value, then that alternative will be chosen.

As was the case with the social-mobility and status-inconsistency frameworks, methodological developments have caused sociologists to question whether there are indeed cross-pressure effects on political behavior resulting from membership in particular combinations of social groups. Again paralleling the fields of social mobility and status inconsistency, the most precise research carried out suggests that nonvoting, like party choice, can be best accounted for by the additive effects of the particular sociological variables under consideration, with no additional increment attributable to cross-pressure.[40]

[39] David R. Segal, "Status Inconsistency, Cross-Pressures, and American Political Behavior," *American Sociological Review* 34 (June 1969), pp. 352–359.

[40] Patrick M. Horan, "Social Positions and Political Cross-Pressures," *American Sociological Review* 36 (August 1971), pp. 650–660.

RELATIVE DEPRIVATION

While the relative-deprivation framework, like the three frameworks discussed above, seeks to identify connections between the allocation of rewards (e.g., acceptance) and deprivations (e.g., rejection) in the social order and political behavior, it differs from these approaches in an important respect. Whereas the status-inconsistency and social-mobility frameworks are rooted in processes associated with the acceptance of an individual by a high status group, and the cross-pressure framework assumes that the individual will himself decide which of his group memberships are most important in a particular political context, the relative-deprivation framework is rooted in processes of social comparison. Unlike the status-inconsistency situation, in which the individual is purported to compare the deference he expects to receive with the deference that he actually receives, the person experiencing relative deprivation compares the rewards he is receiving from the social order with the rewards received by other people making the same investment in the social order that he is, and finds that he is receiving less for his investment.

The concept of relative deprivation was first introduced in a major study of the American military in World War II.[41] Social scientists studying willingness to serve in the armed forces found that married men were more unhappy about being drafted than were single men. It was obvious that the married man was making the same sacrifices as the single man, plus the additional sacrifice of having to leave his family for some period. Moreover, since draft boards tended to be more lenient with married men than with single men, the married draftee was extremely likely to be aware of other married men who had not been drafted. Thus, whether he compared himself with single draftees or with married men who had not been drafted, the married draftee was relatively deprived. It is important to note that the person who feels relatively deprived need not necessarily be objectively deprived in the sense that something has been taken away from him. He need only be able to compare himself with some *reference group*

---

[41] Samuel A. Stouffer, Edward A. Suchman, Leland C. DiVinney, Shirley A. Star, and Robin M. Williams, Jr., *The American Soldier: Adjustment During Army Life* (Princeton, N.J.: Princeton University Press, 1965), p. 125.

and learn that he is not doing as well as are other members of that group.[42]

The major study dealing with the relationship between relative deprivation and politics was a survey conducted in England and Wales in the early 1960s.[43] The author was concerned with the attitudes of Englishmen and Welshmen toward the inequalities in their stratification system. The author suggests that, given a Labour Party that is ideologically socialistic, egalitarian, and working class, if members of the working class feel deprived relative to members of the middle class, they will support that party. If, on the other hand, a member of the working class fails to support the Labour Party, then there is a discrepancy between his position in the social-stratification system and his attitudes toward the distribution of rewards in that system.

The data suggest very clearly that the Conservative Party, which could not elect a government in Great Britain if it did not receive considerable support from working-class voters, does get such support. More importantly, a good deal of this support can be attributed to people in working-class occupations who define themselves as middle class, seem to regard the inequalities of the British stratification system as just, reject the egalitarian ideology of the Labour Party, and vote on that basis. This study, then, attributes votes cast by members of the working class for the Labour Party as, at least in part, a manifestation of the relative deprivation of the working class in British society.

To be thus manifested, however, the inequalities of British society must be recognized by the workers and must be defined as unjust. To the extent that inequalities are either not recognized or are regarded as proper, members of the working class will tend to vote for the Conservative Party, the symbol of the status quo. To the extent that inequalities are recognized, the individual member of the working class becomes aware that not only is he deprived relative to the middle class, but that other members of the working class are deprived as well. He becomes conscious of the common interests of members of the working class—class conscious, in Marxian terms—and his relative deprivation becomes a *fraternal*

---

[42] For a discussion of the concept of reference groups, which also evolved from *The American Soldier* studies, see Herbert H. Hyman and Eleanor D. Singer, *Readings in Reference Group Theory and Research* (New York: The Free Press, 1968).

[43] W. G. Runciman, *Relative Deprivation and Social Justice* (Berkeley: The University of California Press, 1966).

phenomenon. That is, he becomes aware (or comes to believe) that he is disadvantaged in the system of inequality not as an individual, but as a member of a social class.

This same concept of fraternal relative deprivation has been used to explain at least some of the support of George C. Wallace's candidacy for the presidency in 1968.[44] A study of voters in Cleveland revealed that Wallace received a disproportionately high proportion of the votes of working-class men who felt that economically they were doing as well as other members of the working class, but that the working class as a whole was not doing as well as the middle class, at least in terms of economic gains.

COMPLEX STRATIFICATION SYSTEMS AND POLITICAL CONFLICT

Imagine a society based upon the most simplistic reduction of the Marxian model. There would be two economic classes based upon relationship to the means of production: owners (employers) and nonowners (employees). All other elements of social and political life would be wholly determined by which of these classes an individual fell into. In such a society, any conflict that emerged—regardless of the issue—would divide the antagonists into two hostile camps. The camps would always be the same, determined by economic class membership, and the outcome of the conflict would be predetermined, since power would, in such a society, be perfectly correlated with economic class position. There would be a large segment of society—the nonowners—who always found themselves on the same side and always lost. And there would be a small segment of society—the owners—who always found themselves on the same side and always won. It is not difficult to see how, over time, the frustrations of the always-defeated employees would lead them to recognize their common disadvantaged position and would build up to the point where a workers' revolution would be inevitable. This, of course, would be the Marxian expectation. Thus, in such a simple society, increasing degrees of cohesion in economic classes are expected to result in societal conflict. There is a certain irony in the notion that the better integrated one is into one's own social stratum, the

---

[44] Thomas F. Pettigrew, Robert T. Riley, and Reeve D. Vanneman, "George Wallace's Constituents," *Psychology Today* 5 (February 1972), pp. 47 ff.

less healthy society as a whole is. This notion is, of course, only possible if we regard revolution as a symptom of social malaise.

Let us imagine now a second society—one that had a more complex stratification system. There would still be differentiation along economic class lines, but there would also be differentiation in terms of education, social honor, ethnic group status, and so on. Thus, each individual would be assigned places in the stratification system on a multitude of dimensions. In this society, one's position on noneconomic dimensions would *not* be determined by one's economic class position. Let us suppose, however, that in this complex noneconomically determined system, it was nonetheless the case that the correlations between dimensions in the stratification system were perfect, or almost so. This might be due to the entire system's being determined by something other than economic relations, e.g., the system might be wholly ascriptive, or the correlations might be an accidental occurrence during one period of time in a society. Whatever the reason, the alignment of members of the polity would be exactly the same as was the case in the system described above. Since the system would not be economically determined, the issues over which conflicts arose would not necessarily be economic issues. Nevertheless, one set of people, disadvantaged in terms of every dimension in the stratification system, would consistently find themselves on the losing side of conflicts, due to a lack of resources that might be converted into victory. Another set of people, by contrast, could convert their advantages on each dimension into victory, and would forever be on the winning side of whatever dispute led to conflict. The higher the correlation among dimensions of the stratification system, the more likely the people who were disadvantaged all across the social structure would be to form a cohesive, integrated, organized public. And we must again face the irony that the cost of this cohesion, integration, and organization is almost certain to be intense societal conflict.

The irony is further compounded when we think of how things might be otherwise. What if there were discrepancies between peoples' positions across several dimensions of a social stratification system, or if people were not wholly bound to occupy the niches in the economic and social structures that had been occupied by their parents? Here the status-inconsistency, social-mobility, and relative-deprivation frameworks tell us that society might experience major conflicts anyway, and the cross-pressure framework suggests that people might cease to participate in the polity. Which is the lesser evil?

Fortunately, we have already determined that the above-mentioned frameworks do not stand up well under empirical scrutiny. And no industrial nation has seen the revolution of the proletariat that Marxists insist must eventually occur—at least in the form that Marx expected. Indeed, in those nations that have established regimes that call themselves communist, such estab- · lishment has been a means, rather than a consequence, of industrializing, and in none of them has the state withered away and communism been achieved. However, these observations are ancillary to the two major questions we must confront on a theoretical level. Is the degree of correspondence among the several elements of a system of social stratification related to the level of conflict in a society? If so, must this conflict necessarily be interpreted as a sign of the ill health of the society?

THE FUNCTIONS OF SOCIAL CONFLICT

One of the earliest social theorists to deal with the functions of conflict was Georg Simmel. Shortly after the turn of the twentieth century, Simmel included a chapter on conflict in his text on sociology. In it he suggested that the existence of conflict between individuals, while seemingly negative and damaging, might play a more positive role in its larger context.[45] Economic competition between individuals, he argued, was a sign of health in the larger economic system, whatever its effects on the individual competitors. By analogy, we might argue that the more lines of cleavage there are in a political system, and the more conflicts they generate, the healthier the system will be. After all, what is conflict if not competition for power? Indeed, some sociological theory, by positing that power serves as a medium of exchange in the polity just as money serves as the exchange medium in the economy, lends support to this analogy.[46]

For Simmel, conflict was an essential characteristic of social structure and, in combination with processes of social unification, was necessary for social integration. At the very least, the existence of conflict indicated to individuals that they had some

---

[45] See Georg Simmel, *Conflict and the Web of Group Affiliations,* Kurt H. Wolff and Reinhard Bendix, trans. (New York: The Free Press, 1955), p. 17.

[46] See Talcott Parsons, "On the Concept of Political Power," in *Sociological Theory and Modern Society* (New York: The Free Press, 1967), pp. 297–354.

control over their lives. In contrast to the unicausal economic-determinist model of society, Simmel felt that conflicts were not destined to be resolved on the basis of relationship to the means of production. The very complexity of modern social systems, bringing a variety of forces into arenas of conflict, revealed that conflicts were reflections of humans' controlling, or attempting to control, their destinies, rather than signs of social ill-health. While a wide range of resources might be brought to bear to resolve particular disputes, conflicts would continue to exist.

Most of the important theoretical developments on the positive social functions of conflict have been built on the foundation laid down by Simmel. Lewis Coser, on the basis of Simmel's theory, has developed the thesis that, while conflict helps maintain boundaries between groups in the social system (e.g., economic classes) by increasing group consciousness and consciousness of group differences (e.g., class consciousness), it also helps maintain the total social, political, and economic system by creating a balance among the various groups within the system.[47] Conflict provides a safety valve by means of which competing groups can express their hostility toward each other, rather than feeling that they must withdraw from the system to unburden themselves of their hostility. The conflict itself, of course, can threaten the system if it is particularly intense. However, the very complexity of modern society is thought to mitigate against disruptively intense conflict.

Here we have our irony again. The more planes of cleavage that exist in society, and the more arenas of potential conflict that therefore exist, the less intense any given conflict is likely to be. It is almost as though there were a ceiling on the amount of conflict that could take place in a social system, and the more specific conflicts that this amount were divided up among, the more diluted each individual conflict would be. One corollary of this postulate, of course, is that if conflict is resolved in one arena, it will not disappear, but rather will be manifested in other arenas. On the basis of this reasoning, we would not expect the disappearance of antagonisms rooted in economic class differences (if indeed such antagonisms did disappear) to result in a consensual society. We would merely expect the emergence of antagonisms based upon some other kind of group difference.

---

[47] Lewis Coser, *The Functions of Social Conflict* (New York: The Free Press, 1956).

CROSSCUTTING CLEAVAGES

Why should it be that the more planes of cleavage that exist in a system, the less intense conflict along these planes will be? This hypothesized relationship is based upon the assumption that the greater people's involvements are with their social roles, the more intense the conflicts associated with those roles will be. If there is a single plane of cleavage dividing society into two antagonistic economic classes, then the totality of a person's social life is associated with his role as a member of an economic class. Conflicts involving that class membership will be particularly intense because they will involve the total individual. By contrast, in a more complex system in which an individual is a member of religious, racial, and other groups, as well as a member of an economic class, in which he plays roles in all of these groups, and in which these other memberships are not determined by his role as a member of an economic class, his involvement in his role as a member of an economic class will be less. In a situation of conflict between economic classes, to the extent that his other social roles do not become salient, his involvement in his economic role, and hence in the conflict, will be less, and the conflict will be less intense. As Coser has written:[48]

> It may be that one reason for the relative absence of "class struggle" in this country is the fact that the American worker, far from restricting his allegiance to class-conflict groupings and associations, is a member of a number of associations and groupings which represent him in diverse conflicts with different religious, ethnic, status, and political groups. Since the lines of conflict between all these groups do not converge, the cleavage along class lines does not draw the total energies and allegiance of the worker into a single area of conflict. The relative stability of the American class structure (as compared with European class structures) and the failure of Marxian— or Syndicalist Sorelian—attempts to divorce the American worker from nonclass types of allegiances seem to confirm this observation.

Because the intensity of people's involvements with their social roles corresponds directly with the intensity of the conflicts

[48] Ibid., p. 77.

associated with these roles, the social-mobility and status-inconsistency frameworks both lead to the expectation that conflict will become less intense as society becomes more complex. Our argument here, however, involves a different dynamic. The thesis we have presented assumes that an individual is involved in many groups, and that therefore his commitment to any one group is less than total. An extreme example of this process is the cross-pressured individual, who is expected to behave in two or more different ways by two or more groups to which he belongs, and who resolves the inner conflict by behaving in none of the expected ways. The status-inconsistency and social-mobility frameworks, by contrast, argue that the individual who is mobile or inconsistent is uninvolved in the classes, strata, or groups in which he holds nominal membership not because of the number of groups that his commitment is spread across, but because he is not accepted as an equal by the groups in which he aspires to play social roles. Both the status-inconsistency and the social-mobility framework see this rejection leading the rejected person to make demands on the political system, i.e., to generate conflict. Because of the low level of social involvement of the marginal or inconsistent person, the conflict would not be expected to be particularly intense. Moreover, if one assumed that meritocracy was modern and/or good and ascription traditional and/or bad, then one would have to conclude that the conflict generated by the socially mobile or status-inconsistent segments of the population, to the extent that it achieved its desired ends, was good for society, or at least was a modernizing influence. Depending upon the assumptions one made about what constituted the good society, therefore, one could see conflict of this sort as good or bad for society.

It is important to note that, in Coser's formulation, the existence of a multitude of social cleavages is not in and of itself sufficient to limit the intensity of conflict. In addition, the dimensions underlying these cleavages must be relatively uncorrelated with each other. If the correlations among elements of social structure are low, a significant proportion of the population will be cross-pressured and social conflict will be kept down to a level consistent with the long-term stability of the system. Moreover, the conflicts defined by the planes of cross-cutting cleavage must not challenge the basic values of the social structure, which serve as the foundation of social, political, and economic consensus. Rather, these consensual values must remain intact so that they may be used to define the structures within and the rules by which conflicts involving other values are to be resolved. In the polity, this means that the governmental structures and political party structures must remain relatively intact and unchallenged so that the conflict can be resolved within them.

SUPERIMPOSITION AND PLURALISM

The requirement that there be a low level of correlation among the elements of the stratification system is further developed by Ralf Dahrendorf in his attempt to provide a framework for a theory of class relations to supersede Marx's theory.[49] Dahrendorf's thesis is based upon the assumption that in every social organization, some positions are endowed with power and others are not. Thus, every social organization is a potential arena for conflict between the powerful—those holding dominant roles in the organization—and the powerless—those holding subordinate roles. These relations of power come to be regarded as legitimate, i.e., as authoritative, in every form of social organization, but because of the underlying conflict in social organizations, this legitimacy is precarious. Within any given social organization, conflict between the dominant and subordinate strata (which Dahrendorf, rejecting the Marxian notions of class, refers to as *interests)* may not occur at all, may be manifested by a single interest group's emerging from each stratum, or may be manifested by more than one interest group's emerging from each stratum. That is, the formation and definition of parties to the conflict are not wholly determined by the distribution of power in the organization, although they are constrained by that distribution.

What is crucial for understanding the intensity of conflict in any given society in Dahrendorf's formulation is whether the structure of social organization in that society is *superimposed* or *pluralistic.* In the situation of superimposition, one set of people are always in positions of dominance in every social organization, while another set of people always occupy subordinate positions. Thus, people meeting in different conflict arenas will nonetheless always meet in terms of the same relationships. In a situation of pluralism, by contrast, the populations that fill the positions of dominance and subordination in various social organizations are separate. The upper strata of the religious hierarchy, for example, may have no power in the industrial or political arena, and the top

---

[49] Ralf Dahrendorf, *Class and Class Conflict in Industrial Society* (Stanford, Calif.: Stanford University Press, 1959).

political executives might hold subordinate positions in the religious and economic organizations of the society. There may be conflict within each of these organizations, but across organizations the lines of conflict will not be congruent. When organizational structure is pluralistic, no single conflict is likely to become extremely intense because those people who are subordinate in the organization in which that conflict takes place can hold positions of dominance in other organizations. When superimposition exists, however, the several arenas of conflict add to, rather than detract from, each other, potentially leading to one intense and all-inclusive conflict.

The social organizations that Dahrendorf refers to are defined in terms of resources that can, by conversion, be manifested as power. These resources vary from society to society. In all cases, they are material goods or states of being that are both valued and differentially distributed in the social system. That is, they are regarded as beneficial, and some people have a disproportionate share, perhaps all, of them, while others are denied access to them, at least in part, and perhaps totally.

Harold Lasswell has suggested a typology of eight values that either directly represent, or can be converted into, political power.[50] Four of these he defines as *welfare values,* the possession of which is required for the maintenance of the individual: well-being (health and safety), wealth, skill, and enlightenment or knowledge. The other four values are *deference values,* the distribution of which are taken into account in social interaction: power, respect, rectitude, and affection.

Power is obviously a political resource. The remaining values may serve as bases to gain power in the political realm. Persons ranked high on the dimensions of respect, rectitude, skill, or enlightenment, for example, may be called upon to participate in decision-making processes. Persons high in affection may influence decision-makers as friends. Persons high in wealth can exert economic leverage on the political system. And persons high in well-being can use their access to health and safety to coerce elements of the polity. That is, they can use violence.

Lasswell, like most other stratification theorists before him, assumed that people ranked high on one dimension would tend to rank high on others as well. If we take the values suggested by Lasswell to define eight dimensions of a status system, his

---

[50] Harold D. Lasswell and Abraham Kaplan, *Power and Society* (New Haven: Yale University Press, 1950), pp. 55 ff.

assumption is that people tend to be status consistent. Our discussion above, however, suggests that status consistency decreases with economic development. Moreover, we have reason to believe that this is a good thing. On the one hand, theories that see status inconsistency leading to political conflict have not held up well under the weight of empirical data. On the other hand, theories of social conflict suggest that having different individuals and groups advantaged relative to others across the dimensions of a stratification system minimizes the intensity of such conflict.

We saw these processes at work earlier in our discussion of Dahl's study of politics in New Haven, Connecticut. Like every social system in every time, New Haven evidences an unequal distribution of resources. However, its structure of inequality has changed. The distribution of inequality in New Haven at the birth of the republic was cumulative.[51] People who were advantaged in terms of one value were advantaged in terms of other values. They were status consistent, and the correlations among an individual's positions in the stratification system were high. The local elite had the highest social standing (respect), positions of religious (rectitude), political (power), and economic (wealth) leadership, and differential access to educational institutions (skill and enlightenment). We can assume that they had differential access to medical care (well-being), as well. Even if, as seems reasonable, not everyone loved them, they were clearly well placed with regard to seven of the eight values specified by Lasswell.

Were such a situation to persist for a long period of time, we would, on the basis of the theories of social conflict discussed above, expect conflicts of high intensity to disrupt the calm New England air around New Haven. This did not happen. Rather, an entrepreneurial class whose new wealth made it status inconsistent (high in wealth but low in social standing) was nonetheless able to convert power in the economic arena into power in the political arena. Economic change in a very real sense opened the system to social mobility, which served a dual function: producing status inconsistency and reducing the intensity of social conflict.

The industrial revolution spawned a large urban working class in New Haven, and had there been no mobility channels available to the immigrants who comprised this class, the potential for intense conflict might have again increased. In an era of expanding suffrage, however, members of this urban proletariat

---

[51] Dahl, *Who Governs?* p. 85.

had a resource that even the old New England upper class could not have counted upon: popularity with their fellow-immigrant voters (affection). This resource, in turn, was converted into political power, producing a status-inconsistent stratum of politically powerful Catholic immigrants.

New Haven is not a unique case as a social system in which the complexity of social structure mitigated against intense conflict. In a study of communities in stress and conflict, James Coleman found that the presence of cross-pressured citizens minimized involvement in, and thus intensity of, conflict:

> Individuals have many associations in a community, many roles to play, and many attachments to groups and individuals. If these attachments are spread throughout the community as a whole, then the individual has in a sense internalized many different elements in the community. . . .
>
> When a controversy arises in a community, any one of these objects and values can act as a basis of response: if it becomes involved in a controversy, then it "takes with it" the individual who has attachments to it. The individual who has attachments to many elements in the community very often finds himself pulled in opposing directions as the controversy broadens. . . . Unable to commit himself fully to one side or the other, he either withdraws from the dispute, or, taking sides, is still beset by doubts and fears, unable to go "all out" against the enemy.[52]

In communities having complex social structures with crosscutting cleavages, people experienced inner conflicts, and a good deal of controversy took place within groups of friends, but no overriding issue was able to divide any community as a social system into two hostile camps. In communities not characterized by crosscutting cleavages, however, all individuals knew what side of a conflict they were on, groups of friends agreed on their positions, and the communities themselves were divided.

All of this is not to say that each time a new plane of cleavage which crosscuts other planes of cleavage is added to the polity, the intensity of social conflict will necessarily be reduced and the stability of the polity enhanced. Just as there is a body of political theory that suggests that a society, by virtue of too few planes of cleavage, may be too homogeneous to support a stable democratic

---

[52] James S. Coleman, *Community Conflict* (New York: The Free Press, 1957), p. 22.

form of political organization, so is there a body of political theory that argues that too many planes of cleavage, producing too much heterogeneity, will undermine the stability of democratic political organization.[53] These two lines of thought, of course, need not be regarded as mutually exclusive. They can alternatively be interpreted as suggesting that there is some optimal balance of heterogeneity and homogeneity, or some threshold level of crosscutting cleavages that defines the point at which the costs of heterogeneity, in terms of the stability of democratic institutions, begin to outweigh the gains.

This interpretation is the one that has come to the fore. Research has been conducted on the amount of *fragmentation* in political systems,[54] fragmentation being the probability that two individuals drawn at random from a population will belong to different groups. Fragmentation, in turn, has been shown to reflect the level of crosscutting cleavage in a system. If the level of fragmentation on two dimensions of social structure is either very low or very high, the level of crosscutting cleavages must be very low.[55] Thus, the optimal level of crosscutting cleavages exists at some balance of homogeneous and heterogeneous social structures. The two basic propositions we have discussed on the relationships between conflict intensity and crosscutting cleavages, on the one hand, and democratic performance, on the other, have been tested using data from seven nations, and have been supported.[56] The more intense the cleavage was, the more poorly democratic political organization performed; and the higher the level of crosscutting cleavage, the better democratic political organization performed. The underlying assumption of the complex-stratifications-systems model, that higher levels of crosscutting are related to lower levels of conflict intensity, was also supported by the data.

This entire process, in turn, is presumed to operate largely

---

[53] For a discussion of these positions, see Arendt Lijphart, *The Politics of Accommodation* (Berkeley: The University of California Press, 1968), Chapter 1, and his "Typologies of Democratic Systems," *Comparative Political Studies* 1 (April 1965), pp. 3–44.

[54] See Douglas Rae, "A Note on the Fractionalization of Some European Party Systems," *Comparative Political Studies* 1 (October 1965), pp. 413–418.

[55] Michael Taylor and Douglas Rae, "An Analysis of Cross-Cutting Between Political Cleavages," *Comparative Politics* 1 (July 1969), pp. 534–547. See also Rae and Taylor, *The Analysis of Political Cleavages* (New Haven: Yale University Press, 1970).

[56] Harold D. Clarke and Allan Kornberg, "A Note on Social Cleavages and Democratic Performance," *Comparative Political Studies* 4 (October 1971), pp. 349–360.

within the political party system. In a system characterized by crosscutting cleavages, there is no single overriding issue to identify mutually antagonistic publics for opposing political parties. Rather, the parties must aggregate sufficient support to win elections by combining segments of the electorate that are interested in a wide range of issues. Politics of this kind in a complex system is likely to produce strange bedfellows, and the process of defining a party platform must become one of bargaining or compromise. Conflicts will occasionally break out, although with limited intensity, and whatever consensus appears must be regarded as the short-term result of processes of conflict resolution, rather than an enduring condition of the society.

Two caveats must be added to this discussion. First, while there is a good deal of agreement among political sociologists on the principle that crosscutting cleavages contribute to democratic stability, there are dissenting voices and deviant cases. Perhaps the most dramatic of these is the case of Norway. Norwegian society has historically been characterized by a set of cleavages that are congruent rather than crosscutting, and by a political party system based upon these deep-rooted cleavages.[57] Yet Norway has managed to maintain a stable democratic political system. No simple model can explain all of politics, and in the next chapter we shall consider some additional variables that will help us better understand this deviant case.

Second, it must be recognized that the theory of crosscutting cleavages in no way claims that such cleavages will do away with social conflict. We have suggested previously that if conflict is resolved in one arena, it will not disappear, but will merely appear in another arena. In fact, not only may conflict be transferred from one arena of social life to another, but it may also be transferred from the societal level to the group or individual level. Crosscutting cleavages reduce the intensity of societal cleavage at the cost of increasing the inner conflicts of cross-pressured individuals.

[57] See Harry Eckstein, *Division and Cohesion in Democracy* (Princeton, N.J.: Princeton University Press, 1966).

7

Socialization and Social Influence in the Polity

SOCIALIZATION PROCESSES

Political socialization is the dynamic by which an individual learns what political party it is appropriate for him to support. At the same time, it is a complex and continuing learning process that goes far beyond the internalization of identification with a political party, which is merely one element in a large set of political attitudes that an individual will learn. Nor are socialization processes limited to the learning of attitudes. Political action is as much a set of learned traits as are political attitudes. And, as is the case with attitudes, there is a wide range of potential political behavior that an individual may learn to perform, from voting, running for office, campaigning for a candidate, or making a request of a congressman, to bombing government office buildings.

Although much research on various aspects of political socialization took place in the second quarter of the twentieth century, almost in anticipation of the "behavioral revolution" in political science, no major attempt was made until the 1950s to catalog and systematize the findings that were accumulating.[1] In 1959, as one manifestation of the increasing concern with human behavior, Herbert Hyman published the first inventory of research dealing with politics as learned behavior.[2] Hyman was concerned with three areas in which political learning took place: level of participation (activity level, knowledge, etc.), orientation (party choice or position on left-right continuum), and style (authoritarian vs. democratic). We shall preserve these categories, but shall further divide the orientation category by dealing separately with political party preference and ideology.

LEVEL OF PARTICIPATION

Hyman's major findings regarding level of participation were that sex differences and socioeconomic differences in political involvement that had frequently been observed in adult populations were manifested among children as well. Boys were more likely to read about politics and recognize political figures than were girls. Children from high-income families were more likely to pay attention to politics than were children from low-income families. Equally impressive as these differences, however, has been the growing body of data that enables us to chart the incorporation of young people into the political system (or their rejection of that system) as they age. In the four years of secondary education, for example, one study showed an increase of almost 10 percent in the number of students sufficiently involved in electoral politics to wear campaign buttons: 67.8 percent of the freshmen and 77.2 percent of the seniors.[3]

---

[1] The phrase "behavioral revolution" refers to a period of roughly two decades, from the late 1940s to the late 1960s, during which the major thrust of American political science shifted from concern with issues of political philosophy and diplomatic history to a preoccupation with the political behavior of individuals and groups. See David Easton, *A Framework for Political Analysis* (Englewood Cliffs, N.J.: Prentice-Hall, Inc., 1965), especially Chapter 1, "Theory and Behavioral Research." Interestingly, political science now sees itself in a "post-behavioral" era of intellectual maturity, having passed through its behavioral adolescence. See David Easton, "The New Revolution in Political Science," *American Political Science Review* 63 (December 1969), pp. 1051–1061.

[2] Herbert Hyman, *Political Socialization* (New York: The Free Press, 1959).

[3] Robert D. Hess and Judith V. Torney, *The Development of Political Attitudes in Children* (New York: Doubleday & Co., Inc., 1967), p. 12.

In the very early years of life, as children become aware of politics, they tend to see the political function in terms of idealistic symbols. A study conducted in the early 1960s, for example, revealed that, to second-graders, American government was most commonly symbolized by President Kennedy and George Washington. Eighth-graders, by contrast, viewed the act of voting and the institution of the Congress as the best representations of what our government is.[4]

Along with this change in perceptions about what was important in government came an increasing recognition of the imperfections of government. Ninety percent of third-grade students felt in the early 1960s that what went on in government was all for the best. Among eighth-graders, this sentiment was voiced by only 76 percent of the students.[5] Clearly, throughout the years of primary education, students expressed a high level of faith in their government. Nonetheless, by about age thirteen, one out of four students was willing to express doubts about the government's perfection. This willingness was perhaps related to the child's increasing inclusion in networks of political communication and exposure to political discussion as he aged. Between grades three and eight, there was an increase of almost 33 percent in the incidence of students who had talked to their parents about a candidate for political office (52.4 percent to 85.0 percent). At the same time, there was an increase of 40 percent in those who had talked to friends about a candidate: from 49 percent in grade three to 89 percent in grade eight. In grades three and four, children were more likely to talk to family than to friends about politics. Thereafter, however, the peer group seemed to be the most important context for political communication.[6] We should note that these data do not indicate a high level of political knowledge necessarily, but do suggest that a higher level of political discussion existed among schoolchildren than among the adults we have previously discussed.

---

[4] David Easton and Jack Dennis, *Children in the Political System* (New York: McGraw-Hill Book Co., 1969), p. 116. The Easton and Dennis study and the Hess and Torney study both drew on the same research project, which had been directed by Easton and Hess. Easton was primarily concerned with the functioning of political systems, while Hess was interested in child development. Thus, as we have noted in other areas, we have two major research reports that bring different orientations to the same body of data.

[5] Hess and Torney, *The Development of Political Attitudes in Children*, p. 73.

[6] Ibid., p. 81.

ADOLESCENT POLITICAL PARTICIPATION

Studying the attachment of children and adolescents to the national political system can be misleading. As children become aware of the processes of electoral politics, they learn at the same time that they can neither vote nor hold elective office. Thus the institutions and processes of the national political system do not invite their involvement. However, we noted very early in this book that political acts can be performed in contexts other than governmental or electoral institutions. If we take political socialization to mean the internalization of political orientations, the incorporation of them into one's personality, and if we further assume that the personality traits relevant to politics can be manifested in a variety of arenas and contexts, then in dealing with people who are still in school and have not yet attained full citizenship rights, we can focus on that which is political to the individual, rather than on how the individual relates to that which is political in society. To the extent that political socialization remains constant in a variety of contexts and over time, we would expect some relationship between the way an individual relates as an adolescent to politics in his world and the way that individual will relate to politics in society when he attains full citizenship rights. This assumption is important, and we shall deal with it more directly in a later section.

What is political in the social world of the American adolescent? He can be seen as a participant in a multitude of social groups, formally or informally organized. These include the nation-state, the informal web of relationships of adolescent social life, the institutional structure of the high school, including its student government, a wide range of voluntary associations both inside and outside of the high school, and, for those who are employed, the social relations in the place of work. All of these may be conceived of as small social systems. In each, values are allocated. That is, they each have a political function. Within each context, political activity is possible. In the nation-state, although adolescents cannot vote, they may become members of political clubs (e.g., Young Democrats, Young Republicans, Young Americans for Freedom), civil rights groups, etc. They may be informal leaders in their peer groups. They may hold elective or appointive office in student government or in voluntary associations inside and outside of school. If political socialization refers to a set of internalized acts, attitudes, and orientations that persist throughout the life cycle, then all of these patterns of behavior are of interest to us insofar as they are rooted in a set of predispositions that will lead the same individuals who are politically involved as adolescents to be politically involved in their adult life as well.[7]

Using data collected in 1965 by the Survey Research Center of the University of Michigan, I explored adolescent political activity. The data consist of interviews with a sample of 1669 high school seniors attending ninety-seven high schools in the United States. The level of activity reported by the students was surprisingly high. Almost 57 percent of the sample reported having been elected or appointed to an office in a school club or team.

Three qualifications to this statistic must be noted at the outset. First, the sample does not represent at all the 30 percent of American adolescents who in the mid-1960s were dropping out of high school before the spring of their senior year.

Second, the fact that a person is captain of the rifle team in high school gives us no basis for projecting that he will be President of the United States in adulthood, although he may become president of a local chapter of the National Rifle Association. We are interested in the *pattern* of an adolescent's political participation, rather than in his holding office in a single organization. About 2 percent of the high school senior sample were active in four or five different political arenas, and an additional 12.5 percent were active in three arenas. We would expect these to be the most likely to continue high levels of political activity into adulthood.

Third, there was evidence in the data of differences between what we might call "localistic" and "cosmopolitan" political orientations. One group of students reported themselves to be members of the leadership crowd in their adolescent peer groups. Another group reported themselves to be active in organizations like Young Democrats and Young Republicans. There was no overlap between these two groups. Intuition (and little else) suggests that members of the latter group will be more politically active as adults than will members of the former group. We shall deal with the antecedents of political activity among adolescents below. For the present, note simply that there is evidence that adolescents do have a political life. The final determination of the relationship between political activity in adolescence and adult politics awaits a follow-up study of the 1965 high school seniors.

---

[7] This discussion is based upon David R. Segal, "The Socialization of Adolescent Politicians" (Ph.D. diss., The University of Chicago, 1967).

POLITICAL ORIENTATION: PARTY CHOICE

Hyman, in his initial inventory of findings in the field of political socialization, suggested that the family is foremost among the agencies of political socialization.[8] Clearly, when both parents support the same political party, their offspring are likely to support that party as well. In families in which the parents agree on their party choice, their high school offspring tend to agree with them 76 percent of the time.[9] Interestingly, there are differences between parties. The children of Democrats are more likely to agree with their parents (85 percent) than are the children of Republicans (65 percent). However, when children defect from the party choice of their parents, they are most likely simply to voice no preference. In the 1965 high school survey, for example, only about 7 percent of the adolescent respondents expressed support for the party opposing their parents' choice.[10] Of course, children share with their parents many social characteristics associated with party choice (race, religion, ethnicity), so that even if they were unrelated, they would be expected to support the same party. That socialization does not completely determine party choice is demonstrated by the fact that the defection rate from parental party choice observed among adolescents is roughly doubled by adulthood.[11]

What happens when the mother and father disagree about politics? What are the implications of such disagreement for the political socialization of their children? Some literature, and considerably more mythology on sex roles in political life, suggests that when decisions about politics are made in the context of the family, the male dominates the process. A study conducted of voting in the 1940 presidential election in Erie County, Ohio, reported that "the almost perfect agreement between husband and wife comes about as a result of male dominance in political

---

[8] Hyman, *Political Socialization*, p. 69.

[9] Kenneth P. Langton, *Political Socialization* (New York: Oxford University Press, 1969), p. 59.

[10] M. Kent Jennings and Richard G. Niemi, "The Transmission of Political Values from Parent to Child," *American Political Science Review* 62 (March 1968), pp. 169–184.

[11] See Richard E. Dawson and Kenneth Prewitt, *Political Socialization* (Boston: Little, Brown and Co., 1969), p. 113.

situations."[12] Thus, there is political agreement in most families. Moreover, "in those cases where there is disagreement, the tension of the situation leads the family members to make some adjustments. It is usually the women who so adjust. . . . "[13]

The evidence on male dominance of familial political orientation, however, does not go far toward supporting either the theory or the myth, and it contradicts the assumption that, when parents disagree, the political orientation of the father will dominate. A study conducted in 1952 in Cambridge, Massachusetts, found no evidence of paternal domination in the transmission of political party preference from parent to child. When disagreement occurred, daughters were most likely to be influenced by their mothers, and sons were as likely to agree with their mothers as with their fathers.[14] More recent research has similarly found that, of all parent-child pairs, similarity was strongest between mother and daughter.[15] Neither parent emerges as a clearly dominant role-model for the learning of party preference. When differences are observed between parents, however, an increasing number of studies have consistently shown the mother to be slightly more influential than the father.

POLITICAL ORIENTATION: IDEOLOGY

While it is clear that parents play a major role in "teaching" their progeny political party preference, the evidence on the transmission of political ideology from parents to children is less convincing.[16] It would seem that, having had a political party preference transmitted to it by its parents, the ascending generation then, as it matures, seeks reasons for that preference in its own social world. Since each generation grows up in a world that is different from the one in which the previous generation grew up, the reasons that members of two generations find for support-

[12] Paul F. Lazarsfeld, Bernard Berelson, and Hazel Gaudet, *The People's Choice,* 2nd ed. (New York: Columbia University Press, 1948), p. 141.

[13] Ibid., p. 145.

[14] Eleanor E. Maccoby, Richard E. Matthews, and Anton S. Morton, "Youth and Political Change," *Public Opinion Quarterly* 18 (1954–55), pp. 23–39.

[15] Langton, *Political Socialization,* p. 62.

[16] Hyman, *Political Socialization,* p. 74.

ing the same party may differ. Thus, while there are not gross generational differences in party preference, there may well be such differences with regard to ideology.

The proposition that differences exist between the political orientations of a parental generation and those of its children is not new.[17] However, beyond the observation that the rate of social change is an important factor, little research has been carried out to specify the conditions under which such generational differences will appear or will vary in degree.

As the individual matures, his political cognitions and feelings go beyond the party choice that he in all likelihood learned by age seven. He begins to develop an ideology—a set of ideas about political issues that form his view of how the world is and ought to be. There are two senses in which we can question the consistency of such political belief systems. First, we can ask whether issue orientations are consistent with each other. That is, are people who hold liberal attitudes in an area like civil rights liberal with regard to social welfare as well? Conservatism on various issues should also tend to be consistent. Second, we can ask whether people's stands on specific issues are consistent with the stands taken on those issues by the parties they support.

We have already noted Converse's research on belief systems, which disconfirms the first expectation. At the same time, however, Converse's work does provide some confirmation for the second. While there were not consistent attitude structures among members of the mass public, it was precisely in this segment of the population that party choice had some relationship to belief systems. That is, for nonelite members of the public, party choice and issue orientation tended to be mutually constraining, although different issues were important to different people.[18] This constraint, however, might have been due more to the individual's assumption that the party held the same position that he did than to any information on the position that the party really held. In other words, "The strong partisan who lacks any real information permitting him to locate either party on a question of policy may find it relatively easy to presume that his chosen party is closer to his own belief regarding that policy than is the opposi-

[17] See, for example, Rudolf Herberle, *Social Movements* (New York: Appleton-Century-Crofts, 1951), especially Chapter 6, "The Problem of Political Generations."

[18] Philip E. Converse, "The Nature of Belief Systems in Mass Publics," in David E. Apter, ed., *Ideology and Discontent* (New York: The Free Press, 1964), pp. 206–261.

tion."[19] This assumed balance need not be "true" in an epistemo-
logical sense. It need only confirm to the individual that his
choice of political party is correct.

Thus, an individual may select out of the total environment
those few cues that support his party choice, or may even
misperceive elements of the environment in order to find support
for positively evaluating the chosen party. Agreement between an
individual's views on a specific issue and party policy regarding
that issue may be perceived even when no such agreement exists.
Thus, the individual who, as a child, learned his party identification from his parents must, as he matures, extract reasons from the
world around him for maintaining that party choice.

The differing belief systems held by people supporting the
same party, of course, reflect in part the wider range of ideological
alternatives than partisan alternatives available at any one time.
There was a wide range of issues to focus on in 1972, and an
individual could choose any of them to explain his support for the
Democratic or Republican Party. The same choice between political parties existed in 1972 as in 1940, but the issues were very
different.

The import of the time dimensions cannot be overlooked. The
individual builds his political ideology on the basis of the issue
alternatives that are available to him, and these differ from
generation to generation. His party choice, by contrast, is dictated
largely by the partisan alternatives that were available to his
parents, since they transmitted partisan affections to their progeny
early in the life cycle. Englishmen born during the period from
1900 to 1918, for example, were half as likely to deviate from class
voting patterns as were Englishmen born prior to 1900.[20] Working-class voters born prior to 1900 did not support the Labour
Party as heavily as younger workers did, and thus they deviated
more from class voting patterns. The Labour Party did not exist as
a political alternative for these voters until they reached age
eighteen or older, the party having been formed in 1918. Since the
age of partisan decision is much earlier than the age at which one
enters the electorate, this group developed its political attach-
ments before the Labour alternative was available. For that
segment of the English population born after 1918, by contrast, the

---

[19] Angus Campbell, Philip E. Converse, Warren E. Miller, Donald E. Stokes, *The American
Voter* (New York: John Wiley & Sons, Inc., 1960), p. 186.

[20] See David Butler and Donald Stokes, *Political Change in Britain* (New York: St. Martin's
Press, Inc., 1969), pp. 104–122.

deviation from class voting was only one eighth as great as for the 1900–1918 cohorts.

Just as political parties may appear, change, and disappear over time, so do other social institutions, but with considerably greater frequency. Each new generation, then, experiences social institutions and institutional arrangements that did not exist before. Moreover, the unfolding of social change, as noted early in this book, is not a strictly linear process. Rather, the production of new technologies, new institutions, and new relationships might be better described as a parabolic function. Daniel Bell refers to this process as the "speeding-up of the 'time machine,'" and demonstrates it by showing, for example, that

> the average time span between the initial discovery of a technological innovation and the recognition of its commercial potential decreased from 30 years (for technological innovations introduced during the early part of this century, 1880–1919) to 16 years (for innovations introduced during the post-World War I period) to 9 years (for the post-World War II period).[21]

The difference that such a pattern of change can cause in the views of successive generations is suggested by Figure 1. Here the Y axis is environmental complexity and the X axis is time. The parabolic social-change function indicates increasingly wide environmental differences between generations. Thus, the environmental gap between the 1870 generation and the 1900 generation (a) is less than the gap between the 1900 and 1930 generations (b), and that, in turn, is less than the gap between the 1930 and 1960 generations (i.e., a<b<c). Insofar as political differences between generations are rooted in environmental differences, we would expect the gap in political orientation between generations, as manifested in what issues are seen as problematic, to be widening.

Political socialization has not been studied long enough or systematically enough to determine whether the gap has in fact widened. We do have evidence that it exists between two generations. In the high-school-student study mentioned earlier, students and their parents were asked questions such as what the proper role of the federal government was in integrating schools, whether schools should be allowed to use prayers, whether

[21] Daniel Bell, "Notes on the Post-Industrial Society (I)," *The Public Interest* 6 (Winter 1967), pp. 24–25.

FIGURE 1 Environmental Differences Cross-Generationally

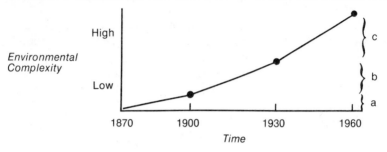

legally elected communists should be allowed to hold political office, and whether people should be allowed to make speeches against churches and religion.[22] The first two issues were extremely salient in the mid-1960s, and the correlations for parent-student pairs were respectable: .34 and .29 respectively. The authors of the study note, however, that "the wonder is not that the correlations are this high, but rather that they are not higher." With respect to tolerance of communists and atheists, however, an area in which presumably more traditional parents who had lived through the Stalin era were compared with offspring who had become politically aware in the post-Korean War years, the correlations for parent-student pairs were .13 and .05 respectively, with the students *more* liberal than their parents.

THE SOCIALIZATION OF POLITICAL STYLE

In his original inventory, Hyman indicated that the bulk of the evidence suggested a somewhat higher level of authoritarianism among children from low socioeconomic-status backgrounds than among those from higher SES backgrounds.[23] He also noted, however, that although authoritarianism seems to increase with age among adults, within any age group the educated are less authoritarian.[24] That is, there seem to be independent effects on authoritarianism attributable to age and to education. What effect would one expect these effects to have on the politics of children,

[22] Jennings and Neimi, "The Transmission of Political Values from Parent to Child."

[23] Hyman, *Political Socialization*, p. 43.

[24] Ibid., p. 134.

who every 365 days are getting a year older and a year more educated?

Among children in grade school, there seem to be clear differences over four grades in the direction of increasingly democratic orientations. Submissiveness to governmental authority rooted in the assumption that the government knows what is best for the people declines markedly between the fourth grade and the eighth grade. Similarly, while fourth-graders regard policemen as among the most influential people, and average citizens among the least influential, in deciding which laws are made for our country, by the eighth grade these positions are reversed.[25] With increasing education, then, submission to political authority seems to decline.

We noted above differences in authoritarianism based upon differences in socioeconomic status. Clearly, this is not based upon differences in years of education between working-class and middle-class ten-year-olds (although it might to some extent be due to differentials in the content of education), because at this age no social stratum has experienced high rates of defection from the educational system. Rather, the relationship between SES and authoritarianism is most commonly seen as rooted in differences between the "power structure" of the working-class family and that of the middle-class family.

There is a body of evidence which suggests that the posture toward authority that one develops in one's family becomes generalized to one's attitudes toward authority in the polity.[26] It has been argued, for example, that dependence on and subordination to an authoritarian father will lead to dependence on and subordination to authoritarian political leaders later in life,[27] and that, especially for that segment of the population with low educational achievement, participation in the family decision-making process is important in creating a feeling of civic competence.[28]

With regard to political activity, we would expect those

[25] Hess and Torney, *The Development of Political Attitudes in Children*, pp. 73–76.

[26] David Easton and Robert D. Hess, "The Child's Political World," *Midwest Journal of Political Science* 6:3 (August 1962), p. 242.

[27] See, for example, Robert LeVine, "Political Socialization and Culture Change," in Cliffort Geertz, ed., *Old Societies and New States* (New York: The Free Press, 1963), p. 296.

[28] Gabriel Almond and Sidney Verba, *The Civic Culture* (Princeton, N.J.: Princeton University Press, 1963), pp. 323–374.

students who participate in the family decision-making process to participate in political processes in other areas of social life as well. This expectation is confirmed by the data on high school seniors. Those who actively participated in family decision-making processes were likely to play active roles in student government, voluntary associations, and other arenas with latitude for adolescent political activity.[29]

While participation in the family context is related to participation in other contexts as well, this extrafamilial participation is not necessarily democratic. There is some evidence that flexibility in cognitive style (what we might call "degree of open-mindedness") is inversely related to parental domination during childhood.[30] The basic argument is that individuals who are more subjected to parental authority are likely to categorize the stimuli in their social environments rigidly, and are likely to react to them in terms of rigid responses that have worked in similarly classified situations in the past. That is, their behavior becomes rehearsed rather than spontaneous.[31]

The adolescents in the high-school-student study were asked whether, in arguments, they usually got their own way, whether they held strong opinions, and whether it was hard to get them to change their minds. The responses to these questions were interpreted to reflect rigidity of attitudes. Interestingly, and contrary to what the literature on family structure and authoritarianism would lead one to expect, those students who had the highest rates of participation in family decision making also had the highest attitudinal rigidity. Thus, while participation in the internal political life of the family seems to "spill over" into other areas of social life as well, there is no reason to believe that the person who manifests such behavior will be the complete democrat, open to all points of view. Indeed, it would be surprising if he were. Even families in which children participate in collective decision making are unlikely to operate on the basis of a one-man–one-vote rule most of the time. The parents tend to dominate regardless of how many children are voting, and the more important the issue, the more likely this is to be the case. Thus,

---

[29] Segal, "The Socialization of Adolescent Politicians," p. 87.

[30] J. Shaffer, S. Mednick, and Judith Seder, "Some Developmental Factors Related to Field Independence in Children," *American Psychologist* 12 (July 1957), p. 395.

[31] Erving Goffman, *The Presentation of Self in Everyday Life* (New York: Doubleday & Co., Inc., 1959).

while children may learn participatory norms in the familial context, they are considerably less likely to learn equality.

What of the assumption that children in working-class families have less chance to participate in familial decision making than do the progeny of middle-class families? There is considerable disagreement on the degree to which working-class families are more authoritarian than middle-class families, if at all, and the structure of family power is complex. There are at least two crucial issues in the determination of familial authoritarianism: the degree to which power is shared by the parents, and the implications of parental use of power for the children.

With regard to the first question, there seems to be a divergence between ideology and reality. Lower-class men concede few rights to their wives, but their wives obtain more than are conceded. Middle-class men concede many rights to their wives, but their wives obtain fewer than are conceded.[32] Ideologically, the working-class man is more likely to subscribe to an authoritarian patriarchal model of family power than is the middle-class man. In reality, the middle-class man wields more power in the familial context than does the working-class man.[33] In both working-class and middle-class families in America, sharing of power between husband and wife is emerging as the modal type.

What are the implications of differing class-based models of family power structure for the political socialization of progeny? The question is difficult to answer from the literature on the sociology of the family, which tends to view such power in terms of how it is shared by husband and wife. For the most part, it is assumed that children do not share in familial power. However, the sharing of power turns out not to be the only important variable. The amount of freedom children are allowed is perhaps equally important, and is relatively unrelated to the sharing of power between husband and wife. Thus, in the patriarchal working-class family, the husband may make decisions on how to spend money, where to go on vacations, where to live, etc., without consulting his wife, but he may have very little interest in the activities of his children, who in turn are relatively free to deal with the world on their own terms. The ideologically democratic middle-class family, by contrast, may be more likely to make

[32] William J. Goode, *World Revolution and Family Patterns* (New York: The Free Press, 1963), pp. 21–22.

[33] Robert O. Blood and Donald M. Wolfe, *Husbands and Wives* (New York: The Free Press, 1950).

demands on its children, to attend more closely to how the children spend their time, and to overprotect them. Such overprotection, in turn, has been found to result in political distrust.[34]

The family, of course, is not the only institution involved in the processes of socialization that help link the emerging citizen to the polity. And it may be that what is crucially important is not the structure of any one of these agencies of socialization, but rather the way that these agencies complement each other.

AGENCIES OF POLITICAL SOCIALIZATION

Hyman's assertion that the family is the foremost agency of political socialization has been challenged, or at least qualified, by research conducted subsequent to his inventory. Doubtless there is a persisting influence of the social environment upon the formulation of political attitudes by the emerging citizen. Neither does it seem reasonable to question the assertion that, at the early stage of life at which party identification is formed, the family constitutes the lion's share of one's social environment. By the time the individual begins to develop a more complex world view and acquire attitudes toward specific political issues, however, the social environment has become more differentiated, parental influence has become less important, and other groups and collectivities have achieved primacy. In fact, even with regard to the early internalized orientation toward political parties, it has been found that, by adolescence, the extrafamilial social environment has become important. High school students tend to identify with the political party that is chosen by the majority of the adult members of the community in which they live, regardless of the party preference of their own parents.[35] Clearly agencies of socialization within the local community other than the family have an impact on political orientation.

The identification of what other agencies of socialization are important is no less difficult than is the assessment of the

---

[34] Frank A. Pinner, "Parental Overprotection and Political Distrust," *The Annals of the American Academy of Political and Social Science* 361 (September 1965), pp. 58–70.

[35] Martin L. Levin, "Social Climate and Political Socialization," *Public Opinion Quarterly* 25:4 (Winter 1961), pp. 596–606. It is important to recognize that there is also a high correlation between the party choice of one's parents and the party choice of other adults in the neighborhood. It is therefore difficult to separate parental and neighborhood effects.

importance of the family. The single agency of socialization that, aside from the family, has received the most attention is the school. In a compendium of research on political socialization published more than a decade after Hyman's inventory, the editor wrote, "Recent research strongly suggests that the public schools are close rivals to the family as major agents of political socialization."[36] The effects of formal citizenship training, however, are minimal. Understanding of the basic principles of democracy does not increase with the number of civics courses taken,[37] and teaching the value of political participation does not get students involved in politics in a participatory manner.[38] Indeed, while we have noted previously that considerable change in political orientation occurs between the fourth and the eighth grades, high school itself seems to have no effect. The political differences between eighth-grade students and twelfth-grade students are minimal,[39] and the high-school-senior data suggest that differences among schools account for less than 15 percent of the variance in adolescent political activity.[40]

What does seem important, however, is that the school is a social system in which students take part. Rather than the formal civics curriculum, what seems to have an effect on students is the set of roles and relationships that they experience within this system, including teaching methods, authority relationships, and extracurricular activities. These factors, in turn, seem to be important only insofar as they complement the roles and relationships in which the students participate in other social contexts.

Perhaps the most underestimated and understudied agency of political socialization is the peer group. In those countries, such as the United States, in which the influence of the family wanes with the coming of adolescence, and in those contexts, such as among college students, in which politics is a legitimate and

[36] Roberta S. Sigel, ed., *Learning About Politics* (New York: Random House, Inc., 1970), p. 311.

[37] Kenneth Langton and M. Kent Jennings, "Political Socialization and the High School Civics Curriculum in the United States," *American Political Science Review* 62 (September 1968), pp. 852–867.

[38] Albert Somit, Joseph Tanenhaus, Walter H. Wilke, and Rita W. Cooley, "The Effect of the Introductory Political Science Course on Student Attitudes Toward Personal Political Participation," *American Political Science Review* 52 (December 1958), pp. 1129–1132.

[39] Sigel, *Learning About Politics*, p. 375.

[40] Segal, "The Socialization of Adolescent Politicians," p. 26.

salient concern for informal peer-group discussion,[41] we know that the peer group exerts great influence on the individual. We do not know the degree to which this influence is internalized rather than reflecting short-term conformity to current group norms. Thus, it might be more precise to speak of the "influence" of the peer group than of its socializing effects. We shall now turn to the continuation of such influence processes through adult life.

THE ADDITIVE EFFECTS OF SOCIALIZATION AGENCIES

We have seen that the effects of the school social system on political socialization are important only to the extent that they complement the social systems of other agencies of socialization. This proposition can be phrased more broadly in the following terms: experience with authority structures in social institutions other than the polity will prepare people for effective citizen participation in the polity only insofar as authority patterns within and without the polity are complementary. This does not necessarily mean that to have a democratic political system, the structures of families must also be democratic. Complementarity does not imply isomorphism. Moreover, since it is highly unusual for families to be democratic, if similarity of authority patterns, rather than complementarity, were a necessary precondition, political democracy could hardly exist.

We must have, then, an alternative to the proposition that democratic families produce democratic citizens. Indeed, the social contexts that we credit with doing the greater part of the job of political socialization are the least likely social institutions to be democratically organized: the family, the school, and the workplace. These social institutions, while not themselves democratic, can complement each other and the government in the process of political socialization through a pattern of *graduated resemblances*.[42] That is, even if institutions at some social distance from the government, such as the family, are undemocratic, an individual can learn to be a competent participant in the polity if other social institutions become increasingly democratic as they

---

[41] See Theodore Newcomb, Kathryn Koenig, Richard Flacks, and Donald Warwick, *Persistence and Change* (New York: John Wiley & Sons, Inc., 1967).

[42] Harry Eckstein, *Division and Cohesion in Democracy* (Princeton, N.J.: Princeton University Press, 1966), p. 239.

are less removed from government. Government in such a context is postulated to receive wide popular support and therefore to be stable. By contrast, a government will not be stable if its authority pattern is substantially different from the patterns in other social institutions, particularly those that are socially proximate to the government, such as the political party structure.

We have here a model that suggests that the structures of the agencies of political socialization are crucial determinants of the stability of the polity. This is a very different approach to political stability from that suggested in the last chapter. There, the pattern of crosscutting cleavages was identified as the major determinant of stability.

In the last chapter, we also noted that Norway is a deviant case in the hypothesized relationship between crosscutting cleavages and political stability. By contrast, the graduated-resemblances hypothesis fits the Norwegian case nicely. Eckstein originally discussed the hypothesis in terms of Great Britain, in which resemblances between authority patterns in government and in other social institutions exist although they decline as one moves away from the governmental sector, and Germany during the Weimar period, in which a democratic political structure was established side by side with existing nondemocratic social institutions. In Britain, a stable democracy has persisted over a long period of time. In Germany, despite evidence that the majority of the German people wanted democracy, the institutional structure of German society could not sustain it because of the gross discontinuity in authority patterns between the government and other social institutions.

Norway is an even more dramatic example of the importance of graduated resemblances. The hypothesis of crosscutting cleavages would lead us to expect Norway to be an unlikely stable democracy, yet it is so characterized. Most social cleavages in Norway, rather than cutting across each other, are superimposed on and congruent with regional and territorial differences. Regional differentiation underlies rural-urban differences, linguistic differences, socioeconomic differences, religious differences, etc. The Norwegian party system, in turn, does not aggregate diverse publics within the electorate, but rather emphasizes the cleavages.[43]

The graduated-resemblances hypothesis suggests that stable democracy is possible even in a system of superimposed cleav-

[43] Ibid., pp. 51 ff.

ages if other social institutions support such a political style so that political consensus can emerge independent of political cleavage. This they seem to do. Norway is a highly organized society in the sense that almost all interests have formal associations to represent them, and working in cooperation with others is a norm in the society. The apparent communalism of Norwegian society has been attributed in part to a homogeneity of authority patterns.[44] The authority patterns in most of the social institutions are modeled on the authority patterns in the governmental structures. Experience in these institutions, in turn, prepares citizens for active participation in the political life of the country.

POLITICAL INFLUENCE IN ADULT LIFE

By suggesting the importance of parallels in authority structure between the polity and other social institutions proximate to it, we have implied that some learning goes on through the life cycle, not merely in childhood and adolescence. Moreover, hypotheses about the effects of social mobility on politics presented in Chapter 6 explicitly assume socialization in adult life.

As we have seen, legal constraints prevent the very young from getting very close to the governmental structure. It is only with the attainment of the age of political majority and citizenship rights that most people experience institutions closer to the center of decision making.

Classical sociological theory has always stressed the important role the primary and secondary social groups to which people belong play in integrating them into the larger society.[45] Such groups, in cases in which memberships are largely overlapping, may serve to integrate the society as a whole by limiting cleavages along class, sectional, or ideological lines. When memberships are superimposed rather than crosscutting, as in the case of Norway, the groups integrate their individual members into society by defining appropriate behaviors and placing constraints upon them. We refer to the effect of these processes as "influence" rather than "socialization" because we have no evidence on how deeply the defined appropriate behaviors are internalized, rather

---

[44] Ibid., pp. 134 ff.

[45] See David R. Segal and Marshall W. Meyer, "The Social Context of Political Partisanship," in Mattei Dogan and Stein Rokkan, eds., *Quantitative Ecological Analysis in the Social Sciences* (Cambridge, Mass.: MIT Press, 1969), pp. 217–232.

than simply responses to felt social pressures. We have no evidence that they are not internalized, but to assume that they are would be to demand too much of available data.

There is no question regarding the proposition that diverse kinds of nonpolitical organizations can serve to integrate people into the polity.[46] Several studies have indicated the importance of primary-group relationships in the formation of political attitudes. These findings show that people in large measure pattern their political beliefs after those of their friends, families, and co-workers.[47]

The community in which one lives also has an effect on one's political orientation. A study of political party choice in nine cities in the northeastern United States indicated that, while only 27 percent of low-socioeconomic-status respondents living in low-socioeconomic-status neighborhoods supported the Republican Party, 47 percent of the low-socioeconomic-status respondents in high-socioeconomic-status neighborhoods were Republicans.[48] That is, there was a tendency to conform to the party choice associated with one's neighbors' social status. This result, among adults, is similar to the finding noted earlier that adolescents tend to identify with the political party choice of the majority of adults in their neighborhood.

In the nine-city study, the more socioeconomically homogeneous the community was, the greater were the effects of the community on individual partisanship. There is some evidence that patterns of voluntary association membership, perhaps more so than informal neighboring patterns, account for the effects of community.[49] That is, when the primary groups to which one belongs do not provide unambiguous specification of the political party one is expected to support, e.g., if one is cross-pressured or status-inconsistent, contacts in secondary associations such as voluntary organizations will have an impact on one's politics. If

---

[46] See Scott Greer and Peter Orleans, "The Mass Society and the Parapolitical Structure," *American Sociological Review* 27 (October 1962), pp. 634–646.

[47] See, for example, Bernard Berelson, Paul F. Lazarsfeld, and William N. McPhee, *Voting* (Chicago: The University of Chicago Press, 1954), Chapter 6.

[48] Segal and Meyer, "The Social Context of Political Partisanship."

[49] Kevin R. Cox, "The Spatial Structuring of Information Flow and Partisan Attitudes," in Dogan and Rokkan, eds., *Quantitative Ecological Analysis in the Social Sciences*, pp. 157–185.

an individual's voluntary organization ties are located within the community of residence, this will accentuate the political influence that his neighbors will wield over him.[50]

THE SOCIALIZATION OF POLITICAL EFFICACY

On the basis of developments in psychoanalytic ego psychology and in animal psychology, an *effectance motivation* has been suggested.[51] This motive force is not a primary drive, nor does it require a source of energy external to the central nervous system. It reflects a seeking, on the part of both animals and humans, for effective or competent interaction with the environment. The experience produced by fulfillment of effectance motivation has been called a feeling of *efficacy.* We know that there is a relationship between feelings of competence in dealing with the environment and political involvement.[52] Specifically, the study of high school seniors that we have discussed above showed that the combination of high levels of personal efficacy with socialization experiences that led the individual to define politics as a relevant arena within which to shape the world, resulted in high levels of political activity.[53]

The combination of the notion of shaping the environment with the assumption that politics is an appropriate arena for such action yields the feeling of *political efficacy.* Political efficacy has been defined as "the feeling that individual political action does have, or can have, an impact upon the political process. . . . It is the feeling that political and social change is possible, and that the individual citizen can play a part in bringing about this change."[54]

Political efficacy is a norm in American society,[55] but a norm

---

[50] Robert D. Putnam, "Political Attitudes and the Local Community," *American Political Science Review* 60 (September 1966), pp. 640–654.

[51] Robert W. White, "Motivation Reconsidered," *Psychological Review* 66 (July 1959), pp. 297–331.

[52] Angus Campbell, "The Passive Citizen," *Acta Sociologica* 6 (1964), pp. 9–21.

[53] Segal, "The Socialization of Adolescent Politicians."

[54] Angus Campbell, Gerald Gurin, and Warren E. Miller, *The Voter Decides* (Evanston: Harper & Row, Publishers, 1954).

[55] David Easton and Jack Dennis, "The Child's Acquisition of Regime Norms," *American Political Science Review* 61 (March 1967), pp. 25–38.

that is differentially internalized as a function of social status. Whereas among third-grade children there is a 7 percent difference between the children of low- and high-status families in the attainment of high political efficacy scores, this difference is increased to 25 percent by the eighth grade. The socialization processes involving the learning of political efficacy favor middle-class children.

As we have noted, processes of social influence later in life may also affect acceptance of normative values. The degree to which individuals subscribe to a norm will be a function of the degree to which they participate in groups in which this norm prevails.[56]

The social status differential in political efficacy persists into adulthood.[57] We can assume, therefore, that middle-class communities have higher aggregate levels of political efficacy than do working-class communities. This was found to be the case in a study in Wayne County, Michigan.[58] Among working-class respondents in the study, however, political efficacy was significantly higher among those who lived in middle-class neighborhoods than among those who lived in working-class neighborhoods, indicating again the impact of community on politics.

In short, political learning continues into adult life. This learning in general does not take place to a great extent in formal institutions of education. Rather, one's political socialization takes place in the groups, formal and informal, voluntary and involuntary, in which one participates throughout the life cycle. These groups, be they as small and structured as the family or as large and amorphous as the community, provide linkages that bind the individual to the polity.

---

[56] Morton Deutsch and H. B. Gerard, "A Study of Normative and Informational Influences upon Social Judgment," *Journal of Abnormal and Social Psychology* 51 (November 1955), pp. 629–636.

[57] Campbell, Converse, Miller, and Stokes, *The American Voter*, p. 479.

[58] David R. Segal and Stephen H. Wildstrom, "Community Effects on Political Attitudes," *Sociological Quarterly* 11 (Winter 1970), pp. 67–86.

8

The Electoral System and Political Movements

THE REPRESENTATIONAL FUNCTION OF PARTIES

In the preceding chapters we have made a simplifying assumption regarding the operation of political parties as a link between the electorate and the government. We have assumed that the interests of the electorate are represented by the parties existing at any given time. Indeed, in the aggregate, this seems to be the case. In most Western nations, most interests seem able to get themselves represented by the existing parties most of the time. Party systems therefore tend to be fairly stable over time. However, in some nations, some interests seem to find difficulty getting the existing parties to represent them some of the time. In these cases in which the parties fail to represent segments of the electorate and thereby fail to link them to the polity, new political movements are likely to form outside of the established party structure. The success of such movements can frequently be measured by the degree to which they are captured, i.e., their interests come to be represented, by established political parties.

THE THEORY OF CRITICAL ELECTIONS

In the mid-1950s, V. O. Key, Jr., made a tentative step toward the development of a comprehensive typology of elections.[1] He suggested that American electoral history was punctuated with "critical elections," characterized by high voter concern and electoral involvement, the results of which revealed a dramatic change in preexisting cleavages within the electorate. This change would then persist for several succeeding elections. The utility of the concept of the critical election was demonstrated by Key himself in an analysis of the results of the 1928 presidential election in the New England states, where Alfred E. Smith, the Democratic presidential candidate, increased the Democratic vote through the mobilization of large numbers of poor, urban, Catholic voters of recent immigrant stock. A more recent piece of research, concerned with critical elections in Illinois, suggests two important modifications to Key's theory.[2] First, it suggests that "critical periods" during which several elections might take place should be the focus of a theory of elections, rather than single critical elections. Secondly, it suggests that, during these critical periods, third-party political movements may serve as "halfway houses" for voters whose allegiances are in the process of being transferred from one major party to the other.

Subsequently, a more refined classification of presidential elections has been developed on the basis of deviations from the "normal" division of the vote.[3] A normal vote is simply a set of electoral returns that coincides with the distribution of partisan sentiment among members of the electorate at the time at which the election is held.[4]

A *maintaining election,* according to this classification, is one in which the previous distribution of partisan sentiment persists and the majority party wins the presidency. If short-term factors affecting individual political involvement, such as candidate personalities, are weak, turnout will be low and the electoral

---

[1] V. O. Key, Jr., "A Theory of Critical Elections," *The Journal of Politics* 17 (February 1955), pp. 3–18.

[2] Duncan MacRae, Jr., and James A. Neldrum, "Critical Elections in Illinois: 1888–1958," *American Political Science Review* 54 (September 1960), pp. 669–683.

[3] Angus Campbell, "A Classification of Presidential Elections," in Campbell et al., *Elections and the Political Order* (New York: John Wiley & Sons, Inc., 1966), pp. 63–77.

[4] Philip E. Converse, "The Concept of a Normal Vote," ibid., pp. 9–39.

returns will approximate the normal vote. If short-term factors are stronger, turnout will be higher and there will be some deviation from the normal vote.

A *deviating election* is one in which the basic division of loyalties remains essentially unchanged, but the influence of short-term forces results in deviations from the normal vote sufficient to cause the defeat of the majority party. Deviating elections are characterized by an absence of major ideological issues and the presence of an especially attractive, perhaps charismatic, candidate.

A *realigning election* is one in which the feelings associated with politics cause some portion of the electorate to change partisan commitments and thus create a new party balance. In the realigning election, the normal vote itself is changed. Such elections tend to be associated with periods of great national crisis.

Thus it may be argued that maintaining elections are decided on the basis of preexisting party orientations, deviating elections reflect candidate orientations, and realigning elections are determined by issue orientations among members of the electorate.

THE ELECTORAL CYCLE AND RECENT AMERICAN POLITICS

A historical study of American election results suggests that a three-phase *equilibrium cycle* has been characteristic of American electoral history, although there have been more deviations from this model in the twentieth century than was formerly the case.[5] The first phase is one of *equilibrium,* characterized by stable party balance and, presumably, by a normal vote. This is followed by a *realignment phase,* distinguished by sharp, short-term oscillations—deviating elections—culminating in a critical, or realigning, election, which is followed by an *ascendency phase.* This last phase continues as long as the conditions that caused the realignment persist, generally a period of one or two elections, after which the ascendant party declines toward equilibrium.

Prior to the 1964 election, the American electorate was considered to be in a moderately pro-Democratic phase approximating equilibrium that had prevailed since the mid-1940s. Since

[5] Charles Sellers, "The Equilibrium Cycle in Two-Party Politics," *Public Opinion Quarterly* 32 (Fall 1965), pp. 441–444.

at least the mid-forties, there had been more Democrats than Republicans in the electorate. The Eisenhower victories of 1952 and 1956 were gross deviations from the normal vote, apparently due to candidate appeal, during a surge of Democratic ascendency, and Kennedy won the presidency in 1960 with a turnout that was below the level of expectation determined by the normal vote.[6] The 1960 and 1964 elections both seem to have been maintaining elections, with victory belonging to the party with which a plurality of the electorate identified.

The characteristics of the campaign leading to the Republican victory on November 5, 1968, clearly suggest that this was a realigning rather than a deviating election. The Republicans did not have a "heroic" candidate, as they did in 1952 and 1956.[7] Moreover, across the breadth of the political spectrum, America was viewed as a nation in crisis. To the right, people were concerned about ghetto riots, agitation on university campuses, and crime in the streets. On the left, the concern was with continued American involvement in Vietnam, the repression of dissent, and the persistence of ghetto squalor in the midst of societal affluence. Concern on the right was manifested by George Wallace's American Independent Party, while on the left dissident groups sprang up within the Democratic Party and a variety of personalities, including Eldridge Cleaver and Benjamin Spock, appeared on the ballot in various parts of the nation as fourth-party candidates. Perhaps the best indicator that 1968 was a realigning election was the outcome of the 1972 election, which yielded a Republican landslide rooted largely in voting groups that had provided the strength of the post-New Deal Democratic coalition: Catholics, Southerners, and organized labor.

PARTY IDEOLOGY AND POLITICAL REALIGNMENT

In Chapter 3 we suggested that a nonideological or "middle-of-the-road" electorate will lead the political parties to adopt a "middle-of-the-road" position as well. It is for this reason that, in the normal maintaining election, the parties are not differentiated

[6] Philip E. Converse et al., "Stability and Change in 1960," *American Political Science Review* 55 (June 1961), pp. 269–280.

[7] See Philip E. Converse and Georges Depeux, "De Gaulle and Eisenhower," in Campbell et al., *Elections and the Political Order*, pp. 292–345.

by the distance between them on issues, and the outcome is largely determined by preexisting patterns of partisan identification. In the realigning election, by contrast, both the existing distribution of party identification and the personalities of the presidential candidates are overshadowed by political issues. For a fleeting moment in political history, the parties present the voters with alternatives that are indeed different from each other. The voters, in turn, responding to these appeals, may leave previous brand loyalties behind in their quest for new and better political products. After the realignment takes place, the losing party will recognize that the voters found the other party more attractive, and will move its own position in the direction that it believes will attract the voters once again. The parties will thus converge ideologically once more. With the decrease in ideological distance between the parties, many voters whose votes deviated from their previous party positions will return to the fold, and equilibrium will be approached.

The realignment of 1968–1972 reflected not ideological divergence on preexisting issues so much as ideological differences on newly emerging issues. With the decline of economic bread-and-butter issues in the affluent society came not consensus, but non–bread-and-butter issues. These taken together have been referred to as the "social issue."[8] This term refers to the congeries of policy questions related to race relations, crime, lawlessness, and civil rights. The social issue, like other issues we have discussed earlier, does not have a traditional liberal vs. conservative dimension. Neither does it appear that political victory is to be found at either extreme of the social issue dimension. Rather, given the distribution of voter sentiment on the issue, success lies at the center, and the market dynamic that leads parties to converge on the center of whatever dimension is relevant to the voters will continue to operate.

THE HALFWAY HOUSE IN POLITICAL REALIGNMENT

As issues come to the fore in the process of political realignment, people are drawn from the party that they have identified with since childhood—an identification that in tem-

---

[8] Richard M. Scammon and Ben J. Wattenberg, *The Real Majority* (New York: Coward-McCann, Inc., 1970).

poral terms alone we must regard as deep-rooted. People seem to find it easier to leave the party with which they have always identified than to take the next step and identify with the party they have always regarded as the opposition. In the short run, a lifelong Democrat who has always regarded the Republicans as the enemy more readily becomes an ex-Democrat than a Republican. Loyalties are easier to abandon than are antagonisms. The emergence of third parties—parties that have not historically been the opposition—makes the transition easier by giving the transient more time. An individual who always identified with Party X and regarded Party Y as the opposition can vote for Party X's candidate for president one year, leave the party and vote for new Party Z four years later, and finally support Party Y eight years after leaving Party X. Eight years, presumably, is sufficient time to forgive Party Y the crimes that were attributed to it in one's childhood once one decides that Party Y is indeed to be forgiven.

Since 1948, there has been a movement away from the Democratic Party in the American South. This movement has been associated with a move through third parties to the Republican Party. In 1968 the movement became nationwide, with George C. Wallace's American Independent Party serving as a halfway house for ex-Democrats and leading to a Republican landslide in 1972. The replacement of economic issues by social issues is dramatically manifested by Wallace's almost populist appeal.

V. O. Key, Jr., in his work on the function of minor parties in political systems, distinguished between parties formed to propagate a particular doctrine, e.g., the Prohibitionist Party, and transient third-party movements.[9] The latter he subdivided into parties of economic protest, e.g., the Populists of 1892, and secessionist parties, e.g., the Dixiecrats of 1948. The doctrinaire parties tend to represent institutional means through which disaffected groups in society express their discontent within the political system. In the United States, parties of this type have little effect on the operation of the polity. By contrast, transient third parties have played an important role in influencing the positions of the major parties on specific issues. For example, in the 1890s the Populist Party exerted leverage on the Democratic Party, moving it from a conservative to a liberal position on economic issues.[10] Similarly, the Dixiecrat revolt of 1948 was

[9] V. O. Key, Jr., *Politics, Parties and Pressure Groups* (New York: Thomas Y. Crowell Co., 1942), pp. 280–309.

[10] See John D. Hicks, *The Populist Revolt* (Lincoln: The University of Nebraska Press, 1961).

instrumental in forcing the Democratic National Convention of 1956 to take a cautious position on civil rights.

More important in terms of voter alignments, as mentioned before, transient parties provide halfway houses for voters in the process of transferring their allegiances from one major party to the other. The La Follette Progressive Party played such a role for ex-Republicans in 1924,[11] and an analysis of Australian politics has indicated that the Democratic Party there may have served such a function for voters moving from the Socialist Labor Party to the Conservative Party.[12] As we have suggested, there is evidence that a large-scale realignment has been occurring since 1948 in the eleven states of the old Confederacy. The sharp increase in Republican strength in this region has been attributed to changes in the urban South, while rural areas have maintained their Democratic loyalties.[13] At the same time, there has been an increase in third-party activity in the South, starting with the Dixiecrat movement in 1948 and continuing through the Wallace movement of 1968. While some scholars have anticipated the emergence of a Dixiecrat-type party as a permanent feature of the political landscape of the South,[14] the more popular interpretation has viewed third parties in the South as temporary phenomena, easing the transition of voters between the Democratic and Republican parties.[15]

We can get some empirical notion of which of these interpretations is most appropriate by considering particular electoral changes in the South. In 1956, the States Rights Party, with Coleman Andrews as its candidate, did quite well in many counties of South Carolina. The Republican Party did relatively well in these same counties from 1956 to 1960. Similarly, an independent slate of electors experienced a relatively high degree of success in many counties of Louisiana in 1960, and the Republicans gained in those counties thereafter. These inferences,

[11] Ibid.

[12] Robert P. Alford, *Party and Society* (Chicago: Rand McNally & Co., 1963), pp. 287–308.

[13] Philip E. Converse, "On the Possibility of Major Political Realignment in the South," in Campbell et al., *Elections and the Political Order,* pp. 212–242.

[14] See Samuel Lubell, *Revolt of the Moderates* (New York: Harper & Row, Publishers, 1956), pp. 178–246.

[15] Alexander Heard, *A Two-Party South* (Chapel Hill: The University of North Carolina Press, 1952), pp. 247–256.

based upon aggregate voting returns, gain some support from survey data as well[16] and support the halfway-house hypothesis.

THE MOBILIZATION OF POLITICAL INTERESTS

We have now moved away from the assumption that the established major parties represent the diversity of interests existing in society and thereby link the people holding these interests to the polity. Instead, we have suggested that the fit between voter desires and party platforms may sometimes be extremely imperfect. At such times, third-party movements may emerge that ease the transition of voters from one party to another and also signal to the major parties where the voters currently stand. Thus, they serve as catalysts for change in the party system. The change that we have allowed thus far, however, still assumes that the party system works, albeit with new parties appearing from time to time to take up slack in the system.

Let us now take another step away from our smoothly running system and admit that, at times, the reciprocal adaptation of a population and its political system cannot be achieved simply by changes in the party system. In such instances, political activity outside of the institutional structure of the party system may well attest to the viability of the polity, although many are likely to view it as a sign of the ill health of the system.

A group unrepresented by the party system may be mobilized to contend for power in the polity.[17] By political mobilization, we mean the utilization of resources available to a social group to influence policy outcomes. At the beginning of this book, we indicated that mobilization is one of the central problems in political development. A wide range of resources may serve as bases for the development of political power. It is important to note that mobilization need not take place outside the established party system.[18] An interest may be mobilized within a political party and compete for power inside the party against other interests which also want the party to represent them. Such

[16] Lewis Bowman, "Political Stability, Political Conflict, and Methodological Artifacts," *South Atlantic Quarterly* 68 (Winter 1969), pp. 109–116.

[17] See Amitai Etzioni, *The Active Society* (New York: The Free Press, 1968).

[18] These ideas were influenced by Charles Tilly's provocative paper, "From Mobilization to Political Conflict," mimeographed (Ann Arbor: Department of Sociology, University of Michigan, 1970).

mobilization is a manifestation of a social movement occurring within the party, e.g., a reform movement. If the movement is successful, the established party then becomes its spokesman in the polity.

Our present concern, however, is with movements that arise outside the structure of the established parties, i.e., third-party movements, or political movements that seek to achieve their collective goals without behaving like parties in the electoral arena at all, e.g., revolutionary movements. Such movements compete with the established parties for power and for the resources upon which power may be based. One might, in fact, categorize contenders for power as being within or outside the polity itself on the basis of whether or not their right to influence the government has become recognized and institutionalized. If they do have such recognition and institutionalization, they are members of the polity. If recognition and institutionalization are lacking, they are not. This is clearly consistent with the distinction between politics and war. Such an approach, of course, assumes that we are defining the polity more in terms of a normative system than in terms of a system of established institutions. The likelihood that a group contending for power will choose to operate nonviolently according to the norms of the political system will depend largely on that group's perception of whether it can achieve just representation if it plays by the established rules of the game.

POLITICAL SEEKERS

Let us now focus on the kinds of people who are likely to join social movements in general, and political movements beyond the pale of the established parties in particular, and on the nature of such movements.

People turn to new behavior patterns when established social institutions fail to provide for them a framework within which they can understand the world, or fail to fulfill needs they feel.[19] To the extent that a number of people come together who share an unfulfilled need and who establish common behavior patterns in seeking fulfillment of that need, a social movement may emerge.[20]

[19] See Hadley Cantril, *The Psychology of Social Movements* (New York: John Wiley & Sons, Inc., 1963).

[20] Orrin Klapp, *Collective Search for Identity* (New York: Holt, Rinehart & Winston, Inc., 1969).

The nature of the movement will be determined largely by the predispositions and orientations of the people who comprise it. Thus the social movement, at a very elementary level, provides a link between the social system and people who exist within it with unmet needs.

One important personal orientation is the arena in which people are predisposed to seek solutions to their problems. One approach to the study of social movements suggests that people see the locus of problems and their solutions either (1) within themselves, (2) in the physical and social world around them, or (3) in supernatural forces or deities.[21] The first are likely to turn to established forms of psychotherapy or, in the extreme, to therapeutic movements to set their world right. The last are most likely to try to find meaning through established religions or, if that fails, to turn to religious movements. Neither, according to this approach, are likely to try to change the world through politics. This task is left to the middle group: those who see problems and their solutions outside themselves but within the boundaries of the present world.

We cannot assert that an individual who sees unfulfilled problems in the world and who prefers extrapunitive but this-worldly solutions will join a political movement to solve them. Neither can we assert that he will be the only kind of person to join a political movement. First, there is an alternative theoretical approach that, in its most simplified form, asserts that a movement is a movement is a movement. This approach denies that people are likely to confine their seeking behavior to either the therapeutic, political, or religious realms.[22] In this view, a person who fails to find fulfillment through therapy or religion might then turn to politics. Alternatively, a person who fails to find fulfillment through a particular political movement might turn then to religion or therapy, rather than to another political movement. The degree to which seekers remain within or travel between arenas is an unresolved issue in the study of social movements.

Second, even if there exists a set of individuals who see the locus of problems and their solutions in the world around them, there is no guarantee that their seeking behavior will be either

---

[21] See John Lofland, *Doomsday Cult* (Englewood Cliffs, N.J.: Prentice-Hall, Inc., 1966), pp. 41-44.

[22] See, for example, Eric Hoffer, *The True Believer* (New York: Harper & Row, Publishers, 1958).

collective or adaptable to eventual incorporation into the polity. Reliance on individual, as opposed to collective, action is a constraint on the formation of any kind of social movement. A single discontented individual who plants bombs in government office buildings does not a social movement make. Neither, in fact, do a number of discontented individuals who act individually in planting bombs in government office buildings, with no coordination or communication among them. There are important organizational components to political movements, and we shall get to these below.

Equally important is the recognition that people can seek, either individually or collectively, to deal with problems in this world that established institutions have not solved for them without operating in the normative political arena at all. They can, for example, seek material well-being through criminal activity.[23] And the frequently mentioned "syndicate" may well represent America's most dramatic example of a large number of people dealing collectively with a problem through means that have clearly become routine, but that, except for alleged payoffs to politicians and occasional campaigns against organized crime that seem to be conducted only during election years, have had few reverberations within the polity. On the other hand, it is interesting to speculate on how much of the demand for the kind of "familial" social services that organized crime is alleged to provide its supporters in return for their loyalty is due to the fact that political parties no longer fulfill these informal welfare functions, and formal welfare institutions have not wholly been able to take up the slack in the system.[24] That is, the "syndicate," operating outside the polity, may have replaced the old-fashioned political machine in this regard, and thereby moved both the allocation of certain resources and the individuals to whom those resources are being allocated outside the polity.

The second behavioral predisposition that concerns us in discussing political movements is whether people who perceive problems in the world are content to improve their own lives and the lives of their immediate communities, or whether they seek to recast the total social order through changes in laws or in institutional arrangements.[25] Individuals with the former orienta-

[23] See Robert K. Merton, *Social Theory and Social Structure* (New York: The Free Press, 1957), pp. 176 ff.

[24] Ibid., pp. 71 ff.

[25] Scipio Sighele, *Psychologie des Sectes* (Paris: M. Giard et Cie., 1898).

tion are likely to seek to improve themselves or to withdraw collectively into isolated enclaves and exert no force on the polity other than that generated by their mere presence. Individuals with the latter orientation, by contrast, are more likely to apply pressure and/or force on the larger society in the interests of reshaping it. These styles of relating to problems seem to be more important than are the problems themselves in determining the membership of political movements. For example, there seems to have been greater overlap in types of membership between the prohibition movement and the abolition movement in the United States than there was between the temperance movement and the prohibition movement. Both prohibition and abolition were concerned with changing legal statutes. Temperance, by contrast, was concerned with pursuing absolute values by making individuals into more moral people. Thus, although temperance and prohibition shared a concern with the use of alcoholic beverages, their styles were different enough to attract different supporters. Abolition, by contrast, although not concerned with alcohol, was stylistically similar to prohibition.

We can see, then, that even when interests and discontents exist in a population that cannot be adequately handled by the established political parties, there are significant limitations on the potential bases of support available for new political movements. Some of the discontented people will choose to act individually, or not at all, rather than participate in a collective enterprise. Among those who are willing to involve themselves in a collective effort to set things right, many will turn to therapy or religion rather than to politics. And among those who favor activity in the political realm, some will choose to isolate themselves from a hostile political world and collectively form their own ideal political system, rather than attempting to change the larger political context. Nevertheless, movements aimed at changing the polity do emerge rather routinely in some societies, and at least occasionally in others.

POLITICAL MOVEMENT ORGANIZATION

Thus far we have largely been concerned with the psychological predispositions of people who are likely to be recruited by political movements. Let us now consider in more general terms the ideologies and organization of the movements themselves.

If we confine ourselves to movements that choose to operate within or upon the polity in order to change it, and recall our earlier discussion of the limited utility of the traditional left-right continuum, one major ideological distinction is important: that between reform movements and revolutionary movements. The former do not seek to change the values and ideals of the system, but rather to bring the realities of the system more into line with those values and ideals. Thus, for example, a movement to bring American life into closer concordance with the Constitution or the Bill of Rights, or the platform of the Democratic Party into closer agreement with the principles of the party, would be regarded as a reform movement and not particularly deviant. The latter type of movement, by contrast, does seek to change basic values and ideals and, indeed, the basic structure of society.[26] Since that which exists tends to be held sacred by many people simply by virtue of tradition, revolutionary movements tend to be regarded as deviant and threatening. Americans seem to forget that they live in a nation born of revolution—a revolution that is celebrated annually.

As with most distinctions in social science, some cases do not fit neatly into one or the other of these categories. For example, there have been revolutionary reform movements. Presentation of the polar types, however, should sensitize the reader to the importance of identifying the degree to which a movement deviates (or is perceived to deviate) from the normative structure of the polity.

This deviation, in turn, is important in understanding the nature of social movement organization. In the abstract, a movement can be defined in terms of an idea, or set of ideas, and individuals whose behavior is influenced by their association with those ideas. We must recognize, however, that political movements, like other sectors of society, are made up of groups of people bound together in some unit of social organization. The nature of the unit is largely influenced by the relationship between the movement ideology and the normative structure of the polity.

Duverger has provided us with the basis for perhaps the most useful typology of political movement organization. He suggests that, as one moves away from the center of the normative structure of the polity, units of organization become smaller, control more

---

[26] Robert E. Park and Ernest W. Burgess, *Introduction to the Science of Sociology* (Chicago: The University of Chicago Press, 1921), p. 934.

centralized, and operations more secretive.[27] Thus, the established political parties, which he calls caucus parties, are organized on the basis of large geographical areas, operate quite openly, and allow for a great deal of membership input. Revolutionary movements at the political extremes, on the other hand, are organized in small units with a very small geographical base, or, as in the case of the ideal communist cell, are based in the workplace rather than a geographical area. Operation is clandestine, and directives originate at the top of the movement hierarchy rather than from the rank and file. We would expect reform movements to be intermediate between established parties and revolutionary movements. That these ideal types are imperfect reflections of the real world is demonstrated by the clandestine and cabalistic behavior of members of the Nixon administration in the Watergate episode.

POLITICAL MOVEMENTS IN THE UNITED STATES AND FRANCE

The United States has had few large-scale political movements since the American Revolution, and none, with the possible exception of the Civil War, ever seemed to have a chance of toppling a political regime, although, as noted earlier in this chapter, movements have influenced the positions of the established political parties. The American case by itself, therefore, is close to the pole of political quiescence over the long run, and in and of itself provides us with a limited range of examples. France lies near the other pole. In contrast to the United States, France has a history of political movements, generally more revolutionary than reform, and frequently successful in overthrowing political regimes.

Let us briefly consider the political history of France through the mid-1950s to highlight this contrast with the United States. France was a monarchy under the *ancien régime* until 1789, when it experienced a revolution establishing the First Republic. The First Republic was toppled in 1799 by a coup, which could be regarded as a particular kind of revolutionary movement,[28] and

---

[27] Maurice Duverger, *Political Parties* (New York: John Wiley & Sons, Inc., 1963), especially Chapter I, "Party Organization."

[28] William Kornhauser, "Revolutions," in Roger W. Little, ed., *Handbook of Military Institutions* (Beverly Hills, Calif.: Sage Publications, Inc., 1971), pp. 375–398.

which established the Napoleonic dictatorship. Napoleon was defeated in war in 1814, and the succeeding Bourbon monarchy was overthrown by revolution in 1830. The July Monarchy was overthrown by revolution in 1848, the Second Republic by a coup in 1851, and Napoleon III's Second Empire by concomitant military defeat and revolution in 1870. The subsequent Third Republic lasted until World War II, but, by the time of the German invasion and the establishment of the Vichy government, the Republic had already been weakened by a withdrawal of middle-class support that was a response to the militancy of the trade union movement supporting the Republic. After the war, the Fourth Republic was established in 1946, to be ended by a military uprising in 1958 establishing the Fifth Republic under Charles de Gaulle.

With this historical sketch as a backdrop, let us consider as exemplary cases two of France's recent political movements: Poujadism (UFF), which might be termed a right-wing revolutionary movement, and Gaullism, a moderate right-wing reform movement.

The UFF was composed largely of social groups that had been loyal to the Republic, but that found themselves under great pressure from the increasing scale of business, labor, and governmental organization in the 1950s: shopkeepers, artisans, small farmers, local and provincial political leaders. The movement started as a pressure group organized by Pierre Poujade, the aim of which was to lighten the tax burden of small businessmen.[29] It evolved into a large-scale movement demanding that: (a) Parlement be closed down; (b) the Estates-General, last convened in 1789 under the *ancien régime,* be convoked; and (c) the leaders of the Fourth Republic be tried before a high court.

The Poujadists were strongest in rural areas, where there was a high density of small businessmen, low revenues, and trends toward decreasing population. The supporters of Poujade were discontent because of increasing tax burdens and dwindling profits. The program of the movement centered around the romantic notion of pulling France backward in time to a world of small enterprise and no taxes. It defined as its enemies the larger industrial corporations, politicians, the state, Jews, and communists.

Poujade himself had both the strength of his convictions and a flair for the dramatic. Wherever he went to give a speech, he

---

[29] See Stanley Hoffman, *Le Mouvement Poujade* (Paris: Colin, 1956).

brought along an audience of his followers in the trucks of the merchants who supported him, and his cavalcade made the cities in which he spoke seem like large open-air markets. In a very real sense, Poujade himself was the movement. There was a notion of organization, but it existed, for the most part, only on paper. Other people in the movement had little chance to develop or utilize organizational or political skills.

The appeals of the movement were popular in an economically depressed France. In the 1956 election, the Poujadists received two and a half million votes, about 12 1/2 percent of the total. This gave them fifty-two seats in the national assembly, and led to the downfall of the movement. Politically and organizationally naive, the Poujadist delegates were unable to function effectively in the legislative context. The movement collapsed as fast as it had arisen. By 1958 it had all but disappeared.

The RPF (Rassemblement du Peuple Français), like the UFF, was largely centered around one man, Charles de Gaulle. However, while it had wide support among agrarian segments of the population and among rural shopkeepers (again like the UFF), it included many technicians, industrialists, engineers, and civil servants in its upper echelons.

One of the most interesting features of the RPF is that it represented De Gaulle's opposition to a government that he himself had headed. After the liberation of Paris, De Gaulle was elected premier as head of a coalition government composed of Communists, Socialists, and De Gaulle's Popular Republican Movement (MRP), a liberal Catholic party. De Gaulle wanted the government to be dominated by the executive, but the left wanted it to be dominated by Parlement. Eighteen months after taking office, De Gaulle resigned, and in April 1947, in a speech at Strasbourg, he outlined his plans for the RPF. By the end of the year, the movement had 800,000 members. Like the UFF, it had a highly centralized authority structure. Unlike the UFF, it was highly organized at the rank-and-file level. To combat the communists, who were organized by workplace rather than by residence, the RPF also developed factory teams and professional organizations. De Gaulle managed to get himself reelected. However, the RPF was opposed by a parliamentary coalition composed of Socialists, Radicals, MRP, and Independents. With Parlement deadlocked, De Gaulle retired in the mid-1950s, although by no means for the last time.

In the French case, then, even discounting occasional revolutions, we have examples of political movements achieving at least short-term success at the national level. The United States has not historically provided such fertile soil for the growth of movements at the political extremes. On the right, we have had two major movements centered on individual leaders: Father Coughlin in the 1930s and Senator Joseph McCarthy in the 1940s.[30] The 1950s and 1960s saw the increased visibility of the John Birch Society, based far more on conservative political principles than on particular leaders. To the right of the Birch Society were a scattering of paramilitary groups such as the Minutemen, and anticommunist propaganda and agitation organs such as the Christian Anti-Communist Crusade. The opposition of these groups to what they saw as the breakdown of the moral fiber of the United States and to communism did not seem to reverse liberal changes in sexual mores or trends toward closer ties with communist nations, although, we may speculate, it might have lengthened American involvement in Southeast Asia.

The radical left in America, if anything, has been less active than the radical right.[31] Among the reasons frequently suggested to explain the lack of persisting large-scale communist or socialist movements have been the absence of a history of class conflict, the expanding frontier, a political system that makes successful third parties unlikely, and a trade union movement that very early decided to work within the institutional context of American politics. Various forms of socialism do persist on a small scale and with virtually no political impact, although during the Depression, under conditions of extreme economic hardship for large segments of the population, both the communists and the socialists did have considerable support.

The more recent "New Left" in the United States reflects different social segments, and has had considerable impact on American politics. This impact has been directed mainly at, and has been felt mainly through, the established political parties. The New Left has not really had a general program or ideology, but rather has focused on different issues at different times. Most commonly through the 1960s the issue was the war in Vietnam. Although some of the activities undertaken by some segments of the New Left have been beyond the pale of what is normatively regarded as appropriate political behavior (e.g., bombing of federal buildings or destroying of records in draft boards), the greater part of the efforts of the movement have been devoted to getting

---

[30] See Bell, *The Radical Right.*

[31] See S. M. Lipset, *Agrarian Socialism* (Berkeley: The University of California Press, 1959).

antiwar candidates into political office through the usual electoral channels. Whatever success the left of the 1960s has experienced, in fact, might best be measured by the degree to which its program has been accepted by both major American political parties.

9

Nonpopular Politics

**MILITARY AND INTERNATIONAL
CONSTRAINTS**

In the last chapter we moved away from a model of democratic politics in which interests get represented routinely by political parties, and considered what happens when established parties fail to provide a linkage between popular interests and the government. This chapter will deal with perspectives that argue that the government either is not or cannot be interested in representing the interests of the electorate, or, as a corollary, that the electorate either is not interested in affecting governmental decisions or is not sufficiently organized to have an impact on governmental policy.

On the one hand, some theorists subscribe to an economic determinist view of the political process, and see political decisions as shaped by a small group of men holding positions of power in three American social institutions: the military, industry, and government. These men are thought to comprise a power elite, or a military-industrial complex. On the other hand, it is argued by some that just as the locus of power shifted from the local to the national level with the coming of industrial society, making the local power structure less important than the national power structure, so in an era of nuclear technology has the international arena replaced the national arena in political importance. In this view, the structures and processes of national government are more highly constrained by the international system than by domestic political demands. We have seen earlier that it is precisely in the area of international relations that the electorate is most poorly represented by its legislature, and there is reason to believe that in general this is the realm in which the popular will has the least influence.

THE POWER ELITE AND THE MILITARY-INDUSTRIAL COMPLEX

At midcentury the American public received warnings from two quarters about an allegedly unhealthy and perhaps conspiratorial concentration of power in the hands of the industrial and military elites. From the university, C. Wright Mills published *The Power Elite* in 1956.[1] In it, he argued that the United States was operating on the basis of a permanent war economy, with power vested in the hands of "the political directorate, the corporate rich, and the high military." He saw this elite as a unified one in terms of social and psychological similarities, frequent social interaction, and coordinated activities among its three components. In 1961, a similar warning came from the White House itself. In his farewell address, President Dwight D. Eisenhower said, "In the councils of government we must guard against the acquisition of unwarranted influences, whether sought or unsought, by the military-industrial complex."

Certain basic dimensions of military-industrial relations are uncontested in the debate on whether American politics are dominated by a power elite, and four of these are primary. First, following World War II, the United States did not decrease the size of its military force as drastically as it had in previous postwar periods. There was some contraction in 1945, but since 1947 it has maintained a large standing army at considerable expense. The movement away from conscription and toward a volunteer army in the mid-1970s is expected to increase rather than decrease the dollar cost of the military establishment, although the size of the active-duty force will shrink.

---

[1] C. Wright Mills, *The Power Elite* (New York: Oxford University Press, 1956).

Second, the emphasis in warfare has shifted in the post-World War II period from manpower to technologically sophisticated firepower. The military has thus become a major consumer of research and development services, as well as of material production by civilian industries. It might be said that the Department of Defense has become American industry's best customer, causing some critics to go so far as to suggest that the large modern corporations are becoming part of the governmental administrative complex.[2] Some civilian corporations have become totally dependent on the patronage of the military establishment.

Third, there is a demonstrable circulation of personnel between the Department of Defense and civilian corporations holding government contracts. During the 1971 fiscal year, 180 military contractors in the civilian sector employed 993 former military officers with the rank of major or above, as well as 240 former Department of Defense civilian employees or consultants who had been employed at or above the GS-13 minimum salary. The largest single supplier of such personnel was the air force, which "recycled" 525 retired senior officers. The aerospace industry, in turn, was the major employer of retired officers. Six major aerospace contractors, for example, employed among them 234 retired senior officers.

Fourth, there have clearly been instances in which members of the Congress and the Senate have attempted to intervene in the defense contract review procedure to get contracts assigned to corporations within their constituencies. Such intervention, of course, takes place with regard to other contracting agencies in the federal government as well.

These parameters do not in and of themselves demonstrate the existence of a power elite, but they do suggest that there is a military-industrial complex, if this phrase is taken to describe a set of interorganizational relationships rather than a conspiracy. In fact, three different perspectives have been suggested for viewing the linkages between the military and industry. These perspectives are not, on the whole, mutually exclusive, but they do contain contradictory elements.

The first and perhaps the dominant position reflected in the literature is the elitist or conspiratorial view following in the tradition of Mills. Its major thesis is that a relatively small group

---

[2] See, for example, Seymour Melman, *Pentagon Capitalism* (New York: McGraw-Hill Book Co., 1970).

of people located at the top of the congressional, military, and industrial hierarchies determine national policy in such areas as foreign affairs and military spending, keeping the American economy in a state of "military capitalism." A major cleavage is presumed to exist between this elite and the rest of the "mass society," and the elite are presumed to be an integrated network of individuals acting in concert. The elite are seen as responsible for placing resources and power in the hands of a corporate structure that is not responsible to the public, for economic inefficiency, and for the nonfulfillment of domestic programs.[3]

Actually, recent work in this tradition has gone well beyond Mills. Historically, Mills saw shifts in the relative importance of the military, corporate, and governmental realms. In the post-World War II period, he saw the military ascendancy as the dominant influence in shaping the power elite. Yet he also recognized that, in terms of education and social origin, the military were not really similar to the rest of the elite, and that the process of promotion through the military hierarchy produced officers who had given up some of their civilian sensibilities. This difference between civilian and military members of the power elite may be seen as an obstacle to the cohesiveness of that elite.[4] Mills in fact suggested that the elite were frequently in some tension and came together only on certain coinciding points.

Other scholars have gone further than Mills in asserting the similarity of social backgrounds and the social cohesiveness of the power elite.[5] The bulk of the data, however, suggest that they are not all that similar. American business leaders tend to be the sons of business leaders, and in general are recruited from the higher strata of society. They tend to come from the Middle Atlantic, New England, and Pacific Coast states, and are likely to have been born in large urban areas. Most tend to be college educated.[6] Military leaders also tend to come from high-status backgrounds, with over half their fathers having been in business and the

---

[3] See Sam Sarkesian, *The Military-Industrial Complex* (Beverly Hills, Calif.: Sage Publications, Inc., 1972), pp. vii–viii.

[4] David R. Segal, "Civil-Military Differentiation in the New Industrial State," *Sociological Focus* 6:1 (Winter 1973), pp. 45–60.

[5] See G. William Domhoff, *Who Rules America?* (Englewood Cliffs, N.J.: Prentice-Hall, Inc., 1967).

[6] See W. L. Warner and J. Abegglen, *Big Business Leaders in America* (New York: Harper & Row, Publishers, 1955).

.professions.[7] Military leaders, however, are far more likely than corporation officials to come from rural areas, and to over-represent the Southern states.[8] In addition, of course, military leaders and corporation executives receive their higher educations at different institutions, the former being predominantly military academy graduates. Thus, civilian and military elites are not held together by old school ties, and they differ in the urbanity and region of their social origins. There are important differences between the two groups of civilian elites, as well. While both U.S. senators and corporation presidents have been shown to be roughly representative geographically, senators tend to come from rural areas while corporation presidents are usually from urban centers. Similarly, although both groups tend to be college educated, the corporation executives are more likely to have gone to Ivy League schools, while senators are more likely to have attended state universities. It has been argued that these background differences lead to disparate images of society and a lack of communication between these groups.[9]

In addition to social background differences, the interchangeability of personnel among the three groups making up the power elite has been challenged. Mills suggested military leaders are like corporation managers and that elite personnel are interchangeable among organizational contexts. This assertion was quickly challenged,[10] but the military sociology of the 1960s saw increasing similarity between military and civilian organization. Ironically, as this convergence was seen as taking place, civilian organization began moving away from the model that military organization was beginning to approach.

CONVERGENCE OF CIVIL AND MILITARY SPHERES

We have previously discussed theories that projected the convergence of social classes in the United States, convergence

[7] W. Lloyd Warner, Paul P. Van Riper, Norman H. Martin, and Orvis F. Collins, *The American Federal Executive* (New Haven: Yale University Press, 1963).

[8] Morris Janowitz, *The Professional Soldier* (New York: The Free Press, 1960).

[9] Andrew Hacker, "The Elected and the Anointed," *American Political Science Review* 55 (September 1961), pp. 539–549.

[10] Janowitz, *The Professional Soldier*, p. 73.

between capitalist and communist societies, and convergence between the American South and other regions of the United States. These theories all assumed that increasing similarity in economic structure would be quickly followed by increasing similarity in social structure. Similarly, the 1960s saw a projected convergence between the civilian and military sectors of American society, bringing theories of the relationship between these structures full circle in an important sense.[11]

Military structure served as a major source of insight for Max Weber's model of rational organization,[12] which in turn has served as the basis for much of the research carried out on complex organizations in the civilian context. Until the 1960s, however, it was assumed by students of formal organization that, because of differences in skill requirements and technologies, military and civilian structures had to have different organizational forms.

The military sociology of the 1960s rejected the theme of structural differentiation and stressed instead observed areas of similarity. Thus, Janowitz has argued that "to analyze the contemporary military establishment as a social system, it is . . . necessary to assume that for some time it has tended to display more and more of the characteristics typical of any large-scale nonmilitary bureaucracy."[13] While this tendency has frequently been referred to in the literature as "civilianization" of the military, the notion of convergence seems more accurately to represent the processes involved. The military was not thought to be adopting organizational strategies from the civilian arena. Rather, both military and civilian organizations were assumed to be adapting to similar environmental conditions and making organizational decisions on the basis of similar principles, with the military frequently making the adaptation prior to similar changes in civilian organizations. With regard to skill distribution, for example, the argument has been made that "change in the military occupational structure appears in certain respects to have anticipated change in the labor force,"[14] while with regard to

---

[11] See Segal, "Civil-Military Differentiation in the New Industrial State."

[12] Max Weber, *Gesammelte Aufsätze zur Sozial-und Wirtschaftsgeschichte* (Tubingen: J. C. B. Mohr, 1924).

[13] Morris Janowitz, *Sociology and the Military Establishment,* rev. ed. (New York: Russell Sage Foundation, 1965), p. 17.

[14] Kurt Lang, "Technology and Career Management in the Military Establishment," in Morris Janowitz, ed., *The New Military* (New York: Russell Sage Foundation, 1964), p. 45.

organizational structure itself, it has been reported that "comparative analysis of military and civilian organization suggests that military organization has reached a stage of bureaucratic development which seemingly anticipates the future movement of other complex systems."[15]

The military sociology of the 1960s, then, asserted the existence of similarities between military and civilian bureaucratic organizations, with the leadership structure of the military paralleling the management structure of civilian complex organizations. This similarity, in turn, could expedite personnel interchange between industrial and military organizations at the management level.

Recent military sociology and organizational sociology, however, refute the convergence theme. Some scholars, such as Janowitz, have argued that the essential difference between military and civilian tasks places limits on convergence; once a certain level of similarity is attained, no further convergence is possible. The assumption here is that some things are so uniquely military that even in an era of complex technology they cannot be completely eliminated, nor can an analogue for them be developed in the civilian sector.[16] A more extreme view is that the trend toward convergence has in fact been reversed, and that the civilian and military sectors of American society are now becoming more dissimilar.[17]

While some students of the military still argue that increasing bureaucratization of the military will lead to civil-military convergence, contemporary theories of economic organization have suggested that the most adaptive model for modern organization may in fact not be the bureaucratic model. Thus, even increased bureaucracy in the military need not portend convergence.

The notion of bureaucracy implies a hierarchical organization through which an individual is promoted on the basis of demonstrated competence at tasks deemed important for the fulfillment of organizational goals. Thus, the successful bureaucratic career is presumed to be based upon expertise with regard to the specific product or service that a specific corporate organization supplies.

---

[15] Oscar Grusky, "The Effects of Succession," in Janowitz, ed., *The New Military*, p. 84.

[16] Morris Janowitz, "The Emergent Military," in Charles C. Moskos, Jr., ed., *Public Opinion and the Military Establishment* (Beverly Hills, Calif.: Sage Publications, Inc., 1971), pp. 255–270.

[17] Charles C. Moskos, Jr., "Armed Forces and American Society," in Moskos, ed., *Public Opinion and the Military Establishment*, pp. 271–294.

This model does seem to fit military careers fairly well, but seems less appropriate for modern large-scale industry. The notion that a bureaucratic career may be dysfunctional for economic organization is not new in organizational theory. At midcentury, economists were pointing out that top management jobs are radically different from the tasks performed by operating executives, and that bureaucratic training produces people who are too narrowly specialized to fill the "generalist" needs of top management, although such people are essential at lower operating levels.[18]

More recent organization theory suggests that in today's highly specialized economy, the task of organizing specialists is becoming so complex within a given corporate structure that specialists on organization will soon be needed to coordinate the activities of the various "technocratic" specialties within the enterprise.[19] A more extreme formulation suggests that the rate of change and the development of new organizational problems in the modern economy are making bureaucratic organizations obsolete. It argues that the routinized responses of bureaucratic structures do not provide sufficient organizational flexibility. This formulation proposes that bureaucratic agencies be replaced by temporary working groups, bringing together people with specific skills to solve specific problems and disbanding once the problems are solved. The job of top management in this setting becomes that of building an organizational climate which fosters growth and development. The manager's substantive expertise regarding a particular topic becomes far less important than his understanding and possession of skills regarding collaboration and coordination.[20]

Of course, it may be argued that the military operates in the same socioeconomic climate as does industry, and that, especially if we take seriously the argument that under military capitalism the defense industries operate as quasi-agencies of the government, common constraints should lead to similar management structures in the military and in industry. The data suggest, however, that the top levels of military command are not made up of specialists in organization, but rather, and not surprisingly, of specialists in warfare.

[18] See Peter F. Drucker, *The New Society* (New York: Harper & Row Publishers, 1950).

[19] See John Kenneth Galbraith, *The New Industrial State* (Boston: Houghton Mifflin Co., 1967).

[20] Warren G. Bennis and Philip Slater, *The Temporary Society* (New York: Harper & Row, Publishers, 1968).

The U.S. Air Force, as the newest of the American armed services and the one with the most complex technology, might be expected to be the most adaptive branch and the most likely to adopt new organizational principles. However, promotion to general officer grades in the air force comes through performance of mission-oriented activities, i.e., flying aircraft, rather than through attainment of managerial skills.[21] Similarly, the U.S. Navy, which, as the ranking service in terms of the social backgrounds of its officers, is the most likely to contribute personnel to a power elite, promotes personnel to flag (admiral) rank on the basis of combat rather than management training.[22] Given different management structures and skills in the military and in industry, Mills' notion of the interchangeability of leadership personnel does not stand up. This is not to deny that a considerable number of retired military officers do find employment with corporations that hold large contracts with the Department of Defense. Indeed, such personnel interchange is to be expected, given that most professional officers finish their military careers in early middle age and then undertake a second career, and that these retired officers have some expertise in the needs of the clients of defense contractors.[23] What is crucial is that only in very rare cases do these retired officers find themselves at the topmost levels of the hierarchies of large corporations. Retired generals and admirals do not automatically become corporation presidents or chairmen of boards of directors.

A third set of criticisms of Mills' model has challenged the dominant position that Mills assigned to military leaders, seeing them ascendent over the civilian members of the power elite.[24] In the light of these criticisms, more recent attempts to demonstrate the existence of a power elite in the United States have come to view the military as a junior partner in the elite structure, frequently participating through cooptation rather than coopera-

---

[21] Segal, "Civil-Military Differentiation in the New Industrial State."

[22] David R. Segal and Mady W. Segal, "Models of Civil-Military Relationships at the Elite Level," in M. R. Van Gils, ed., *The Perceived Role of the Military* (Rotterdam: Rotterdam University Press, 1971), pp. 277–292.

[23] See Albert D. Biderman, "Retired Soldiers Within and Without the Military-Industrial Complex," in Sarkesian, *The Military-Industrial Complex*, pp. 95–124.

[24] See, for example, Paul M. Sweezy, "Power Elite or Ruling Class," and Herbert Aptheker, "Power in America," in G. William Domhoff and Hoyt B. Bullard, eds., *C. Wright Mills and the Power Elite* (Boston: Beacon Press, 1969), pp. 115–132, 134–164.

tion, and serving rather than shaping the interests of an assumed upper class.[25]

THE PLURALIST VIEW

The second major perspective on relations between the military and industry is the pluralist position.[26] In this view, the military is seen as an interest group attempting to influence political decisions. Similarly, industries producing goods for the military are viewed as an economic interest group. This approach concedes that, when the interests of the military and industry converge, the two might form a coalition and/or coordinate their lobbying efforts. It also concedes that the Congress may at times be responsive to the demands of these groups. It asserts, however, that the military and military-related industries are not powerful enough to consistently dominate the national political scene. Rather, it views them as two elements in a large and diverse set of interests, some manifested as organized groups and others as a more diffuse public opinion, that from time to time exert or attempt to exert leverage on the policy-making process.[27] It further asserts that the Congress is no more responsive to military interests than to other interests in the long run. Rather than assuming the concentration of power in the hands of a relatively small group of elite, this approach assumes the incremental building of pluralities in support of policy. This difference has implications for the policy process itself. Rather than making sweeping policy changes, as a unified power elite might do, the decision-makers in a pluralistic system evolve policy through a series of small steps in what they perceive to be the desired direction, pausing at each point to evaluate the effects of what they have done.[28]

[25] Domhoff, *Who Rules America?*

[26] See, for example, Arnold M. Rose, *The Power Structure* (New York: Oxford University Press, 1967), and Robert A. Dahl, *Pluralist Democracy in the United States* (Chicago: Rand McNally & Co., 1967).

[27] See V. O. Key, Jr., *Politics, Parties, and Pressure Groups* (New York: Thomas Y. Crowell Co., 1964), and *Public Opinion and American Democracy* (New York: Alfred A. Knopf, Inc., 1965).

[28] See, for example, Robert A. Dahl and Charles E. Lindblom, *Politics, Economics and Welfare* (New York: Harper & Row, Publishers, 1953), and Charles E. Lindblom, "The Science of 'Muddling Through,' " *Public Administration Review* 29:2 (Spring 1959), pp. 79–88.

VETO GROUPS AND COMPENSATING
STRATEGIES

The third perspective on power relationships involving the military and defense industries shares with the pluralist perspective an assumption of a multiplicity of interests which compete for power. However, these are seen as existing primarily at elite levels in the social hierarchy, and the role of public opinion and popular interests is deemphasized.

At about the time that Mills' theory of the power elite appeared, a book by David Reisman called *The Lonely Crowd* was attracting a great deal of attention. Little discussion, however, was devoted to Reisman's theory of power in America, which was very different from that of Mills.[29] Where Mills saw a unified power elite taking aggressive action in the polity to further its own interests, Reisman saw power in America being exercised by many veto groups which, rather than being expansive, operated primarily to defend their interests. The problem of American politics, for Reisman, was not that one group would come to dominate the entire system, but rather that a multiplicity of groups, each cancelling out to some extent the efforts of other groups, might completely immobilize the polity so that nothing would be accomplished. In this view, the power of the military-industrial complex was highly constrained by nonmilitary or nonindustrial interest groups.

An alternative approach, related to the notion of veto groups, but not rooted in an assumption of defensive posturing, is that of compensating strategies. From this perspective, it is possible for interest groups to influence policy in such a way that the policy will not reflect plurality interest even when the government is not controlled by a power elite. It is assumed that different policies have different degrees of salience for different interests. Thus, one segment of the American business community can involve itself greatly in policy debates regarding military expenditures, while other existing interests disregard the debate because they can derive financial (or other) benefits from other policy areas. Each interest group is seen as seeking to maximize its own net gain, and if it can increase its gains at low cost by entering an alliance with another interest, it will do so. Consequently, political decisions in an area such as military expenditure may well reflect "the intense

---

[29] David Reisman, *The Lonely Crowd* (New Haven: Yale University Press, 1961), pp. 213–217. See also William Kornhauser, " 'Power Elite' or 'Veto Groups,' " in Seymour M. Lipset and Leo Lowenthal, eds., *Culture and Social Character* (New York: The Free Press, 1961).

concern of a minority of interests coupled with the support obtained from other segments whose major interests are found elsewhere."[30] As long as interests other than the military or defense industries can increase their gains by influencing legislation involving factors such as taxes or labor law, they will not involve themselves deeply in matters of military spending, but may well ally themselves with military and defense-industry interests by providing moral support, in return for which they expect similar support when their own interests are at stake. However, should it come to pass that they cannot make gains in other areas because of the magnitude of defense spending, these interests are likely to enter the defense-spending debates in opposition to the military-industrial complex; if they are in the dairy business, they will try to persuade the Congress to buy butter instead of guns.

THE GARRISON STATE

While the perspectives discussed above foresee the militarization of civil society and the domination of domestic politics by military interests arising primarily out of power politics at the national level, an alternate approach anticipates the militarization of society as a response to pressures largely independent of domestic political concerns. In Chapter 4, in the course of our discussion of convergence in the international system, we noted that some theorists see both communist and capitalist societies evolving into military bureaucracies, and that, prior to the development of "end of ideology" arguments, scholars had noted that in both the USSR and the industrial nations of the West the values of totalitarianism, militarism, conflict, and aggression were gaining ascendency over democracy and internationalism.

These propositions, taken as projections, are interesting because, while they portend a high level of interpenetration between the civilian and military sectors of society and the military dominance of this interrelated system, they do so without postulating the economic determinism of Mills and of others concerned with the military-industrial complex. Were the capitalist interests of defense industries, whether free-enterprise capitalism or Pentagon capitalism, responsible for the presumed dominance of the

---

[30] Stanley Lieberson, "An Empirical Study of Military-Industrial Linkages," *American Journal of Sociology* 76 (January 1971), p. 577.

military in American politics, there would be no reason to posit such dominance in the Soviet Union. Indeed, in the light of its lower level of industrialization, the relative absence of the profit motive in industry, the relatively low availability of consumer amenities, and the centralized control of the Soviet economy, one would probably expect the Soviet government to devote its industrial resources primarily to capital expansion and consumer production, rather than to defense-related activities, as a means of improving both its economic position in the international system and the legitimacy of its regime in the eyes of the population. The allegation of military dominance in communist systems suggests that it is not the profit motive of defense industries that explains this dominance. Rather, we are forced to fall back on definitions of national interest and perceived threats to national prestige as possible explanatory variables. Such variables, in turn, might be regarded as forms of ideology, although not necessarily defined in terms of a highly structured and coherent set of beliefs. And if support exists for such an explanation, then at a minimum it is premature to argue that the age of political ideology has ended. [31]

Indeed, Harold Lasswell, in his formulation of the garrison-state concept, anticipated that the emergence of such a state would be associated with one or another of the major existing ideological patterns: democracy, national socialism, communism. [32] Where Robert Lane saw the decline of politics as rooted in the modern technology of administration, Lasswell saw the ascent of military bureaucracy as rooted in the modern technology of war. On the basis of the Sino-Japanese War experience, [33] Lasswell anticipated the emerging but short-lived military philosophy based initially on air power and later on first-strike nuclear potential. The major technical condition for the emergence of the garrison state was air power, which produced a new distribution of danger in society. With the coming of aerial warfare, the risk differential between civilian and military roles diminished, or perhaps was reversed. Airborne weapons may inflict greater casualties on large and highly concentrated civilian populations than on military formations.

[31] For an insightful discussion of the inability of the American government to seek a rapproachment with the communist bloc, and with China in particular, through the 1960s, see David Halberstam, *The Best and the Brightest* (New York: Random House, Inc., 1972).

[32] Harold D. Lasswell, "The Garrison State," *American Journal of Sociology* 46 (January 1941), pp. 455–468.

[33] See Harold D. Lasswell, "Sino-Japanese Crisis," *China Quarterly* 11 (Fall 1937), pp. 643–649.

As a concomitant of this "socialization of danger," Lasswell anticipated the increasing permeability of the boundary between the military and civilian sectors of society, with the management of the new combined civil-military enterprise vested in the hands of military men. This was not to suggest that the ideal of political democracy would be rejected. Indeed, the symbols of democracy were expected to continue under the garrison state, as well as certain basic democratic values such as respect for human dignity. Decision making in the garrison state, however, was expected to be centralized and autocratic, although perhaps legitimized through ritual acceptance by an elected legislature and sold to the population as public opinion through the instruments of communication and propaganda.

A quarter of a century after developing the garrison-state construct on the basis of the Asian experience, Lasswell examined its applicability to a bipolar Cold War world.[34] He noted that, while skill in the management of violence played a prominent role in modern politics, it was still subordinate to other bases of political power. Nonetheless, for advocates of participatory political democracy, the prognosis was pessimistic. Lasswell saw the totalitarian nations of the Soviet bloc already approximating the garrison-state model, and he saw processes at work in the industrialized democracies of the West which he anticipated would lead to the reification of the model in those nations as well. To the extent that the populations of the nations of the world recognized the threat to themselves generated by the socialization of danger through military technology and responded to it by demanding peace at any price (the slogan "Better red than dead" comes quickly to mind), Lasswell anticipated that the utilization of police powers by the state to control such subversion would be increased. That is, if the nonelite became more internationalistic and pacifist, the elite would respond with heightened levels of nationalism. By refusing to identify with national political structures, the nonelite would elicit garrison-state responses from the political elite.

There is evidence accumulating of the decrease in popular identification with national political institutions,[35] and the in-

---

[34] Harold D. Lasswell, "The Garrison-State Hypothesis Today," in Samuel P. Huntington, ed., *Changing Patterns of Military Politics* (New York: The Free Press, 1962), pp. 51–70.

[35] See David R. Segal and Gerald Kent Hikel, "The Emerging Independent" (Paper prepared for the 1973 meeting of the American Sociological Association, New York, August 1973).

cidence of mass arrests at political demonstrations and of military intelligence agencies being used to monitor the activities of civilian groups in the United States during the Vietnam War clearly bespeaks garrison-state tactics. At the same time, we cannot assert that the repressive tactics were caused solely by antiwar activities. Indeed, it may well be that much of the American alienation from government during the early 1970s was a response to, rather than a cause of, the garrison-state policies of the government. At a minimum, the relationship is reciprocal rather than unidirectional.

The intelligence function played by the military is especially crucial in Lasswell's formulation because this is, for him, the first phase in the decision-making process. Since specialists in violence are also participants in the definition of what is deviant and in the application of policy, and since in the crisis period of the 1960s the role of the military in decision making was expected to (and did) expand, the projection of an increasingly narrow sharing of power, an ever widening scope of power, and the formation of a self-perpetuating elite concerned with the utilization of violence in both the domestic and international arenas is reasonable.

Whether the garrison-state emerges as a reality in the Western democracies in the coming years seems to Lasswell to depend upon two processes internal to each individual nation: the socialization of ascending generations to either accept or reject the military model of society, and the ability or inability of civilian institutions in society to "civilianize" the military.

With regard to the first point, Lasswell is concerned about the subordination of other social values to military potential in crisis periods.[36] In such periods, when the expectation of violence is routinized and national ideologies demand personal sacrifice for the common good, the military man may well appear as the personification of social values and an ideal role model. It is interesting to note that, while in recent years the liberal academic community has regarded the profession of arms with some disfavor, at the peak of the Cold War a captain in the regular army had the same prestige, in terms of occupation, as an instructor in a public school—somewhat less than a sociologist and somewhat

---

[36] Harold L. Wilensky discusses this problem, and suggests a means for overcoming it, in "Intelligence, Crises, and Foreign Policy," in Richard H. Blum, ed., *Surveillance and Espionage in a Free Society* (New York: Praeger Publishers, Inc., 1972), pp. 236–266.

more than an accountant.[37] The prestige equation of military officers with schoolteachers is certainly an important datum if we are to be concerned with the military as role models for youth.

With regard to the potential for encouraging "civilianism" within the military, Lasswell sees at least a baseline for hope. He views the current structure of the American elite in terms of shifting coalitions formed within the context of a plurality of interests. While the inertia of international relations may over time favor the military, the rules of the game nonetheless legitimize the presence of civilian interests within the elite coalition that rules at any given time.

Another aspect of civilianism in the garrison state may well be more problematic. This is the input of civilian sensibilities into the military institution itself. The history of the American army has been one of high personnel turnover, with the effect of having a large number of men within the military who did not consider themselves career soldiers. Conscription, whatever its costs, had the benefit of linking the military with civilian society at the enlisted ranks. To the extent that the volunteer army replaces personnel turnover with careerism at the enlisted ranks, this input is lost. Similarly, noncareer officers, such as those commissioned through ROTC, have also been an important link—perhaps more important than conscripts—between military and civilian worlds. To the extent that programs like ROTC are cut off and the military becomes more dependent on its own academy graduates and on career-oriented personnel to staff its officer corps, the level of civilianism within the military can be expected to decrease and the military will operate with a more monolithic militaristic ideology within the broader political arena.

Lasswell's garrison-state construct was perhaps the dominant theory of civil-military relations in post-World War II America. However, in no way was it universally accepted. In particular, critics pointed out that it equates the military with war and violence. Contemporary perspectives more commonly deal with the peacekeeping function of the military in an age of nuclear technology—the constabulary concept of the military.[38] Moreover, Lasswell's view reflects a belief that the world must exist in

---

[37] See Robert W. Hodge, Paul M. Siegel, and Peter H. Rossi, "Occupational Prestige in the United States," in Reinhard Bendix and Seymour Martin Lipset, eds., *Class, Status, and Power*, 2nd ed. (New York: The Free Press, 1966), pp. 322–334.

[38] See Morris Janowitz, "Military Organization," in Roger W. Little, ed., *Handbook of Military Institutions* (Beverly Hills, Calif.: Sage Publications, Inc., 1971), especially pp. 46–48.

a state of either unified peace or total war. The possibility of a continuing and relatively constant level of international tension, requiring neither international unification nor another world war, is ruled out.[39] Finally, while military-industrial-complex theorists agree with the garrison-state approach in seeing the fusion of civil and military structures, even the most extreme warnings of the evils of government control of defense industries do not demonstrate such control across the broad spectrum of the American economy.[40]

MASS SOCIETY

In Chapter 2 we introduced briefly the notion of a mass society. In such a society, rank-and-file members of the polity are not integrated into the fabric of society through linkages to other rank-and-file members of the system. In the absence of such linkages, members of the polity are held together only by responsibility to a common political authority. These linkages, in turn, are provided primarily by the media of mass communications.[41]

In order for Mills' power elite, or Reisman's veto groups, or Lasswell's garrison state to dominate the political scene for any appreciable period of time in opposition to the will of the people, it would seem that a condition approximating mass society would have to exist so that either the elite could use the mass media to convince society that it wanted to live under a war economy or at least groups opposing the elite would be unlikely to form. The former strategy involves the elite's actively controlling the population by forming rather than following public opinion. The latter does not require initiative on the part of the elite, because the nonelite would be controlled simply by their inability to organize an effective opposition movement.

Some variant of the mass society was assumed by Mills, Reisman, and Lasswell. For Mills, "the transformation of public into mass . . . has been . . . one of the major trends of modern

---

[39] See Samuel P. Huntington, *The Soldier and the State* (Cambridge: Harvard University Press, 1957), pp. 346–350.

[40] Benjamin S. Kleinberg, *American Society in the Post-Industrial Age* (Columbus, Ohio: Charles E. Merrill Publishing Co., 1973), pp. 85–89.

[41] William Kornhauser, *The Politics of Mass Society* (New York: The Free Press, 1959).

societies."[42] This is not to say that the United States had become, for Mills, the ideal-typical mass society. However, on a continuum running between a society of engaged publics at one pole and a mass society at the other, Mills saw America closer to the latter than to the former. The mass media in America have become more important than interpersonal discussion in political communication, and public opinion has become a reaction to media content. The broad base of the American population has become fragmented, and voluntary associations have ceased to integrate people into the body politic.

Reisman, while he did not argue for the control of the mass media by the political elite, and in fact pointed out that the media are critical of politics, nonetheless saw the rank-and-file member of society playing a passive role as a political consumer, unsure of what he wants or expects from politics, but accepting the picture of politics presented by the media.[43] In the worlds of Mills and Reisman, opposition to power elites or veto groups is unlikely to emerge.

Lasswell, even more than Mills, saw the managers of the garrison state manipulating symbols through the mass media as a means of maintaining popular support. At the same time, he was far more optimistic than Mills or Reisman regarding the degree of fragmentation and the social isolation of individuals in the population.[44] Indeed, he saw a need, from the perspective of the managers of the garrison state, to utilize force and violence to control elements of the population that are not swayed by the media. And from the perspective of democratic elements in the population, he saw potential for civilianizing the garrison state.

THE MILITARY-INDUSTRIAL SOCIETY

A major part of this book has been concerned with identifying units of social organization in modern industrial society that provide linkages between individuals and the larger political order. While the quality of such traditional forms of social relationship—the family, the peer group, the neighborhood, the

[42] Mills, *The Power Elite*, p. 301.

[43] Reisman, *The Lonely Crowd*, pp. 190 ff.

[44] Harold D. Lasswell, "Does the Garrison State Threaten Civil Rights?" *Annals of the American Academy of Political and Social Science* 275 (May 1951), pp. 111–116.

ethnic group, etc.—may be changing, the social bonds embedded in these relationships are not weakening. Neither in the United States nor in any other Western democratic nation have the masses been kept "atomized," "fragmented," or "isolated."[45] How, then, can we account for the role played in American politics by the military establishment and the defense industries? While scholars debate the magnitude of this role, no one denies that it is a major factor in the politics of the nation.

The proposition that American society has been transformed into a system of "military capitalism" need not be based upon the assumption that certain strategic elites in America have been able to impose their will on society and reshape society in pursuit of their interests. Rather, one can argue that the inertia of the past has gradually built a system of military capitalism in response to changing international conditions, and that American society has come to support this system primarily on the basis of inertia. Social systems are conservative. They tend to prefer what is to what might be. The larger the social system, the longer it takes to change. And change itself is threatening.[46] Thus, a society is destined to carry with it the results of its own history.

The major application of this argument to the alleged militarism of American society goes further, suggesting that the military posture that has been developed in the United States is supported by three basic values in the American ethic: that, in foreign affairs, efficacy is more important than principle; that private property is preferable to collective property; that the current form of constitutional democracy in the United States is superior to any other form of government.[47]

The first point is a specification of a more general principle contributed to political sociology by Max Weber, that politics is a business of pragmatism rather than of idealism.[48] The means of dealing with international cleavages pragmatically is through military preparedness. Of course, the doctrine of efficacy demands

---

[45] Harold L. Wilensky, "Mass Society and Mass Culture," in Bernard Berelson and Morris Janowitz, eds., *Reader in Public Opinion and Mass Communications* (New York: The Free Press, 1966), p. 297.

[46] Regarding this assumption, see Eric Hoffer, *The Ordeal of Change* (New York: Harper & Row, Publishers, 1964).

[47] Marc Pilisuk and Thomas Hayden, "Is There a Military-Industrial Complex Which Prevents Peace?" *Journal of Social Issues* 21:3, pp. 67–117.

[48] Max Weber, "Politics as a Vocation," in H. H. Gerth and C. Wright Mills, eds., *From Max Weber* (New York: Oxford University Press, 1958), pp. 77–128.

efficiency in military preparedness. It is not, therefore, surprising that much of the criticism of the military-industrial complex in the halls of government is aimed not at dismantling the complex, but at making it run more efficiently through elimination of cost overruns and the like.

The argument that American militarism is supported by the placing of a higher valuation on private property than on collective property is an especially interesting one, given that most scholars concerned with the military-industrial complex characterize the economic consequences of its existence as an expansion of government control over industry. The counterproposition is that, given the dependence upon military production that has been built up over the years, a massive conversion to peacetime economic activity would require far greater governmental involvement in the economy because of the massive dislocation that would result.

The commitment to "our" system of government reflects the level of ideology that might be required to generate popular support for Lasswell's garrison state. Thus, this approach argues "not that American society contains a ruling military-industrial complex . . . [but] that American society *is* a military-industrial complex."[49] The groups involved in the formation of policy fluctuate greatly over time, but the membership of the top stratum of the power structure at any moment is unimportant. The structure of the system and its history dictate that any combination of interests comprising the governing group will produce essentially the same policies. The existence of a military-industrial complex as a set of institutional relationships becomes not a matter of conspiracy, but of consensus. The last three major military engagements in which the United States participated (World War ii, Korea, and Vietnam) saw, in their early stages, the incumbent president increasing popular support for his policies by adopting a hard-line military posture.[50]

Just as the development of linkages between the military establishment and industrial bureaucracies can be seen as a popularly supported, natural stage in the unfolding of the modern history of industrial nations, rather than as a drastic break with the past, so can theories of the power elite and the military-industrial complex be seen as a natural step in the development of

---

[49] Pilisuk and Hayden, "Is There a Military-Industrial Complex Which Prevents Peace?"

[50] Robert B. Smith, "Disaffection, Delegitimation, and Consequences," in Moskos, *Public Opinion and the Military Establishment,* pp. 221–251.

theory in political sociology. While some "sociologists of sociology" attribute a renaissance of radicalism and Marxism in sociology to Mills' formulation,[51] the power-elite notion is well rooted in and naturally developed from traditions in political sociology that are both nonradical and non-Marxist. In particular, the political theories of Machiavelli, which see cleavages between economic classes replaced by cleavages between elites and masses, and the organizational theories of Weber, for whom power could be rooted in formal leadership positions as well as in capital ownership, are as important as those of Marx, if not more so, for understanding the dynamics of even the most conspiratorial formulations of the military-industrial complex.[52]

[51] Cf. Jack L. Roach, "The Radical Sociology Movement," *The American Sociologist* 5:3 (August 1970), pp. 224–233.

[52] See Charles C. Moskos, Jr., "The Military-Industrial Complex," in Sarkesian, ed., *The Military-Industrial Complex*, pp. 3–23.

10

Differentiation and Integration

POLITICAL PLURALISM AND SOLIDARITY

Two complementary perspectives have framed the ideas presented in this book. The first deals with the great plurality of interests resulting from social differentiation which are characteristic of a modern industrial nation. This perspective is perhaps dominant in modern political sociology, and is firmly embedded in the classics of European sociology: the works of Marx, Weber, Mosca, Machiavelli, and Pareto. Sociological studies of conflict adopt this perspective to the virtual exclusion of other points of view. In our analysis, the issue of political pluralism resulting from social differentiation has appeared in discussions of class politics, status politics, political differences among regional, cultural, or religious groups, and cleavages both between elites and masses and among competing elite groups.[1]

We have tried to balance attention to social differentiation against an emphasis on social integration and solidarity. The issue

[1] For a general discussion of the differentiation theme in the context of the United States, see Robert A. Dahl, *Pluralist Democracy in the United States* (Chicago: Rand McNally & Co., 1967).

is basically one of order. Given the plurality of interests existing in a modern industrial nation, each making claims on the resources of that nation, how does society deal with these demands so that violent conflict is kept to a minimal level and the nation can survive?

Interestingly, integrative solidarity was not a primary focus in the classical literature of European political sociology, although it clearly was central to other areas of general sociological thought. Auguste Comte, considered by many to be the father of sociology, urged the study of solidarity early in the nineteenth century, but it was not until much later in that century that Emile Durkheim and Ferdinand Toennies developed a sociology of solidarity. More recent work in the tradition of Durkheim and Toennies has been fairly distant from the field of political sociology.[2]

The emphasis on conflict rather than consensus in American political sociology comes largely from its European antecedents. European political analysis has been recorded largely in the rhetoric of conflict, and has focused on opposition to the established order as a social problem, albeit frequently from a socialist perspective.[3] American sociology, on the other hand, has viewed society in terms of a shared, middle-class, Protestant way of life.[4] Where the basic policy issue for European social scientists has been how to generate and manage fundamental changes in society, the prime issue for American social scientists has been how to share their middle-class way of life with groups not yet acculturated. We have seen in Chapters 4 and 5 that only recently has American social science challenged the assumption that political integration in a multi-ethnic society is achieved through the assimilation of minority ethnic groups. Indeed, only in the last three decades have such groups asserted their group identity on a large scale. As Bramson says, "The twentieth-century American sociologists . . . were concerned with maintaining the American norm. . . . The European sociologists emphasized ultimate and irreducible conflicts of classes which would hasten the reorganization of the entire social system on a new economic and social basis."[5] Note that the American emphasis on consensus has

[2] See, for example, the papers on Durkheim in *American Journal of Sociology* 78:3 (November 1972).

[3] See Leon Bramson, *The Political Context of Sociology* (Princeton: Princeton University Press, 1961), pp. 27–44.

[4] Ibid., pp. 47ff. See also C. Wright Mills, "The Professional Ideology of the Social Pathologist," *American Journal of Sociology* 49 (1943–44), pp. 165–180.

[5] Bramson, *The Political Context of Sociology*, p. 51.

not been limited to sociology, but is characteristic of post-World War II American historians as well. Only recently has American history, with a present-minded bent worthy of Turner and Beard, rediscovered cleavages in the American past that are reflected in the present state of the nation.[6]

The difference between the perspectives of traditional European political sociology and the newer American strain of the discipline, the one emphasizing cleavage and the other solidarity, reflects a real difference in the political styles found on the two continents. In Europe, political cleavage has generally been defined in terms of issues rooted in social class concerns, and studies have repeatedly shown class to be an important basis of party choice in those nations.[7] By contrast, the incidence of class voting is much lower in the United States, and is almost completely absent in Canada.[8]

As we have seen, the absence of class-based politics is not proof of a consensual style, and thus the issue of political order remains problematic even in the absence of class conflict. Interestingly, the very social differences that produce social cleavages and therefore make politics a *necessary* institution in society seem to define social groups that bind the individual to the state and thus make politics a *viable* institution in society.[9] As sociologists, we assume that people are social animals: they seek the company of other people. By virtue of their seeking each other's company and coming together, people form groups. An individual does not necessarily need the groups in which he is currently a member, but in a more general sense he needs groups. The groups with which he is affiliated, in turn, help make the government responsive to him *as a group member* in a way that it would be unlikely to respond to him as an individual. Social institutions respond to other social institutions, not to individuals. Some scholars have pointed this out as an alienating trend in modern society, and others have praised it for helping postpone the arrival of mass society. For good or ill, it seems to be the way that social systems work.

[6] See Barton J. Bernstein, ed., *Towards a New Past: Dissenting Essays in American History* (New York: Pantheon Books, Inc., 1965).

[7] Seymour Martin Lipset, *Political Man* (New York: Doubleday & Co., Inc., 1963), pp. 230ff.

[8] Richard Lewis Ogmundson, "Social Class and Canadian Politics" (Ph.D. diss., The University of Michigan, 1972).

[9] See Robert M. MacIver, *The Web of Government*, rev. ed. (New York: The Free Press, 1965), especially Chapter 13, "The Unit and the Unity," pp. 303–334.

That the same social phenomenon, differentiation, should produce both political cleavage and political integration is not a new idea. Almost all political ideologies view cleavage and conflict as bringing about integration.[10] For Marx and other utopians, conflict exists before, and is the cause of, the revolution of the proletarians. The conflict reaches its zenith during the revolution and is afterward replaced by integration and solidarity. In place of this temporal ordering of cleavage and consensus, modern political sociology sees the two as necessarily coexisting. Cleavages are manifested in political demands and must exist if society is to change. Consensus is necessary if society is to be able to persist and deal with the demands.

In Chapter 2 we discussed communication as an integrative force in the polity, and now we shall return to it. While social groups provide the structural linkage between the individual and the state, it is communication, in a multitude of forms, that serves as the process by which the groups themselves are integrated into society and linked to the polity. Influence and power are meaningless concepts if they refer to phenomena that cannot in some way be transmitted and communicated. We may therefore view the state as a cybernetic system. The government is linked to other groups and institutions within the polity by the information that flows between them.[11] At a minimum, demands and requests must flow to the government and decisions from it. Much of this interchange is informal and unofficial, and a good deal of it is symbolic. A confrontation on a university campus that results in death and injury may communicate a greater intensity of feeling about an issue to a government official who was not involved in the confrontation than will the most strongly worded petition directed to that official.

In all societies, communication is important in the political process. As the technologies of communication become increasingly complex and diverse, new avenues for political expression are opened up. The student activist in 1950 would give a speech as soon as a few people gathered to hear him. The 1970 activist would wait until a battery of microphones, and hopefully a television camera, were in place. While corporations such as Xerox and IBM could scarcely be regarded as major institutional supporters of countercultures, technological advances in decreas-

---

[10] See Maurice Duverger, *The Idea of Politics* (Chicago: Henry Regnery Co., 1970), especially Part III, "From Conflict to Integration," pp. 161–220.

[11] See Karl W. Deutsch, *The Nerves of Government* (New York: The Free Press, 1963).

ing the capital investment and unit cost of older printing processes helped provide highly politicized but low-budget groups with
access to wider audiences. Even in the days of mimeograph
technology, much of the revenue of anticapitalist groups on
college campuses wound up in the coffers of A. B. Dick. We can
now only begin to imagine the potential political uses of public
access requirements being written into cable television legislation.

With the revolution in communications technology in the
1960s came a renewed awareness of the implications of communication. Where past research on the effects of mass communication
had focused on media content and found little if any effect,[12]
contemporary scholarship has begun to focus on the media
themselves and has suggested that the very existence of particular
communications technologies has an impact independent of
media content.[13] And modern communications have left an
indelible imprint on politics. John F. Kennedy won the presidency largely because of the impact of television on the 1960
election.[14] His opponent, Richard M. Nixon, subsequently became
the first candidate to be packaged for a campaign run primarily by
means of telecommunications technology.[15] The twentieth-
century candidate can reach a much larger constituency than his
nineteenth-century counterpart, and yet he need not and cannot
know his constituents as intimately.

Communication involves the manipulation of symbols—an
activity that has always been central to politics. In a sense, in the
age of telecommunications, politics has become a metamedium,
utilizing particular communications technologies for particular
tasks in the processes of resource allocation and political integration. It is not simply the case that politics is the content of media
of mass communications. It is far more appropriate to say that
politics largely determines the content of the media, thereby using
them for political ends.[16] Few news stories appearing in local

---

[12] See Joseph T. Klapper, *The Effects of Mass Communication* (New York: The Free Press, 1960).

[13] See Marshall McLuhan, *Understanding Media* (New York: McGraw-Hill Book Co., 1964).

[14] See Bernard Rubin, *Political Television* (Belmont, Calif.: Wadsworth Publishing Co., Inc., 1967), especially pp. 43–103.

[15] See Joe McGinnis, *The Selling of the President, 1968* (New York: Trident Press, 1969).

[16] See Murray Edelman, *The Symbolic Uses of Politics* (Urbana: The University of Illinois Press, 1964), and *Politics as Symbolic Action* (Chicago: Markham Publishing Co., 1971).

papers in the United States are written by employees of those newspapers (reporters or correspondents). Most are centrally produced by the wire services and purchased by subscription. The wire services, in turn, generally report information transmitted at press conferences or contained in press releases. What is revealed about the government in the newspapers, therefore, is largely what agencies of the government have said about themselves. The student activist shares with the president of the United States, albeit to a lesser degree, some control over what will be said about him in the local press. To varying degrees, the same model holds for other media of communication as well. It is important to note that the centralization of the news production function does not place control over the media in the hands of formal governmental agencies, but it does place the media under the influence of any political interest (including governmental agencies) that has the technology and staff necessary for producing press releases and that is associated with a cause sensational enough to attract attention.

The major American contribution to political sociology, then, has been the recognition, both theoretical and empirical, that integration, or solidarity, is an important component of political systems, and that pluralistic systems need not be regarded only as conflict systems. An emerging framework of political sociology views social structures in terms of networks, or sets of linkages among people.[17] From this point of view, many of the social groups with which we have dealt earlier, e.g., classes and ethno-religious groups, are useful objects of analysis only insofar as they are solidary, or have an internal network linking their members. Political differences can exist between groups that have minimal overlap in their network structures. At the same time, the networks bind their members to the polity. As a dramatic example of this phenomenon, one may view the military-industrial complex as a social network, without whose linkages individual members of the political, military, or industrial elites might not only have limited leverage on the political system, but indeed might not be involved in it at all. In like manner, local community power structures may also be viewed as social networks.[18] What is important is that we have balanced the European concern with

[17] See, for example, Edward O. Laumann, *Bonds of Pluralism* (New York: John Wiley & Sons, Inc., 1973).

[18] For example, see Edward O. Laumann and Franz Urban Pappi, "New Directions in the Study of Elites" (Paper presented at the 1972 meeting of the American Sociological Association).

forms of cleavage in society against American social science perspectives which attempt to identify the social ties that weave individuals into the fabric of society. These perspectives have identified a wide range of objects of analysis, including reference groups,[19] significant others,[20] and opinion leaders.[21] They have in common the assumption that people in communication with other people contribute to system stability.

THE CONVERGENCE THEME

Within the framework set by the perspectives of cleavage and solidarity, we have considered a large number of substantive concerns of political sociology. Among these, two have recurred repeatedly: the convergence theme and the theme of ideology. Both are centrally important because they reflect on the balance of cleavage and solidarity in society. They are also highly related to each other.

On the basis of a deterministic model of society, the convergence theme projects a decrease in the incidence of social cleavage (although not necessarily an increase in social solidarity) at various levels of social organization. We have noted that, at the international level, some theorists have suggested a structural convergence between communist and capitalist nations (usually exemplified by the Soviet Union and the United States) because of the impact of industrialization on these nations. Different variants of these convergence theories foresee different outcomes of convergence. With regard to the political role of the military, for example, one polar view regards warfare as an artifact of pre-industrial society that will disappear when mature industrialization is achieved. The opposing viewpoint sees all modern industrial powers evolving into garrison states, each dominated by its own military-industrial complex. What is crucial is that, while industrialization has indeed had some effects in common on the USA and the USSR, these nations have not converged, nor do they seem about to do so. Over a century after the birth of the industrial

---

[19] See Theodore M. Newcomb, "Attitude Development as a Function of Reference Groups," in Harold Proshansky and Bernard Seidenberg, eds., *Basic Studies in Social Psychology* (New York: Holt, Rinehart & Winston, Inc., 1965), pp. 215–225.

[20] See Harry Stack Sullivan, *Conceptions of Modern Psychiatry* (Washington, D.C.: W. A. White Psychiatric Foundation, 1940), especially pp. 18–22.

[21] See Elihu Katz and Paul F. Lazarsfeld, *Personal Influence* (New York: The Free Press, 1955).

revolution in Europe, we still live in a pluralistic international system.

While the debate on international convergence took place primarily in the early to mid-1960s, the debate on intranational, regional convergence peaked in the late 1960s and early 1970s. The logical structure of the argument, however, was the same. Given historical differences between the Southern United States and the rest of the country in both political style and level of economic development, it was projected that, as the South came to increasingly approximate the rest of the country in level of economic development, the two regions would converge politically as well. Again, regional differentiation remains a characteristic of American politics.[22]

What is rarely recognized is the similarity between the theories of international and interregional convergence of the 1960s and 70s and the theories of ethnic political assimilation rooted in the sociology of the 1920s and 30s. The units of analysis differed: theories of political assimilation focused on individual members of ethnic communities, rather than on territorial units. The dynamics of determinism, however, were the same. Immigrants and their families, as a result of being successfully caught up in the advancing processes of industrialization, were expected to lose that which was culturally unique about themselves and become politically similar to the other workers in the melting pot of an expanding capitalist economy. And again, the data suggest that advanced industrialization has not decreased the ethnoreligious pluralism of American politics.

The convergence theme has also appeared in discussions of the decreased polarization of economic classes in modern industrial society. As we noted in Chapter 4, the same processes of industrialization that were expected to lead the communist and capitalist worlds to converge were also expected to produce a convergence between the working class and the middle class in America. While the data fail to support the convergence theme in this realm as well, some scholars still anticipate the embourgeoisement of the proletariat or the proletarianization of the bourgeoisie. At the present time, differences in level of income and in life-style still exist between the working and middle classes, and members of the latter group are significantly more likely to regard themselves as Republicans than are members of the former.

[22] David Knoke, "A Causal Model for the Political Party Preferences of American Men," *American Sociological Review* 37 (December 1972), pp. 679–689.

The most recent manifestation of the convergence theme has been in the area of civil-military relations, and here the social sciences seem to have learned a lesson from their own intellectual history. By the late 1960s, military sociologists were recognizing that, despite the technological modernization of the military, there was still something uniquely military in the function of armies. The management of violence is sufficiently different from other industries that military organization can never be just like any other large-scale organization in America. Indeed, while the trend in the past has been in the direction of increased similarity between civil and military organizations, the consensus is now that this trend has been either halted or reversed. The difference between the two remains. In the absence of a fusion between the two, the maintenance of civilian control over the military in a democratic polity remains problematic, and the existence of the military as an interest or set of interests within that polity, making demands upon its resources, must be recognized. At each level of social organization, with the failure of the prophesized convergence, a plurality of interests remain to make demands on the resources of the system. Many of these demands, in turn, are justified on the basis of differing ideologies.

THE IDEOLOGY THEME

The role of ideology in the sociology of politics is problematic. Indeed, the very meaning of the concept "ideology" is problematic. In Chapter 3 we mentioned Converse's research on belief systems. Why did Converse use the term "belief system" rather than "ideology"? "A term like 'ideology,' " he writes, "has been thoroughly muddied by diverse uses."[23] As if in support of that assertion, Robert Lane, in his own study of political ideology, prepares his reader for what is to follow by citing nine definitions of the term.[24] We have suggested repeatedly that most Americans do not have highly structured political belief systems, nor do they devote much thought to politics at all. We have also suggested, however, that while extremist political ideologies have experienced some attrition among their believers, the age of ideological

[23] Philip E. Converse, "The Nature of Belief Systems in Mass Publics," in David E. Apter, ed., *Ideology and Discontent* (New York: The Free Press, 1964), p. 207. See also David W. Minar, "Ideology and Political Behavior," *Midwest Journal of Political Science* 5 (November 1961), pp. 317–331.

[24] Robert E. Lane, *Political Ideology* (New York: The Free Press, 1962), pp. 13–14.

consensus has not dawned. Somewhere between the ideal-typical poles defined, on the one hand, by a situation in which all citizens have highly structured belief systems and, on the other, by the end of ideology lies the reality with which we are concerned here: the linkage between the world of political ideas and the world of political action.

Rather than trying to define the concept "ideology," let us simply say that we are concerned here with people's political ideas, to whatever extent they have such ideas. More specifically, there are two classes of ideas that are of greatest concern to us: ideas that justify the continued participation of individuals or groups in the polity, thereby maintaining the existence of the polity, and ideas that lead some individuals and groups to make demands of the polity that are different from the demands being made by other participating individuals and groups.

The first type of ideas serve as the roots of political legitimacy. Lane has pointed out, on the basis of an intensive study of the political ideologies of a group of working-class men, that such men tend to believe in popular sovereignty. Although they

> find themselves politically impotent on most specific issues, do not petition or write letters with any frequency, are dubious of the wisdom of the electorate . . . , see elections as only partially successful instruments for imparting instructions to candidates, find themselves often confused by the complexity of public affairs, and tend to think of the elected officials as better judges of policy than they themselves are,[25]

the men studied nonetheless felt that they were politically important. Because they had personal ties with people who were involved in local politics, because they did not see local politics as less important than national politics, and because the electoral process gave them a sense of importance quite independent of their understanding of what was going on, these men saw themselves as "the people." Without having developed a sophisticated theory of democratic politics, they nonetheless accepted the proposition that the welfare of the people was the primary criterion on which governmental policy decisions were based.

While Lane's subjects in no way comprised a random sample of the American population, there is reason to believe that, at least through the mid-1960s, their views were shared by a majority of

[25] Ibid., p. 165.

their fellow Americans. We argued at the beginning of this book that the state can function smoothly and in a noncoercive manner only to the extent that the people have faith in it—and "faith" is perhaps a better term here than "ideology." Until recently, this condition was met in American society. Research conducted by the Survey Research Center of the University of Michigan in 1964 indicated that 62 percent of the public had a high level of faith in the government. By 1970 that figure had declined to 35 percent. We shall discuss below some of the implications of this decline. Let us for the moment note it as a fluctuation, and return to our discussion of ideology.

Assuming that some level of consensus exists on the ideological justification for continued participation in the polity, there will exist, within this framework of consensus, ideological justifications for making competing demands on the resources of the polity. Research in the area of political socialization has taught us something of the development of political ideas, but it has not led us to the principles on the basis of which personal political ideologies evolve.

Robert Lane followed his study of the political ideologies of working-class men with an intensive analysis of the political thinking of twenty-four college students, in an effort to identify the motivational bases of political ideology. Lane's analysis reflects his belief that American society is moving in the direction of more rational politics, perhaps because his subjects were middle- and upper-class students at a private, elite university.[26] In Chapter 4 we suggested that Lane's view of the knowledgeable society is at minimum premature. At the same time, his view that political ideas are manifestations of personal needs—the need to be liked, the need to feel moral, the need for autonomy or competence or efficacy—reflects a renaissance rather than a birth of clinical thinking in the behavioral study of politics.

In 1948 and before, Harold Lasswell had already suggested that political behavior could be viewed as the displacement of private motives on public objects. The motivation that he originally placed primacy on was a quest for power.[27] Subsequent

---

[26] Robert E. Lane, *Political Thinking and Consciousness* (Chicago: Markham Publishing Co., 1969).

[27] See Harold D. Lasswell, *Power and Personality* (New York: W. W. Norton & Co., Inc., 1948). See also Arnold A. Rogow, "Toward a Psychiatry of Politics," *Politics, Personality and Social Science in the Twentieth Century* (Chicago: The University of Chicago Press, 1969), pp. 123–145.

empirical tests of this proposition revealed that political office-holders do not stress power,[28] and Lasswell reconceptualized his formulation and suggested that political officeholders use power not as an end, but as a means to the maximation of other values or motives.[29] With the "behavioral revolution" in political analysis in the 1950s came an emphasis on survey research that undermined the neonatal field of political psychiatry both because of a disbelief that personality factors were important in political behavior and because of a related inability to arrive at clinical judgments on the basis of survey data.[30] The "postbehavioral" late 1960s saw a reemergence of interest in political ideology and behavior as manifestations of personality needs and values,[31] as well as attempts to measure these underlying personality factors with survey methods.

Lane has viewed the personal values that influence political orientations in terms of a hierarchy of needs.[32] Influenced, but not bound, by the thinking of psychologist Abraham H. Maslow, Lane suggests that safety needs are the first for which satisfaction is sought.[33] Thus, people sometimes compete for shelter or food. Once safety is assured, people strive to fulfill social needs (affection) and self-esteem needs (dignity), and these quests for fulfillment may again involve competition for scarce resources. Once these deficiency needs are satisfied, at least at a minimal level, people seek self-actualization, and, in seeking to grow as people, may generate new sets of demands on the political system.

We can view the difference between political generations discussed in Chapter 7 in these terms. The emergence of a "counterculture" among members of the ascending generation in

---

[28] Rufus P. Browning and Herbert Jacob, "Power Motivation and the Political Personality," *Public Opinion Quarterly* 28:1 (Spring 1964), pp. 75–90.

[29] Harold D. Lasswell, "The Selective Effect of Personality on Political Participation," in Richard Christie and Marie Jahoda, eds., *Studies in the Scope and Method of the Authoritarian Personality* (New York: The Free Press, 1954), pp. 197–225.

[30] See Rogow, "Toward a Psychiatry of Politics," Roy A. Grinker, Sr., "Psychoanalysis and the Study of Autonomic Behavior," and Robert Rubenstein, "The Study of Political Processes in Psychiatric Illness and Treatment," in Rogow, ed., *Politics, Personality and Social Science in the Twentieth Century.*

[31] See Fred I. Greenstein, *Personality and Politics* (Chicago: Markham Publishing Co., 1969), and Leroy N. Rieselbach and George I. Balch, eds., *Psychology and Politics* (New York: Holt, Rinehart & Winston, Inc., 1969).

[32] Lane, *Political Ideology*, p. 339.

[33] See A. H. Maslow, *Motivation and Personality* (New York: Harper & Row, Publishers, 1954).

modern industrial nations involves young people making demands on the political system which are different from the demands made by earlier generations and which are rooted in a quest for self-actualization.[34] Much of the attention paid to the counterculture phenomenon has assumed that the counterculture stresses opposition to the bourgeois capitalist materialism of the parental generation, and values humanism and a return to the earth. The ecological costs of modern economic technology are assumed to have been recognized by supporters of the counterculture, and have been ruled too expensive—an ideological transformation that Charles Reich has labeled "Consciousness III."[35]

Inglehart has explored the value priorities of youth in industrial society and the political implications of these priorities. Research in six European nations revealed a slight shift away from "acquisitive" materialistic values and toward "postbourgeois" humanistic values in younger cohorts as a function of economic security in the cohorts' formative years. The projected possible political results of this new orientation include the development of new political parties appealing to the interests of the growing postbourgeois electorate (e.g., parties concerned with ecology or consumerism) and a realignment of the social bases of support of existing parties. "In terms of . . . value priorities . . . ," Inglehart explains, "upper-status respondents are far likelier than lower-status respondents to support a set of postbourgeois principles which seem more compatible with parties of movement than with parties of order."[36] It is important to note that this shift in personal values across generations is not likely either to accelerate the rate of social change or to lead to a denial of materialistic interests. On the one hand, the shift is gradual. The majority of the children of the European acquisitive middle class are themselves acquisitive. On the other hand, the trend toward the increased incidence of postbourgeois humanism does not reject the materialism of the parental generation, but rather takes it for granted. It is only because security needs have already been fulfilled that the ascending generation can seek kinds of fulfillment that its parents, concerned with bread-and-butter issues, did not have time for.

---

[34] Theodore Roszak, *The Making of a Counter Culture* (New York: Doubleday & Co., Inc., 1969).

[35] Charles Reich, *The Greening of America* (New York: Random House, Inc., 1970).

[36] Ronald Inglehart, "The Silent Revolution in Europe: Intergenerational Change in Post-Industrial Societies," *American Political Science Review* 65 (December 1971), p. 1009.

ECONOMIC DEVELOPMENT, SOCIAL
SOLIDARITY, AND POLITICAL DECAY

In Chapter 2 we argued that economic development may undermine the stability of a polity if it is not accompanied by the development of integrative social institutions, especially those that facilitate communication among diverse groups. Let us now return to this theme in more general terms.

In discussions of political development or modernization, it is common to assume, at least implicitly, that some nations are already "developed" or "modern." Depending on the level of chauvinism and the nationality of the theorist, the prototype for that which is modern may be limited to the United States, or it may be extended to include Western Europe and/or the Soviet Union. The assumption, of course, is incorrect. The more developed nations of the world are themselves still developing. Indeed, they are developing at a more rapid rate than are the less developed nations, thereby widening the development gap between themselves and the "third world."[37] If development per se has any impact on political integration, then this impact should be felt in the more developed nations perhaps more strongly than anywhere else. The processes of economic development are themselves a shock to the integrative function of society,[38] and, as de Tocqueville has noted, "If men are to remain civilized or to become so, the art of associating together must grow and improve in the same ratio in which the equality of conditions is increased."[39]

Sociologists have long recognized that economic development is related to changes in the quality of social solidarity. In simple, homogeneous systems, individuals do not have highly differentiated role sets; they relate to each other as total personalities, rather than in the context of specific social or economic exchanges. Such societies are characterized by high levels of affective investment in one's interpersonal relations.[40] In more developed, complex societies, by contrast, individuals have high-

---

[37] See Gunnar Myrdal, *Rich Lands and Poor* (New York: Harper & Row, Publishers, 1957).

[38] See Samuel P. Huntington, *Political Order in Changing Societies* (New Haven: Yale University Press, 1968), especially Chapter 1, "Political Order and Political Decay," pp. 1–92.

[39] Alexis de Tocqueville, *Democracy in America*, vol. 2 (New York: Alfred A. Knopf, Inc., 1955), p. 118.

[40] See Ferdinand Tonnies, *Community and Society*, C. P. Loomis, ed. and trans. (East Lansing: Michigan State University Press, 1957).

ly differentiated role sets, and relate to each other in the context of these roles, rather than as total personalities. Such relationships tend to be constrained by the temporal and spatial limits associated with specific roles. They are functionally related to the roles being played, and are characterized by relatively low levels of intimacy and affect. This differentiation and compartmentalization of social roles has two important implications for social solidarity. On the one hand, it puts people into contact with a wider, more heterogeneous set of others, and these wide social networks facilitate the flow of information through society. On the other hand, the cost of this openness is a weaker set of affective ties linking individuals to the social system.[41]

Can the more developed societies afford the costs in social solidarity of these weak ties? From one perspective, the negative effects of affluence on political stability can be defined in international terms. The United States, accepting the hypothesis that economic development promotes political stability, exported economic assistance to less developed nations, thereby shaking their political stability without threatening its own.[42] Not surprisingly, this perspective recognizes that economic development and political stability need not go hand in hand. Thus, it can regard the United States as never having gone through a revolution of political modernization, which the nations of Western Europe have. Indeed, it views the American polity as one built on a Tudor base, exported by a colonizing Europe which itself departed from the Tudor model.[43] Ironically, the eminence of the United States in the twentieth century could conceivably influence Europe to adopt a neo-Tudor style.

This point of view overlooks the implications of building a political system to which people are not closely tied affectively, but rather are linked primarily through established political parties. The American experience suggests that the effect of the recent American policy of exporting economic assistance and thereby contributing to foreign political instability was dysfunctional, particularly with regard to the Vietnam War. The American people, having borne the cost of exporting economic aid, saw it contribute to political turmoil. Many Americans developed a

---

[41] See Mark Granovetter, "The Strength of Weak Ties," *American Journal of Sociology* 78 (May 1973), pp. 1360–1380.

[42] Huntington, *Political Order in Changing Societies*, p. 6.

[43] Ibid., Chapter 2, "Political Modernization: America vs. Europe," pp. 93–139.

distrust of the policy and, in the absence of strong linkages to the government, a broader lack of trust in the government itself. Between 1964 and 1970, the percentage of the American population having a high level of faith in the government declined from 62 percent to 35 percent. Distrust of the government, in turn, has been shown to be related to opposition to the Vietnam War.[44] The political parties, which provide the tenuous linkage between the American people and their government, have also suffered. In the 1950s and early 1960s, the percentage of the electorate that did not identify with a political party varied between 15 and 25. By the early 1970s, approximately a third of the electorate considered itself to be independent. And the most politically sophisticated members of the electorate were overrepresented among the independents.

A widespread and deep-rooted sense of partisan identification has been regarded as in large measure responsible for the relative stability of the American political system.[45] Indeed, Converse has suggested that, as a political party system reaches maturity (within about three generations), the level of party identification in its electorate reaches an equilibrium point of about 72 percent and does not drop below that.[46] Other scholars have noted more recently that party identification in the United States has dropped below the equilibrium point in Converse's model, and suggest that a process of dealignment, which portends even lower rates of partisanship in the future, is taking place.[47] This dealignment implies neither depoliticization nor deideologization of the electorate. Rather, it may be seen as a manifestation of dissatisfaction with current political parties and the limited range of ideological positions that they represent. Political consumers are demanding products not currently available in the partisan marketplace.[48]

[44] Andre Modigliani, "Hawks and Doves: Isolationism and Political Trust," *American Political Science Review* 66 (September 1972), pp. 960–978.

[45] Philip E. Converse and G. Dupeaux, "Politicization of the Electorate in France and the United States," *Public Opinion Quarterly* 26 (Spring 1962), pp. 1–23.

[46] Philip E. Converse, "Of Time and Partisan Stability," *Comparative Political Studies* 2 (July 1969), pp. 139–171.

[47] Ronald Inglehart and Avram Hochstein, "Alignment and Dealignment of the Electorate in France and the United States," *Comparative Political Studies* 5 (October 1972), pp. 343–372.

[48] Segal and Hikel, "The Emerging Independent."

This dealignment does not reflect a need for political revolution in America, although some analysts have interpreted it in that way. Rather, the imbalance between the level of differentiation in the population and the ability of political and social institutions to integrate the polity may be viewed as a short-term phenomenon to which the homeostatic processes in society will adapt. In the party system, the most likely adaptations are the development of greater ideological differences between the major parties or the increased incidence of minor parties. Minor parties are more likely to proliferate at the local than at the national level, and, while they are unlikely to dominate the electoral arena, they might well have a major impact on the nature of American politics. At the level of national government, the United States might well shift its priorities from the international scene to the domestic arena. Such a shift might increase the power of the Congress, as against that of the president, in the decision-making process. The reassertion of the power of the representatives of the people might go far toward restoring faith in government. And in the population at large, we shall see old cleavages and hostilities fade away, new cleavages emerge, and new coalitions form, binding diverse segments of the population to each other, if only weakly and briefly.

Selected Readings

The study of political sociology is rooted in the assumption that there is something political in every social system. An overview of the field is presented in Morris Janowitz, "Political Sociology," in *International Encyclopedia of the Social Sciences,* vol. 12 (New York: The Macmillan Co., 1968), pp. 298–307. A more developmental perspective on politics is presented in Morton H. Fried, *The Evolution of Political Society* (New York: Random House, Inc., 1967). The role of politics in the life of nations is dealt with on a comparative basis by Gabriel A. Almond and Sidney Verba in *The Civic Culture* (Princeton, N.J.: Princeton University Press, 1963).

There is no single "systems" perspective on the study of politics. The cornerstone of systems analysis among political scientists is probably David Easton, *A Systems Analysis of Political Life* (New York: John Wiley & Sons, Inc., 1965), while among sociologists, Talcott H. Parsons' essays on "Structure and Process in Political Systems," published as Part 3 of *Structure and Process in Modern Societies* (New York: The Free Press, 1960), have been influential.

The concepts of power, authority, and legitimacy are discussed widely. Basic theoretical statements can be found in Hans Gerth and C. Wright Mills, *From Max Weber* (New York: Oxford University Press, 1958), pp. 159–266.

Political anthropology has tended to emphasize the political process in less developed nations, although contemporary anthropologists are concerning themselves increasingly with the modern world. Traditional political anthropology is well represented by L. P. Mair, *Primitive Government* (Baltimore: Penguin Books, Inc., 1962), and by M. Fortes and E. E. Evans-Pritchard, eds., *African Political Systems* (New York: Oxford University Press, 1940). A multitude of studies conducted by political sociologists and political scientists concerned with political development have been influenced by, but have departed from, the anthropological approach. Among the important works in this tradition are Reinhard Bendix, *Nation-Building and Citizenship* (New York: John Wiley & Sons, Inc., 1964), A. F. K. Organski, *The Stages of Political Development* (New York: Alfred A. Knopf, Inc., 1965), and David E. Apter, *The Politics of Modernization* (Chicago: University of Chicago Press, 1965).

There are a wide range of theories of democracy that purport to describe how democratic politics should operate, or to explain how democracy does or does not function. The presentation in this book utilizes the market analogy to the political system as a pedagogic tool, and the reader interested in this approach may turn to Anthony Downs, *An Economic Theory of Democracy* (New York: Harper & Row, Publishers, 1957). An alternate formulation, which explains political outcomes more in terms of the activities of the upper strata of society than by the sentiment and ideologies of the mass of voters, is Peter Bachrach, *The Theory of Democratic Elitism* (Boston: Little, Brown and Co., 1967). An interesting summary of data on the degree to which politics is a participatory process is James David Barber, *Citizen Politics* (Chicago: Markham Publishing Co., 1969).

The importance of communication in political development is discussed in Lucian W. Pye, ed., *Communications and Political Development* (Princeton, N.J.: Princeton University Press, 1963), Richard R. Fagen, *Politics and Communication* (Boston: Little, Brown and Co., 1966), and Karl W. Deutsch, *Nationalism and Social Communication* (Cambridge, Mass.: M.I.T. Press, 1953). An insightful presentation of the utilization of communication by elites is presented in Satish K. Arora and Harold D. Lasswell, *Political Communication* (New York: Holt, Rinehart & Winston, Inc., 1969). Hugh Dalziel Duncan treats communication as a vehicle for relationships of both equality and dominance in *Communication and Social Order* (New York: Oxford University Press, 1968).

Ideology has emerged as a central concept in political sociology. For an attempt to define the concept as it appears in political analysis, see George Lichtheim, *The Concept of Ideology* (New York: Random House, Inc., 1967). A fine collection of studies that have attempted to use the concept in empirical analysis (with varying degrees of success) is *Ideology and Discontent,* ed. David E. Apter (New York: The Free Press, 1964).

The ways in which legislative bodies serve as vehicles by which the demands of public opinion become transformed into public policy have been empirically explored less fully than have many other areas of political sociology. For views on the impact of public opinion on the choosing of legislators, see the essays on William N. McPhee and William A. Glaser, eds., *Public Opinion and Congressional Elections* (New York: The Free Press, 1962). A technical discussion of a study of the ways in which voting blocs align in the legislative process is presented in Duncan MacRae, Jr., *Dimensions of Congressional Voting* (Berkeley: University of California Press, 1958).

The relationship between social stratification and politics has been an enduring concern of political sociology. Robert Alford's *Party and Society* (Chicago: Rand McNally & Co., 1963) presents a review of this research tradition coupled with an empirical investigation of the relationship between class and politics in the Anglo-American nations. The readings in *The Search for Community Power* (Englewood Cliffs, N.J.: Prentice-Hall, Inc., 1965), ed. Willis D. Hawley and Frederick M. Wirt, present an overview of the past debate and probable future direction of research on stratification and politics in the context of American communities.

The hypothesized convergence of classes in modern industrial nations which characterizes one school of political sociology has been the subject of considerable debate and little resolution in the literature. Two of the more interesting positions in this debate are presented by Harold L. Wilensky, "Class, Class Consciousness and American Workers," in William Haber, ed., *Labor in a Changing America* (New York: Basic Books, Inc., 1966), pp. 12–28, and Richard F. Hamilton, "Income, Class, and Reference Groups," *American Sociological Review* 29 (August 1964), pp. 576–579. The debate on the end of ideology, which is seen by many as a cultural correlate of structural convergence, is nicely summarized in Mustafa Rejai, ed., *The Decline of Ideology* (Chicago: Aldine Publishing Co., 1971).

Among the works done on political consensus, see Ulf Torgersen's paper "The Trend Toward Political Consensus," in Erik Allardt and Stein Rokkan, eds., *Mass Politics* (New York: The Free Press, 1970), pp. 93–124. The cleavage side of the consensus-and-cleavage equation is treated by Seymour Martin Lipset in "Political Cleavages in 'Developed' and 'Emerging' Polities," pp. 23–44 in the same volume. Lipset's paper also appears in Part 1 of Erik Allardt and Yrjo Littunen, eds., *Cleavages, Ideologies and Party Systems* (Transactions of the Westermarck Society, vol. 10, Turku, Finland, 1964), and both volumes, which reflect the work of the Committee on Political Sociology of the International Sociological Association, will be of interest to the reader. A somewhat different approach to the issue of cleavages is presented in Douglas W. Rae and Michael Taylor, *The Analysis of Political Cleavages* (New Haven, Conn.: Yale University Press, 1970).

The role of religion in politics is discussed in Gerhard Lenski, *The Religious Factor* (New York: Doubleday & Co., Inc., 1963). The importance of religion for behavior has been the subject of much dispute in sociology, and a replication of Lenski's work, although concerned more with economics than with politics, might be of interest to the reader. See Howard Schuman, "The Religious Factor in Detroit," *American Sociological Review* 36 (February 1971), pp. 30–48. Ethnicity and politics are well covered in Raymond E. Wolfinger, "The Development and Persistence of Ethnic Voting," *American Political Science Review* 55 (December 1965), pp. 896–908. A good sense of the impact of race on American political patterns is presented in Donald R. Matthews and James W. Prothro, *Negroes and the New Southern Politics* (New York: Harcourt Brace Jovanovich, Inc., 1966), while persisting elements of traditional Southern politics are discussed in V. O. Key, Jr., *Southern Politics* (New York: Random House, Inc., 1949).

The literature on how the complex cleavages that occur in modern societies combine to influence political patterns appears largely in professional journals, rather than in books. Three exceptions to this rule are noteworthy. On the issue of relative deprivation and politics, see W. G. Runciman, *Relative Deprivation and Social Justice* (Berkeley: University of California Press, 1966), and on the impact of social mobility, see James Alden Barber, Jr., *Social Mobility and Voting Behavior* (Chicago: Rand McNally & Co., 1970). The impact of crosscutting cleavages is discussed in Harry Eckstein, *Division and Cohesion in Democracy* (Princeton, N.J.: Princeton University Press, 1966).

Reading in the area of political socialization should start with Herbert Hyman's original synthesis of the field, *Political Socialization* (New York: The Free Press, 1959). Subsequent research has been summarized in several compendia. The most comprehensive of these, to my thinking, is Roberta S. Sigel, *Learning About Politics* (New York: Random House, Inc., 1970). Where Sigel, reflecting the major tendency among researchers in the field, focuses primarily on normative socialization (political learning supportive of the political system), other scholars have been concerned with learning opposition to the established order. Edward S. Greenberg, in his edited volume *Political Socialization* (New York: Lieber-Atherton, Inc., 1970), presents the debate on the learning of discontent and nonsupport, and Anthony M. Orum has edited a collection of papers on the socialization of student activism entitled *The Seeds of Politics* (Englewood Cliffs, N.J.: Prentice-Hall, Inc., 1972).

While most research carried out in the field of political socialization has been concerned with the system-level consequences of this process, i.e., with the implications of socialization for the political system, increased attention has been paid in recent years to the individual being socialized. Fred I. Greenstein, in *Personality and Politics* (Chicago: Markham Publishing Co., 1969), reviews the field and provides an insightful discussion of personality as a dependent variable in political analysis. Along more empirical lines, Robert E. Lane, in *Political Thinking and Consciousness* (Chicago: Markham Publishing Co., 1969), probes the bases of political orientation with materials gathered from intensive clinical interviews with twenty-four young men.

The linkage between American voters and policy, through the Congress, is dealt with in Milton C. Cummings, Jr., *Congress and the Electorate* (New York: The Free Press, 1966). A broader picture of the relationship between elections and political institutions is presented in Angus Campbell, Philip E. Converse, Warren E. Miller, and Donald E. Stokes, *Elections and the Political Order* (New York: John Wiley & Sons, Inc., 1966). Walter Dean Burnham presents a view of the theory of critical elections in the context of political institutions in *Critical Elections and the Mainsprings of American Politics* (New York: W. W. Norton & Co., Inc., 1970). An alternate view of realignment in the American electorate is suggested in Richard N. Scammon and Ben J. Wattenberg, *The Real Majority* (New York: Coward-McCann, Inc., 1970).

An early sociological view of the impact of social movements on politics is presented in Rudolf Herberle, *Social Movements* (New York: Appleton-Century-Crofts, 1951). Roberta Ash in *Social Movements in America* (Chicago: Markham Publishing Co., 1972) focuses on the historical impact of movements on American politics. In an edited volume, *Protest, Reform, and Revolt* (New York: John Wiley & Sons, Inc., 1970), Joseph Gusfield brings together much of the social movement literature relevant to an understanding of politics.

On the theme of political dominance by members of the political, military, and industrial upper strata, see the contrasting views presented by C. Wright Mills in *The Power Elite* (New York: Oxford University Press, 1956), David Reisman in *The Lonely Crowd* (New Haven, Conn.: Yale University Press, 1961), and Arnold M. Rose in *The Power Structure* (New York: Oxford University Press, 1967). The garrison-state model is discussed in Samuel P. Huntington, *The Soldier and the State* (New York: Vintage Books, 1964), and the mass-society model in William Kornhauser, *The Politics of Mass Society* (New York: The Free Press, 1959). The most current collection of research on the military-industrial complex is Steven Rosen, ed., *Testing the Theory of the Military-Industrial Complex* (Lexington, Mass.: D. C. Heath & Co., 1973).

Views of social and political systems as social networks are presented in Robert M. MacIver, *The Web of Government*, rev. ed. (New York: The Free Press, 1965), Karl W. Deutsch, *The Nerves of Government* (New York: The Free Press, 1963), and Edward O. Laumann, *Bonds of Pluralism* (New York: John Wiley & Sons, Inc., 1973). Political change in modern societies is dealt with in Robert A. Dahl, *Polyarchy* (New Haven, Conn.: Yale University Press, 1971), and Samuel P. Huntington, *Political Order in Changing Societies* (New Haven, Conn.: Yale University Press, 1968).

The reader interested in the influence of politics on sociology will find much to think about in Leon Bramson, *The Political Context of Sociology* (Princeton, N.J.: Princeton University Press, 1961).

Index